OVAL OFFICE

STORIES OF PRESIDENTS IN CRISIS FROM WASHINGTON TO BUSH

OVAL OFFICE

STORIES OF PRESIDENTS IN CRISIS FROM WASHINGTON TO BUSH

EDITED BY NATHANIEL MAY

SERIES EDITOR CLINT WILLIS

Thunder's Mouth Press
New York

Oval Office: Stories of Presidents in Crisis from Washington to Bush

An Adrenaline Book®

Published by
Thunder's Mouth Press
An Imprint of Avalon Publishing Group Incorporated
161 William Street, 16th floor
New York, NY 10038

Book design: Sue Canavan

frontispiece photo: Oval Office, © Bettmann/Corbis

Library of Congress Cataloging-in-Publication Data is available.

ISBN: 1-56025-435-1

Printed in Canada

Distributed by Publishers Group West

for my grandmother, Frances Bell

contents

photographs

introduction

The stories in this book tell of 13 men who, having made their way to the top of the American political ladder, found that the job of President was bigger than they were. Thrust into war, political scandal, domestic unrest and international conflict, these men responded in ways that helped to define their presidencies.

Some presidents were more successful than others. Lincoln is remembered for his steadfast leadership during the Civil War. Roosevelt led the nation through the Great Depression and World War II. Nixon sealed his administration's fate with lies. Clinton's personal behavior tarnished his political achievements.

Politicians always have been subject to criticism from their constituents, but only in recent years have they been scrutinized so closely. The information age has been hard on public officials, especially presidents. Yet we persist in holding these men to high standards of achievement and character. We expect from them charm, wisdom, integrity—above all, success. We hold them responsible for virtually everything in the public sphere—from crime to the strength of the dollar. Meanwhile, the office's authority and power continue to be limited by our system of checks and balances—and the men who hold it are merely human.

Are our expectations too high? Thomas Jefferson wondered as much in his first inaugural address, delivered March 4, 1801:

> Sometimes it is said that man can not be trusted with the government of himself. Can he then, be trusted with the government of others?

Our presidents are not perfect, but many of them have been good men. In times of crisis, they often have done what they deemed right, sometimes paying a political price for their actions. Their stories remind us that presidents are human beings subject to foibles that range from memory lapses to incompetence—who on occasion demonstrate virtues that over the centuries have included wisdom, compassion, and courage.

—NATHANIEL MAY

from Patriarch

by Richard Norton Smith

George Washington (in office 1789–1797) feared that farmers' 1794 revolt against the whiskey tax was a serious threat to the country's young republican government. Biographer Richard Norton Smith (born 1953) describes Washington's response to the Whiskey Rebellion—a response that helped determine the power of the federal government over regional interests.

A lust for land represented only part of Washington's complex love affair with the American West. None of his countrymen thought on so continental a scale. To be sure, Jefferson might talk learnedly with European philosophers about the unique zoological attributes of the trans-Appalachian West (some in the Old World believed that dogs actually lost their bark in the thin American air). But no one could claim, as did Washington, to have actually tramped the forests and taken the measure of this vast trackless empire in the making. Nor could anyone match his strategic and emotional grasp of a region that served simultaneously as granary, marketplace, buffer zone, and battlefield.

Above all, Washington was sensitive to the area's delicate political balance. "The western states," he had written after the war, "stand as it were on a pivot; the touch of a feather would almost incline them any way." What he was referring to, of course, was the complex rivalry of European powers, each seeking to establish its domination over the trans-Appalachian region. England, France, and Spain all nurtured territorial ambitions. So did the native tribes for whom Washington's migrating countrymen posed an imminent threat to their hunting grounds and way of life. This intuitive reading of western hopes and doubts helps to explain the administration's repeated military forays against the frontier tribes, its wooing of Spanish courtiers who might favor more liberal access to the Mississippi, and the president's measured response to the first wave of grass-roots resistance to Hamilton's excise tax back in the summer of 1792.

Since then, Congress had taken steps to pacify agrarian discontent, but they were half measures at best. Paying nine cents' tax on a gallon of distilled rye liquor seemed as onerous to this generation of Americans as a two-cent tax on British stamps had to their fathers. Even those willing to swallow their opposition to the tax in principle gagged on the means by which it was enforced.

On July 15, 1794, a federal marshal named David Lenox unwittingly struck a spark that engulfed the whole region in flames. Attempting to serve writs on more than sixty tax evaders, he succeeded only in panicking the residents into believing that their friends and loved ones were being hauled off to appear in a Philadelphia courthouse. The next day, an angry militia went to Bower Hill and attacked the home of John Neville. As the government's well-fed tax collector, Neville symbolized everything offensive to frontier dwellers trapped in virtual peonage. Shots rang out; one of the insurgents fell mortally wounded. That night a mass meeting heard demands for Neville's head. This was Pennsylvania, however, not Paris, and the tax man was in any event disinclined to gratify his vengeful neighbors.

Neville was powerless, however, to halt a much larger force from setting a torch to his property the next day. After an exchange of gunfire in which two of the attackers were killed, Neville was lucky to escape with his life. Rebels seized the feckless David Lenox and forced him, on penalty of death, to recant his support of the tax. In the ensuing days, liberty poles sprouted throughout Washington, Fayette, Westmoreland, and Allegheny counties. Mock trials condemned local respectables to imaginary guillotines. Talk of secession mingled with threats of violence. The Whiskey Rebellion was on.

Delegates meeting at Mingo Creek on July 23 produced an unlikely Daniel Shays in David Bradford, a thirty-four-year-old deputy attorney general for Washington County and vice president of its Democratic Society, allied with the state organization of the same name. At the time of his election, the only violence Bradford engaged in was rhetorical, but three days later he led a raiding party that held up an eastbound mail coach. Inside were found letters from conservative townspeople, petitioning Philadelphia for help in restoring law and order.

Bradford's call for area militia to assemble at Braddock's Field, outside Pittsburgh, on August 1 caused prosperous residents of the little city, dubbed "Sodom" by the rebels, to hide what valuables they were unable to spirit away. Those remaining behind were easily cowed by a ragged line of 7,000 "white Indians" that snaked two miles through apprehensive neighborhoods. At the head of this improvised army rode Bradford, resplendent in a plumed hat and with a glittering sword at his side. One of his soldiers stuck his own, more modest headgear on a rifle barrel and hoisted it high in the air. "I have a bad hat now, but I expect to have a better one soon," he crowed.

When word of the skirmish at Bower Hill reached Philadelphia on July 25, horrified conservatives reacted predictably. At first glance both the government and the rebels stood on familiar ground: it was 1792 all over again. Closer examination revealed significant differences between this uprising and the earlier, mostly verbal, protest. Two years of bitter charges and countercharges had poisoned the political climate, as European hatreds were reflected among Federalists and Republicans who had come to question their opponents' patriotism. In 1792 there had been no Democratic Societies to alarm Washington and other friends of the Constitution. Citizen Genêt was unheard of, Philip Freneau but a mild irritant.

Congress in that year had enacted legislation defining the conditions under which the executive might be empowered to call up troops. Now, in holding to the law, Washington asked justice James Wilson of the Supreme Court to certify a state of near anarchy in the alienated region around Pittsburgh. Making judicial sanction even more critical was the refusal of Governor Thomas Mifflin, no friend of the president's, to mobilize his state's forces. A stalemate threatened at the end of July, when a stretch of hot dry weather rekindled memories of the previous summer's epidemic of yellow fever. As a precaution, the first family retreated to the stone house in Germantown that Washington had used during the most lethal months of 1793. After paying Colonel Isaac Franks a rent of $201.60, the president had two wagonloads of furniture hauled out from the city to make the place habitable.

The Washingtons took naturally to the semirural ways of Germantown. The first lady was seen leaning out a window to chat with her neighbor, a blacksmith's wife. Young Wash irregularly attended classes at Germantown Academy while his sister rose before dawn each day to perfect her Italian. So attached did Nelly Custis become to the place that she teasingly refused to return to Philadelphia except on her nag, Rozinante, at the head of a "grand cavalcade." By the first week of August, it looked as if her grandfather might soon be leading a cavalcade of his own. At a pivotal conference on the second, Washington decried the western unrest as an ax aimed at the root of constitutional government. Mifflin was unconvinced. By questioning how many Pennsylvanians would take up arms against their fellow citizens and insisting that nothing would drive wavering moderates into the rebel camp faster than overreaction on the part of federal authorities, the governor planted doubts in Washington's mind.

Conflicting advice snowed the president's desk. On the one hand, Hamilton and Knox insisted that 12,000 men were needed to crush the uprising, reassert federal supremacy, and avoid the specter of national dismemberment. "Government can never be said to be established until some signal display has manifested its power of military coercion," argued Hamilton. Opposing him, Randolph, Mifflin, and Attorney General Bradford were unanimous in counseling delay. As Randolph put it, "The strength of a government is the affection of the people." Why destabilize an already fragile situation, alienating responsible elements who might rally behind the administration given time and a conspicuous display of moderation?

Washington cast his lot with administration doves by appointing Attorney General Bradford, his former colleague on the state's supreme court Jasper Yeates, and Senator James Ross to a peace commission. But the president also kept his powder dry. Should David Bradford and his ragtag army fail to negotiate in good faith, a proclamation on August 7 commanding all the insurgents to disperse peaceably by the first day of September hinted at stronger actions. During the period of watchful waiting that followed, the putative peace commissioners tested attitudes on the other side of the mountains. The alarmist reports they relayed back, based largely on secondhand observations, did little to advance a negotiated solution.

Chafing against his self-imposed limits, Washington privately chastised the troublemakers belonging to Genêt-inspired Democratic Societies who were "spreading mischief far and wide either from *real* ignorance" of the government's intentions or in hopes of discrediting the Federalist system. Painful as it was to contemplate "such violent and outrageous proceedings" as held the deluded Pennsylvanians in their grip, the president expected far worse unless his government operated to remove the canker of sedition. "If the laws are to be trampled upon with impunity, and a minority (a small one too) is to dictate to the majority, there is an end put, at one stroke, to republican government."

Throughout August the administration talked peace while preparing for war. Cabinet officers discussed the mechanics of stockpiling arms and supplying a large force in the field. On August 17 Henry Lee tendered his personal services in suppressing the rebellion, whose representatives were reputed to have contacted the British and Spanish ministers in Philadelphia. Thoughts of western treachery were very much on his mind when Washington told Lee, "I consider this insurrection as the first *formidable* fruit of the Democratic Societies. I early gave it as my opinion to the confidential characters around me that, if these Societies were not counteracted (not by prosecutions, the ready way to make them grow stronger) . . . they would shake the government to its foundation." The president castigated frontier agitators for "the most diabolical attempt to destroy the best fabric of human government and happiness that has ever been presented for the acceptance of mankind."

It is easy today to dismiss the threat to Washington and his government in the summer of 1794. Even its name has given the Whiskey Rebellion a faintly comic tinge among historians who have arraigned the administration for employing military force absurdly disproportionate to the handful of malcontents ranged under David Bradford's banner. More recent scholarship has cast doubt on the traditional depictions of impoverished farmers staging a landlocked version of Boston's Tea Party. Yet almost no one has asked the question essential to understanding Washington's behavior during the crisis, indeed, throughout his presidency. Simply put, how much faith did the first president have in the ability of his countrymen to govern themselves?

Daniel Shays's 1786 uprising in western Massachusetts had occasioned a rare but unmistakable airing of doubt. "We have probably had too good an opinion of human nature in forming our confederation," Washington had written in obvious distress during the gravest crisis of his brief postwar furlough at Mount Vernon. "Experience has taught us that men will not adopt and carry into execution measures the best calculated for their own good, without the intervention of a coercive power." The retired general could be forgiven his wary assessment of humankind. Having sparred with Robert Dinwiddie in his youth, outwitted the revolutionary usurper Charles Lee, and stared down the Newburgh Conspiracy that threatened civilian supremacy in the new republic; having experienced personal betrayal and political chicanery at all levels of government, Washington knew at first hand the levers of power and the petty intrigues that attended their use.

As president, he harbored none of the modern reformer's illusions about human perfectibility. Nor did he ever confuse republicanism with pure democracy. Even indirect democracy assumed a virtuous citizenry as the bulwark of popular liberties. Washington had said as much in his first inaugural address, insisting that "there is no truth more thoroughly established than that there exists . . . an indissoluble union between virtue and happiness; between duty and advantage." His was a highly practical idealism, more Roman than Greek in its antecedents, with little of Rousseau's unquestioning celebration of natural man and much of Tidewater Virginia's noblesse oblige.

Still, if he lived apart from most of his fellows, it was at a distance that lent surprising charity to his judgment. "It is to be regretted, I confess, that democratical states must always *feel* before they can *see*," he told Lafayette a year before Shays's insurgency shook his confidence, adding, "It is that that makes their governments slow, but the people will be right at last."

The people, yes, but hardly *vox populi vox Dei*.

Philosophical abstractions aside, Washington had compelling reasons for fearing the whiskey rebels and the leveling impulse they represented. He was only human. He had spent a lifetime climbing the social ladder of respectability, escaping his modest origins, sacrificing personal serenity and physical comfort to win a brutal war and found a nation. With an aristocrat's sense of entitlement, he expected both gratitude and intellectual deference from the cheering masses. For all his assertions of individual modesty, by 1794 Washington regarded himself as the surest interpreter of the Constitution to which he had given sanction and in whose defense he was now prepared to risk bloodshed.

On the personal level, he took umbrage at democrats who questioned his truthfulness while putting harshly critical words about him in the mouths of others. Jefferson, for example. Washington refused to credit a report from the tattling Henry Lee that the former secretary of state was describing the president to friends as a British tool. Jefferson could not possibly think such a thing, Washington countered, "unless . . . he has set me down as one of the most deceitful and uncandid men living." To demonstrate continued faith in his friend, he proposed sending him to Madrid. Who better to pry open the Mississippi—or quiet secession talk in restive Kentucky—than Jefferson, the West's most ardent champion?

There was only one problem. Having been coopted before to support offensive policies, Jefferson had no intention now of forsaking his little mountain for the squalid arena of politics. Pleading a bad case of rheumatism, the Sage of Monticello ruled out any return to public affairs. "I thought myself perfectly fixed in this determination when I left Philadelphia," he told Randolph, "but every day and hour since has added to its inflexibility." Patrick Henry proved no more willing to cross the ocean and test his oratorical powers on Spanish diplomats. Washington, disappointed, finally moved Thomas Pinckney from London to Madrid. At the end of August, the president gave fresh instructions to Jay, urging him to punish any Canadian agents who had incited Indian attacks on the American frontier and vowing that if King George wished to be at peace and to enjoy the benefits of trade with his former colonies, he must vacate the northwestern posts promptly. Washington was adamant: war would be the inevitable price, he insisted, of Britain's failure to implement the yellowing treaty signed eleven years earlier.

Judging by the latest reports from western Pennsylvania, the president may have thought himself transported to revolutionary France. At a stormy meeting of western representatives on August 28, Albert Gallatin strongly argued for accepting the terms posed by Washington's peace commissioners: amnesty for all lawbreakers and forgiveness of uncollected taxes. Gallatin ridiculed the idea that western Pennsylvania could exist either as an independent nation or as a vassal state of Britain or Spain. But David Bradford dismissed this cautionary appeal, insisting that water-gruel Easterners would prove no match for Appalachian sharpshooters. When the roll was called, Bradford's supporters mustered 23 votes against 34 in favor of Washington's offer, not enough to prevail but more than enough to dash hopes for a peaceful settlement.

Quick to perceive his opportunity, Alexander Hamilton was quicker still to seize it. Hamilton was hungry for glory and feeling even more than usually combative that summer. With Henry Knox away from the capital trying to save his overextended Maine investments from ruin, the secretary of the treasury was free to enact his favorite fantasy, that of the avenging man on horseback. To prepare the public for military adventures, he took to the gazettes to pound the ragged sans culottes of western Pennsylvania, by his jaundiced estimate a tiny fraction of the population. He defined the issue in stark terms: "Shall the majority govern or be governed?"

Hamilton had not been noticeably concerned about majority rule in the past. Washington, on the other hand, paid close attention to public opinion as the guiding light of republican government. Far from being Hamilton's tool, as often alleged, the president through his initial conciliatory response went directly against his secretary's advice. Before confronting the rebels with muskets, Washington would attempt to isolate them with words. If force must be used, it would be only after weeks of patient negotiation had demonstrated to the public's satisfaction that no alternative existed.

By the beginning of September, the Whiskey Rebellion had spread to twenty counties in four states. Sedition flourished at Pigeon Creek, Pennsylvania, Isle of Wight, Virginia, and Hagerstown, Maryland. The authority of Washington's government was openly challenged in Washington County, Ohio, as well as Washington County, Pennsylvania. Ragged men intoxicated with rhetoric and whiskey tarred and feathered treasury agents and obstructed the recruitment of militia. With rebellion metastasizing along the nation's Appalachian spine and his War Department unable to send payment to Wayne's Legion for fear that highwaymen would pick the federal pocket, Washington faced a choice between moving forcefully during the weeks of Indian summer or permitting insurgents to use the coming winter to gain fresh credibility.

On September 11, thousands of Pennsylvanians took a loyal oath, but others refused, stranding moderates who added their voices to the chorus demanding federal intervention. Governor Mifflin, relieved of public responsibility for summoning the Pennsylvania militia by Washington's highly visible leadership, came around with a belated call to arms that produced an enthusiastic response from the same countryside held to be of doubtful loyalty just days earlier. The way was cleared for Washington to issue a final proclamation, lamenting that "the well-disposed . . . are unable by their influence and example to reclaim the wicked from their fury." His anger at the Democratic Societies had not cooled, judging from a letter of September 25 blasting the notion that "self-created bodies, forming themselves into *permanent* censors," could arrogate the right to pick among the laws deserving of obedience.

Having come this far, Washington now chose to lend his personal prestige to the federal army in the making by joining the march to Carlisle; from there he could weigh crossing the mountains and invading the heart of the disaffected region. Shortly after ten o'clock on Tuesday morning, September 30, Washington boarded a carriage outside 190 Market Street, with Hamilton on his left and Bartholomew Dandridge on his right. Off they went, general and generalissimo, until they reached the tiny German settlement of The Trappe, their overnight destination. It was close to midnight when the furious pounding of hooves announced Major John Stagg, Knox's chief clerk. Washington's face brightened and his spirits soared as he read Stagg's news, a graphic account of Anthony Wayne's violent encounter with Little Turtle and his confederates.

On the hot, misty morning of August 20, Wayne's Legion had collided with 2,000 warriors from the Shawnee, Wyandot, and Ottawa tribes supplemented by small contingents of English, French, and Canadian Tories. The Indians occupied a high ridge within sight of the British garrison at Fort Miami, their lines stretching for nearly two miles in the twisted remains of a forest blown down years earlier in a tornado. This natural fortress, made seemingly impregnable by additional breastworks, gave the ensuing battle its name: Fallen Timbers. At first it looked to be a repetition of earlier disasters visited on American armies. A few minutes after ten o'clock, an advance party came hurtling back from its forward position pursued by shrieking tribesmen. This was the signal for Wayne to execute his carefully devised plan of attack, deploying well-drilled troops in a double line, with mounted volunteers taking up positions to the front and on the left while the Miami River protected the American right.

Now it was the red men who were exposed, tied to a fixed line of defense and forced to fight a conventional battle. Wayne ordered a bayonet charge to flush the enemy from behind protective stumps and the tall grass of the prairie. As the American cavalry rounded the Indians' left flank, an Ottawa chief named Turkey Foot climbed on top of a prominent boulder and promised his men that the Great Spirit would give them the courage to prevail. Then he fell, mortally wounded by an American bullet. Less than an hour after it began, the battle degenerated into an uneven contest between the horse's hoof and the moccasin. Brightly painted faces made conspicuous targets. Sharp as the blades that cut down fleeing Indians was the betrayal of the tribes' supposed friends, the British. Warriors retreating to the stout walls of Fort Miami found the outpost shut up like a turtle in its shell. Desperate pleas for admission fell on deaf ears, so the murderous chase continued for seven miles along the banks of the bloodied Miami. It was a race the Indian could not win. Some of the defeated tribesmen kept on running until they reached Canada.

Fallen Timbers was marked by savagery on both sides. Among Wayne's reported forty-four dead was an officer hacked into pound pieces as retaliation for the quartering of a young Shawnee chief. The Indians' losses were far more severe. By the time the firing sputtered to a halt, the myth of the red man's invincibility in forest warfare had been punctured. So had his alliance of convenience with the British. The triumphant general moved quickly to consolidate his gains, wiping out several Indian villages and laying waste to 5,000 acres of corn before moving on to decimate the stores of Britain's agent for the region. No stronger message could be sent to the foreign ministry in London that it had better deal seriously with John Jay.

Before the bloody encounter, Little Turtle had warned his fellow chiefs that Wayne was not to be confused with the pedestrian Harmar or indolent St. Clair. This soldier played for high stakes, all right, but without neglecting the unending drills and the thousand routine but vital details that turn a rabble into an army. Wayne deserved the title given him by a respectful adversary: "General who never sleeps." So did his commander in chief. Tossing on his cot during the early hours of October 1, Washington could hardly envision Wayne's Treaty of Greeneville, signed in the summer of 1795, under which the defeated tribes would cede 25,000 square miles in present Indiana, Michigan, and Ohio for $20,000 outright and the promise of $10,000 annually, conditional on their behavior toward the expansive republic now firmly established on the west bank of the Ohio. But the president quickly grasped the implications of Fallen Timbers on both sides of the Appalachians—and both sides of the Atlantic.

With this triumph, Wayne handed Washington a key capable of unlocking the northwestern frontier to thousands of land-hungry American settlers *and* of imprisoning the rebels in Pennsylvania who were trying to dissolve the ligaments of republican government. If the decisive victory did not render Washington's invasion of rebel country anticlimactic, it dramatically shifted the psychological odds against David Bradford and his supporters. Like Wayne, Washington had won his campaign before ever firing a shot. For months he had restrained his urge to smash the rebels militarily. He had skillfully maneuvered public opinion until it crystallized behind tough action and nerved reluctant warriors like Thomas Mifflin. Merely by appearing in the inflamed region, Washington's peace commissioners had enhanced the administration's credibility and exposed radical elements hoping to contest federal might on the field of battle. The resulting split between moderates of Albert Gallatin's stripe and militants itching for blood was skillfully exploited by Washington's advisers. So were scattered (and grossly exaggerated) reports of rebel atrocities.

As the fog cleared around the chief protagonists, ordinary men and women came to realize with the force of revelation that what they confronted was no longer simply a question of internal taxation, noxious since colonial days. As important as the principles being contended for were the rival personalities who had come to symbolize order versus disorder. By the beginning of October 1794, Americans were being asked to choose between George Washington and David Bradford.

The first part of Washington's western march took him through the rich agricultural country between Philadelphia and Harrisburg. In this prosperous region, heavily populated by German immigrants, the president admired a profusion of Lutheran churches, neat stone barns, and orderly fields. He observed abundant rockfish in the rivers and "a fish which they call salmon." On the morning of October 4, driving his own coach, he forded the Susquehanna at a point where it stretched three quarters of a mile from shore to shore. The only confrontation that day pitted the militias of Pennsylvania and New Jersey against each other for the honor of welcoming the chief executive to Carlisle. By leaving town two hours before dawn, the Philadelphia Light Horse took the prize.

Word of Washington's arrival filtered quickly through the ranks. "The horse marched down the road about two miles," one who was there remembered, "followed by the Jersey cavalry in great numbers. We were drawn up on the right of the road, when our beloved Washington approached on horseback in a traveling dress, attended by his secretary, etc. As he passed our troop, he pulled off his hat and in the most respectful manner bowed to the officers and men." A swelling train of admirers accompanied him into Carlisle, whose streets were clogged with soldiers struck dumb by his presence. Said an onlooker, "Every heart expands with joy except the whiskey boys." Looking out over 3,000 men and sixteen guns, the president declared it the most respectable army he had ever seen. At dinner that night he offered a confident toast: "A happy issue to the business before us."

His optimism was well placed. At Presbyterian services the next morning, the eminent visitor heard "a Political sermon" against the insurrection. On the subject of drunken army officers and mutinous enlisted men the loyal preacher was less outspoken. Yet the so-called Watermelon Army hastily assembled to put down an even more ragtag force reflected society's divisions as much as its collective will. Aristocratic regulars made no secret of their disdain for impoverished or foreign-born volunteers of questionable sentiments and unappeasable hunger. Green soldiers might uncover in the presence of Great Washington, but an hour later they were likely to be foraging for chickens and chopping up fences for firewood.

Washington planned on accompanying this motley army as far as Bedford, there to choose between continuing with them over the mountains or returning to Philadelphia for the reconvening of Congress. Until then, the War Department was advised to send only such articles as were "absolutely necessary" for the president's table, including beef and bread supplied by army contractors. Since Washington was about to enter whiskey country, Bart Dandridge reported, "he proposes to make use of that liquor for his drink." At sixty-two, the fabled equestrian could no longer spend a full day in the saddle and so covered most of Pennsylvania's roads in his carriage. Undiminished, however, was Washington's hold over his fellow citizens. Thousands of Carlisle's residents cheered a courthouse transparency proclaiming WASHINGTON IS EVER TRIUMPHANT. A second banner conveyed local viewpoints held with equal fervor. THE REIGN OF THE LAWS, it read on one side, WOE TO ANARCHISTS on the other.

No anarchists being present, on the morning of October 7, Washington met with the next best thing when two emissaries from the rebel camp presented themselves. Congressman William Findlay was a Republican originally from Ireland, now living in Westmoreland County; his countryman David Redick was a lawyer in Washington County and the former vice president of Pennsylvania. Washington listened carefully as the men described a mass conversion taking place among their constituents. Civil authority was reestablishing itself throughout the region around Pittsburgh, Findlay insisted, although only after a tense period during which friends of the government had slept with firearms at their side. Just as fever animates a sick man, giving him a false sense of strength, so few among the insurgents had actually believed a federal army would take the field against them. Once Bradford's allies recognized their miscalculation, arrogance gave way to terror.

Fearing that a vengeful army might punish residents inclined to accept the administration's offer of amnesty, Findlay and Redick requested time for the moderates to regain firm control of the situation. Washington promised to hold those arrayed under the federal banner strictly accountable to the laws they enforced. Any soldier disobeying orders or taking reprisal against civilians would "be discharged with infamy." Toward the rebellion itself, however, the president was firm. Too much money and effort had been invested for anything "short of the most unequivocal proofs of absolute submission" to forestall the armed columns from moving west.

Before leaving Carlisle on October 12, Washington entrusted command of the army to Lighthorse Harry Lee. Governor Mifflin received second place, despite his questionable politics and alcoholic buffoonery, while behind him ranked New Jersey's governor Richard Howell, whose musical talents had produced a rousing anthem sung in recruiting offices and in the rain-lashed hollows of western Pennsylvania:

> To arms once more our hero cries
> Sedition lives and order dies,
> To peace and ease then bid adieu,
> And dash to the mountains, Jersey Blue.

One did not have to wear a uniform to pick up the song's infectious spirit. On the night of October 13, lights blazed in every window in Williamsport in honor of the visiting chief executive. Crossing into Virginia the next day, Washington paused at the warm springs to which, nearly forty years earlier, he had taken his dying half-brother Lawrence. The roads deteriorated as the presidential party neared Cumberland, the assembly point for the militia of Virginia and Maryland. Swelling the population were 3,200 men in uniform, among them Major George Lewis, one of five Washington nephews in the federal army. Eight hours away by carriage lay Bradford, the common destination for volunteers from New Jersey and Pennsylvania. Here fresh units of artillery, horse, and infantry were lined up for official review. Following a conference on the morning of the twentieth, Washington gave orders for the entire force, 13,000 strong, to begin a final march within seventy-two hours.

He would not go with them, for political battles in Philadelphia now claimed his attention. In a farewell address, he praised the men for their patriotic zeal and unselfish devotion to constitutional government. But he also reminded them of their ultimate duty "to support the laws." It would be a gross violation of trust, he said, for any soldier to disregard that which he was sworn to protect. "The essential principles of a free government confine the provinces of the military to these two objects: 1st to combat and subdue all who may be found in arms in opposition to the national will and authority; 2nd to aid and support the civil magistrate in bringing offenders to justice. The dispensation of this justice belongs to the civil magistrate and let it ever be our pride and our glory to leave the sacred deposit there unviolated."

Early on the twenty-first, Washington climbed into his carriage, leaving Hamilton behind to tie up loose ends. Ahead stretched a week's journey through the glorious plumage of autumn and long hours in which to ponder the origins and lessons of the rebellion so thoroughly crushed. Washington arrived home on the twenty-eighth, still searching for the right words with which to impress Americans of their narrow escape.

His recent triumph in the field did not incline the president to magnanimity. To Hamilton, still chasing a phantom army in remote hamlets like Jones's Mill and Budd's Ferry, he expressed a desire to send Bradford and other ringleaders to Philadelphia for the winter "by Hook or by Crook." Although Bradford managed to escape to

Louisiana, Hamilton rounded up 150 scruffy prisoners and trotted them across the frozen mud of western Pennsylvania. Falling temperatures, inadequate provisions, and taunts from their captors provided a grim escort, as did a victorious general who vowed to chop off the head of any other rascal attempting escape.

The capital was spared the grisly spectacle so familiar to Parisians, but 20,000 Philadelphians turned out anyway to jeer a wretched handful of insurgents who marched through the city with paper cockades in their hats and chains on their ankles. Official juries proved more lenient than the self-appointed judges of the street, acquitting all but two of the accused men, whom Washington later pardoned as mental defectives. Even so, the president approached his forthcoming speech to Congress in a score-settling mood. The more he brooded, the more he convinced himself that the Democratic Societies had seriously miscalculated in provoking the abortive uprising. While the rebels may have changed their language, he told Jay, "their principles want correction," and he intended to set them straight when he addressed Congress.

More than revenge guided his pen. Washington knew that quite apart from its impact on domestic politics, the rebellion had international repercussions—on Jay's mission and Pinckney's looming talks with the Spaniards over western access to the Mississippi. The slightest hint of American disunity would make the work of these diplomats all the more difficult. Better to tell his own story in his own words, Washington concluded, "than to let it go naked into the world, to be dressed up according to the fancy or inclination of the readers, or the policy of our enemies."

On November 19, Philadelphians expecting a dramatic performance packed the House of Representatives. Washington did not disappoint his audience. After sketching the history of the original excise act, the steps taken to enforce it, and the violent opposition they had aroused, the president lashed out at "certain self-created societies," an obvious reference to the Pennsylvania Democratic Society and its ill-mannered offspring. Most Americans had accepted the tax, however grudgingly. But a few counties in western Pennsylvania had combined to frustrate its collection. Disgruntled agrarians had openly defied the law, detained a federal marshal behind bars, and destroyed the property of a revenue collector. Unwilling to temporize with incipient anarchy, the administration had sought and won judicial sanction to move forcibly against the rioters.

The decision to use force against other Americans had not been an easy one. "On this call, momentous in the extreme, I sought and weighed what might best subdue the crisis," said Washington. "On the one hand, the judiciary was pronounced to be stripped of its capacity to enforce the laws; crimes, which reached the very existence of social order, were perpetrated without control; the friends of government were insulted, abused, and overawed into silence." Yielding to such behavior "would be to violate the fundamental principle of our constitution, which enjoins that the will of the majority shall prevail."

Reluctant to incur the embarrassment of a revolutionary government marching to snuff out a rebellion by its own people, the president had postponed hasty action. Commissioners had been sent into the troubled area offering pardons on no other condition than satisfactory assurances that the laws would be obeyed. But "the vicious and turbulent" had spurned his offer, leaving Washington no choice but to summon an army to protect law-abiding citizens and punish miscreants. The subsequent outpouring of volunteers convinced him beyond doubt "that my fellow citizens understand the true principles of government and liberty; that they feel their inseparable union; that notwithstanding all the devices which have been used to sway them from their interest and duty, they are now as ready to maintain the authority of the laws against licentious invasions, as they were to defend their rights against usurpation."

He would not soon forget, said Washington, the exhilarating sight of Americans from all classes serving side by side in "the army of the constitution," undeterred by jagged mountains, country roads that were little more than icy gashes in the steep terrain, and unceasingly hostile weather. He contrasted the instinctive patriotism of the enlisted man with that of the guileful Westerners, who had set themselves up, like a modern Caesar's Legion, in opposition to the people's elected representatives. "And when in the calm moments of reflection, they shall have retraced the origin and progress of the insurrection," the president said of his countrymen, "let them determine whether it has not been fomented by combinations of men who, careless of consequences and disregarding the unerring truth—that those who rouse, cannot always appease a civil convulsion—have disseminated . . . suspicions, jealousies, and accusations of the whole government."

Washington's audience sat immobilized, the stillness in the crowded chamber broken only by muffled sounds of weeping from the galleries. In weathering the challenge, he had fulfilled his sacred oath to preserve, protect, and defend the Constitution. Now he proclaimed, with undisguised emotion, that "on you, Gentleman, and the people by whom you are deputed, I rely for support."

Among the opposition members in Congress Hall were many who squirmed in embarrassment for the aging hero. Could he really be so out of touch with popular sentiments? Had the sound of cheering crowds dulled his instincts or drowned out the distress cries of peaceably assembled farmers? Madison declared Washington's unbridled attack on the Democratic Societies the greatest political blunder of his life. More perceptively, he reminded lawmakers that "the censorial power is in the people over the government and not in the government over the people."

A fierce debate erupted over the House's official response to the executive. Republicans, half defiant, half apologetic, moved to repudiate the most extreme of Washington's claims by striking out the inflammatory phrase "self-created societies." Tempers flared as Madison's allies identified numerous such organizations flourishing in the United States. There were the Sons of Tammany, they reminded anyone who would listen, and the Society of Friends; even that prideful bastion of old soldiers whose taste for rank mirrored the titled society against which they had fought and won a revolution, the Society of the Cincinnati. Moreover, said William Branch Giles, with a sly dig at the aristocratic Senate meeting upstairs, if the chief offense of the Democratic Societies was that "they began their business after dinner, bolted their doors and voted in the dark . . . is there no other place where people bolt their doors and vote in the dark?"

Washington's speech and its stormy sequel strained old friendships. Thomas Jefferson, for one, was moved to personal condemnation. Already recorded in opposition to the administration's military campaign ("An insurrection was announced and proclaimed and armed against, but could never be found"), the great champion of free speech and free thought apprehended in Washington's strident words confirmation of his worst fears—the monocrats had at last captured the president. What a tragedy, thought Jefferson, that George Washington, the symbol of man's age-old desire to taste the fruits of liberty, should now permit himself to become an instrument in the suppression of basic rights to discuss and dissent and publish.

In this, Jefferson misread his former chief, although no more than Washington himself underestimated the chilling effect of his emotionally charged sentences. As the president saw it, nothing less was at stake than the survival of a central government strong enough to defend the republican system adopted in 1787 and since confirmed by the voting public. While others formed ranks around party standards or economic systems or European alliances, Washington planted his banner where he had always stood, upon a Constitution whose delicate balance was threatened by the ancient enemies of republics, domestic factionalism and foreign influence.

The House was just as resolute in its opposition. Ten days later, Washington listened politely as Speaker Frederick Muhlenberg delivered a mild rebuke in the parlor of 190 Market Street. Pointedly missing from his comments was any mention of "self-created societies," the deleted catchphrase. A far more welcome sound lured Washington from his desk on a frosty December afternoon when the shrill fifes of a company of Jersey Blues led by Major William MacPherson marched into Philadelphia for an impromptu homecoming parade. The president reviewed the column from his doorstep with unconcealed pride. A reporter observing the scene wrote that "the father of his country expressed in his countenance more than can be described." The look on his face was answer enough to Washington's growing body of critics.

from Polk and the Presidency

by Charles A. McCoy

James K. Polk (in office 1845–1849) campaigned for the presidency on an expansionist platform. His views appealed to the many Americans who believed in Manifest Destiny—the idea that the U.S. had a divine right to become a transcontinental nation. Historian Charles A. McCoy (born 1920) describes Polk's efforts to expand the nation beyond the borders of the Louisiana Purchase.

On March 4, 1845, when Polk assumed the duties of President of the United States, he was faced with a rapidly deteriorating relationship with the Republic of Mexico. Relations between the two nations had been strained for a number of years, in fact, ever since the United States had recognized the Republic of Texas as an independent nation. Another almost equally thorny issue was the matter of claims of United States citizens against the Mexican Republic which Mexico, although recognizing the validity of the claims, had been unable to pay. Mexico, furthermore, had repeatedly warned that the annexation of Texas by the United States would be regarded as a warlike act. When President Tyler, two days before his term of office ended, signed the joint resolution of annexation, Mexico broke off all diplomatic relations with the United States. Of even greater concern to Mexico than the annexation of Texas was the claim by Texas that its boundary, which as a province of Mexico had never extended beyond the river Nueces, now extended all the way to the Rio Grande.

If the United States were to insist upon this boundary, then in addition to the loss of Texas, which after all had had an independent existence from Mexico for nine years, Mexico stood to lose still further territory. It is with this background that the new President took over the task of directing the nation's foreign policy toward Mexico.

Our relations with Mexico during the Polk Administration can be subdivided into two distinct phases. During the first phase, lasting less than a year, Polk endeavored, by a mixture of diplomacy and force, to secure for the United States the additional territory of New Mexico and California. The second phase can be identified with the existence of war between the two nations. Its object was to bring about a peace without losing the ultimate goal of adding California and New Mexico to our nation. The attempts to secure peace took some unusual turns, including the negotiations with the exiled Santa Anna, negotiations which certainly had the net result of prolonging rather than shortening the war, and the Gilbert-and-Sullivan-like Trist mission, which in spite of its peculiar circumstances did produce the desired settlement in the Treaty of Guadalupe Hidalgo.

The joint resolution which provided for the annexation of Texas gave Polk the opportunity which he sought, as the resolution left to the President the task of adjusting the ultimate boundary of Texas. Using this as a wedge, the President hoped to be able to purchase the territory of California and New Mexico from Mexico. His desire to commence such negotiations was hampered by the fact that diplomatic relations had been broken off between Mexico and the United States during the last days of the Tyler Administration, when Tyler had signed the joint resolution for the annexation of Texas. Polk, however, wasted no time. The same ship which bore the Mexican minister back to his country carried a secret agent of the United States with instructions to convince the Mexican officials that the United States, though determined on the reunion of Texas, was desirous of friendly relations. The secret agent was to determine whether the Mexican government was willing to receive an envoy from the United States. Finally, on August 26, Parrot, the secret agent, wrote to Buchanan that he thought Mexico ready to receive an envoy and added, "An Envoy possessing suitable qualifications for this Court might with comparative ease settle *over a breakfast* the most important national question. . . ." Upon receipt of this message on September 16, Polk called his Cabinet together and disclosed to them the objective of his planned Mexican negotiations:

> One great object of the Mission, as stated by the President, would be to adjust a permanent boundary between Mexico and the U. States, and that in doing this the Minister would be instructed to purchase for a pecuniary consideration Upper California and New Mexico . . . The President said that for such a boundary the amt. of pecuniary consideration to be paid would be of small importance. He supposed it might be had for fifteen or twenty millions, but he was ready to pay forty millions for it, if he could not be had for less.

Acting upon the advice of his secret agent, Polk prepared to send a minister to Mexico, selecting Mr. Slidell for the task. Polk's instructions to Slidell were to remain as the official position of the Administration toward Mexico throughout the negotiations. The same demands were included in the instructions sent with Trist a year and a half later. Slidell was to negotiate for New Mexico and California, using the claims of American citizens against Mexico, which Mexico had previously recognized as valid, as a bargaining tool. Slidell was authorized to state that the United States would assume liability for the claims and pay in addition twenty-five million dollars for California.

Polk's expectation that Mexico was willing to receive a minister from the United States was not fulfilled because, for the existing government in Mexico, to do so would be tantamount to acknowledging that its threats about war—if Texas were annexed—were only empty gestures. Mexico's refusal to negotiate was used as justification by the President to deploy his military forces so as to occupy the country in dispute between the Nueces and the Rio Grande. Slidell remained in

Mexico from November, 1845, until the following spring in the hope that he might eventually be received, but in spite of a revolution in Mexico and a change in administration Slidell was never received by the Mexican Government. On the eighth of April, 1846, the President received the final news that Slidell had asked for his passport and was returning to Washington.

From that time on Polk was determined to gain by force what he had failed to win by negotiations. On May 9, 1846, the Cabinet met to consider sending a message to Congress asking for a declaration of war. The President said, "that in my opinion we had ample cause of war, and that it was impossible that we could stand in *status quo*, or that I could remain silent much longer. . . ." Four hours after the Cabinet meeting adjourned the President received the long-awaited message from General Taylor that the Mexican forces had attacked, an event which Reeves characterized most aptly as "one of those strange happenings that result in the concealment of man's real motives."

On the thirteenth of May, 1846, the day Congress declared war on Mexico, Polk held a meeting with his Cabinet which he described thus: "The discussion to-night was one of the most earnest & interesting which has ever occurred in my Cabinet." The substance of this discussion was a proposal by Buchanan that the French and British governments be advised that the United States had no territorial designs upon Mexico. Polk countered by saying: "though we had not gone to war for conquest, yet it was clear that in making peace we would if practicable obtain California and such other portions of the Mexican territory as would be sufficient to indemnify our claimants on Mexico, and to defray the expenses of the war which that power by her long continued wrongs and injuries had forced us to wage." Buchanan replied that to follow such a course would surely involve us in a war against both France and England and would prevent the settlement of the Oregon boundary dispute. Polk responded with righteous indignation: "I told him that before I would make the pledge which he proposed, I would meet the war which either England or France or all the Powers of Christendom might wage, and that I would stand and fight until the last man among us fell in the conflict. I told him that neither as a citizen nor as President would I permit or tolerate any intermeddling of any European Power on this Continent."

The President eventually closed the discussion, which had lasted for more than two hours, by going to his writing desk and drafting a substitute, which he instructed Buchanan to use in his dispatch in place of Buchanan's own message.

The subject of war aims lay dormant for about a month, but on the thirtieth of June Buchanan once again returned to the subject. This time in a heated exchange with the Secretary of the Treasury, Walker, Buchanan maintained that the United States must renounce any territorial claims or win the animosity of the world. Polk, after listening to the heated exchange between his two Cabinet members, stated that as a minimum "we must obtain Upper California and New Mexico in any Treaty of Peace we would make," a position constantly maintained throughout the war.

Polk's efforts to negotiate a peace continued throughout the war, and this desire to terminate hostilities as soon as possible led him into one of the most unusual affairs in our nation's history. As early as February 13, 1846, three months prior to the declaration of war, Polk had a conversation with Colonel Atocha, a confidant of the exiled Mexican leader Santa Anna. Colonel Atocha stated that Santa Anna, if only he were in control in Mexico, would be willing to settle all boundary questions between the United States and Mexico for a sum of thirty million dollars. He went on to say that only through a show of force would it be possible to persuade Mexico to settle the boundary question. That this conversation had a decided effect upon the President is indicated by the fact that he discussed the meeting with his entire Cabinet on the next day and decided to adopt a firmer policy toward the Mexican Government. On the day that Congress recognized that a state of war existed between Mexico and the United States, orders were issued to the American naval commander in the Gulf not to obstruct the passage of Santa Anna from his exile in Cuba back to Mexico. These instructions were followed by the dispatching of a personal representative, Alexander

Slidell McKenzie, a naval officer, to confer with Santa Anna in Cuba. Santa Anna impressed McKenzie with his desires for peace and with his willingness to settle on terms agreeable to the United States, and in return McKenzie informed Santa Anna of the arrangements which had been made to pass the Mexican General through the American blockade.

Santa Anna accepted the opportunity and arrived in Veracruz early in August, where he received a hero's welcome; by the middle of August he was in control of the entire country. Buchanan immediately made an overture to begin the peace negotiation which General Santa Anna just as promptly refused. The net result of these unusual negotiations was to provide the Mexicans with their ablest military commander and to prolong the war for an indefinite period.

In most constitutional matters President Polk was a strict constructionist. Regarding the collection of duties in Mexico, however, Polk adopted a broad constructionist view. He insisted that the Army collect import duties on all goods shipped to the ports of Mexico which were under United States' control. The revenue from such duties was to be used to defray the expenses of the war. In this manner the President, without authorization from Congress, established a system of duties and expended the monies collected in that manner for the prosecution of the war. He justified his action as follows:

> . . . that such duties should be collected, as a condition upon which foreign commerce as well as commerce from our own country should be admitted at such ports as were in our military possession. The imposition of such duties results as one of the incidents of war belonging to the conqueror of a town or province. They are not to be imposed under our constitution and laws, but under the power which belongs to a belligerent over a conquered town or place.

This justification certainly provides the President with an ample degree of latitude in dealing with a conquered nation or territory and admits of no legal or constitutional restrictions whatever. In the area of foreign relations, Polk evidently subscribed to a doctrine of "inherent powers."

In the spring of 1847, the President began considering the desirability of assigning to the army in Mexico someone with authority to negotiate a treaty should the Mexicans be willing to do so. The President, with his usual political adroitness, felt that it would be best to appoint a commissioner who, if the mission should prove successful, would not be able to make too much political capital out of his success. He recorded in his diary: "The embarrassment in carrying it out consisted in the selection of a suitable commissioner . . . who would be satisfactory to the country. This was a great difficulty. Such is the jealousy of the different factions of the Democratic party in reference to the next Presidential Election towards each other that it is impossible to appoint any prominent man. . . ." It was for this reason that Polk turned to Nicholas P. Trist, chief clerk in the Department of State. Trist had a long record as a reliable Democrat. He had married Jefferson's granddaughter, studied law under his tutelage, been named an executor of Jefferson's will, and much later had been a secretary to Andrew Jackson. Certainly this was a record to satisfy the most partisan Democrat; and in addition Trist brought to the task a knowledge of Spanish.

After being instructed with the intent of his mission and the necessity for the utmost secrecy, Trist departed for Mexico. Within a week after his departure difficulties began to beset the mission. The press had learned of the secret mission. Polk suspected everyone and although the leak of news to the press did not directly affect the success of the mission it did serve as a basis for the breakdown of confidence between the President and his emissary.

The difficult circumstances under which the mission had begun soon grew worse. Almost immediately after Trist's arrival in Mexico a complete rift in relations between General Scott and Trist occurred. In fact, for weeks the two men never met but carried on an acrimonious campaign of letters. Finally, in the first week of July, after a lapse of over two months, Scott and Trist met for the first time and as suddenly as the quarrel had begun it ended and they became the strongest of friends. Polk, during this period, became more and more exasperated at both men. In August, Trist met with the Mexican commissioners to discuss peace terms, but it soon became apparent that Mexico was unwilling at that time to sign a treaty which would extend the boundaries of Mexico from the river Nueces to the Rio Grande. Trist's instructions had made the boundary line of the Rio Grande *sine qua non* on any settlement. Therefore, when Trist agreed to submit the Mexican proposal for the Texas boundary to Washington, Polk decided that he had exceeded his usefulness as well as his authority, and ordered him recalled.

Buchanan, in advising Trist of his recall, left the door ajar just a bit to further negotiations by adding in his letter that if he, Trist, had a treaty written when he received his notice of recall he might bring the treaty back with him. Buchanan followed this official letter with a personal one which assured Trist of Buchanan's kind personal regard and said, too, that the Secretary of State wanted him again in the Department. What Buchanan and Polk did not know was that while they were dismissing Trist as a negotiator, Mexico City had fallen and the fighting was all but over.

Trist, after some hesitancy, decided to ignore the order of recall and remain in Mexico City and negotiate a peace if that were at all possible. Perhaps he was encouraged by the tone of Buchanan's personal letter and by the knowledge that Polk had once expressed a willingness to accept a treaty even if it were negotiated by an American newspaper man in Mexico.

This unusual event—an American newspaper reporter negotiating a peace treaty—occurred at the time Buchanan was preparing the instructions for the Trist mission, and it is quite probable that Trist had knowledge of the situation. The facts were that in April, 1847, Buchanan read to Polk a letter which he had received from Moses Beech of the New York *Sun*. The letter was written in Mexico City and indicated that the Mexicans were ready to sign a treaty and that he, the newspaper reporter, would negotiate it. The reporter had been made a secret agent of the American Government but was not given any diplomatic power. Polk's reaction to this information was as follows:

> It is clearly to be inferred from his letter that he will make a Treaty with them if he can. Should he do so, and it is a good one, I will waive his authority to make it, and submit it to the Senate for ratification. It will be a good joke if he should assume the authority and take the whole country by surprise & make a Treaty. Mr. Buchanan's strong impression is that he may do so.

Whether it was Trist's knowledge of the reporter-peace-treaty incident or Buchanan's encouraging letter, or perhaps both, that decided Trist to remain in Mexico is uncertain. Trist, of course, gave his own reasons for disobeying the order of recall. He felt that his action was justified by his belief in four contingencies: (1) that his government still desired peace, (2) that time was of the utmost importance, (3) that Mexico would not surrender any more territory beyond the boundary which his original instructions had called for, and (4) that the President had ordered his recall through a lack of awareness of the situation.

The President, quite naturally, became very indignant upon hearing of Trist's decision to remain in Mexico and negotiate a treaty in spite of his order of recall. Polk expressed his amazement and indignation in no uncertain terms:

> His [Trist's] despatch [*sic*] is arrogant, impudent, and very insulting to his Government, and even personally offensive to the President. He admits he is acting without authority and in violation of the positive order recalling him. . . . He has acted worse than any man in the public employ whom I have ever known. His despatch [*sic*] proves that he is destitute of honour or principle, and that he has proved himself to be a very base man. I was deceived in him.

• • •

Yet in spite of these strong terms the President less than a fortnight later stated that he would not automatically reject a treaty submitted by Mr. Trist, but would decide that question only after seeing the treaty.

This debate over whether a treaty signed by Trist could or should be accepted continued in the Cabinet until the treaty of Guadalupe Hidalgo was received in Washington on February 20, 1848. By that time the lines in the Cabinet were clearly drawn, with Buchanan and Walker opposing the treaty—both advocated seizing more Mexican territory—and Marcy, Mason, Johnson, and Clifford favoring the treaty. Polk, in his third annual message to Congress, had expressed himself as opposed to seizing all of Mexico: "It has never been contemplated by me, as an object of the war, to make a permanent conquest of the Republic of Mexico or to annihilate her separate existence as an independent nation. On the contrary, it has ever been my desire that she should maintain her nationality, and under a good government adapted to her condition be a free, independent, and prosperous Republic."

Polk, however, did not commit himself on the treaty on the day it arrived, but summoned his Cabinet together again on the next day. He then informed them of his decision to submit the treaty to the Senate. He stated his reasons for his decision as follows:

> I assigned my reasons for my decision. They were, briefly, that the treaty conformed on the main question of limits & boundary to the instructions given to Mr. Trist in April last; and that though, if the treaty was now to be made, I should demand more territory, . . . yet it was doubtful whether this could ever be obtained by the consent of Mexico. I looked, too, to the consequences of its rejection. A majority of one branch of Congress is opposed to my administration; they have falsely charged that the war was brought on and is continued by me with a view to the conquest of Mexico; and if I were now to reject a Treaty made upon my own terms, as authorized in April last, with the unanimous

> approbation of the Cabinet, the probability is that Congress would not grant either men or money to prosecute the war. Should this be the result, the army now in Mexico would be constantly wasting and diminishing in numbers, and I might at last be compelled to withdraw them, and thus loose [*sic*] the two Provinces of New Mexico & Upper California, which were ceded to the U.S. by this Treaty. Should the opponents of my administration succeed in carrying the next Presidential election the great probability is that the country would loose [*sic*] all the advantages secured by this Treaty. I adverted to the immense value of Upper California; and concluded by saying that if I were now to reject my own terms, as offered in April last, I did not see how it was possible for my administration to be sustained.

After the President concluded his statement, Secretary of State Buchanan took issue with him, and remarked that the United States ought to reject the treaty in favor of securing a settlement which would give the United States greater territory. Polk reminded Buchanan of his previous stands in which he, Buchanan, had urged the necessity of the President's making a declaration to the countries of the world that the United States had no intention of securing any territorial concessions from Mexico. Buchanan acknowledged that he had so advised but stated that he had now changed his opinion. Polk took accurate measure of Buchanan's motives and recorded in his diary the following:

> My conversation with Mr. Buchanan was unpleasant to me, but I thought I ought to rebuke him, and let him understand that I understood the motive that governed him. He wished to throw the whole responsibility on me of sending the Treaty to the Senate. If it was well received by the country, being a member of my administration, he would not be injured by it in his Presidential aspirations, for these

> govern all his opinions & acts lately; but if, on the other hand, it should not be received well, he could say, "I advised against it."

Two days after this tempestuous Cabinet meeting on February 23, President Polk sent the treaty to the Senate for ratification. From the twenty-third of February to the tenth of March Polk made comments daily in his diary on the progress of the treaty, generally to the effect that its acceptance by the Senate seemed very doubtful. He often recorded having spoken with various senators to urge them to support the treaty. When the chairman of the Committee on Foreign Relations called to inform the President that, although the Committee approved of the substance of the treaty, they were going to recommend that it be rejected because it was drafted by Mr. Trist after his recall, Polk informed the chairman, Senator Sevier of Arkansas, that he strongly disapproved that action. Polk wisely observed that the treaty might be defeated by the union of two opposing forces: those who did not want the United States to gain any territory and those who wanted the United States to take over the whole of Mexico. He stated the axiom that "Extremes sometimes meet and act effectively for negative purposes, but never for affirmative purposes." But, as the days passed and the President continued to count the number of votes which he felt the opposition might get, he gradually became more confident that the treaty would be ratified. He felt that perhaps eight, ten, or even as many as twelve Democrats might oppose the treaty and that they might be joined by as many as six or eight Whigs. With only nineteen opposing senators necessary for defeat of the measure, it is possible to understand his great concern. On the tenth of March, Polk received the news that the treaty had been ratified by a vote of 38 to 14 with four senators not voting.

Polk capped this victory when he was able to persuade the chairman of the Senate Foreign Relations Committee to resign from the Senate and take the treaty to Mexico to secure that nation's ratification. It is a measure of the importance he attached to the successful conclusion of this treaty that, when Senator Sevier became ill and could not depart for

Mexico immediately, Polk persuaded his Attorney General, Mr. Clifford, to resign his Cabinet post and take the treaty to Mexico.

The commissioners did their work well and on June 9, 1848, Polk learned that Mexico had ratified the treaty on May 25. Peaceful relations with Mexico were once more established and the President had realized his dream of adding the territory of New Mexico and California to the domain of the United States. He had remained faithful to this end throughout the long negotiations with Mexico. First, he had seized upon the wording of the joint resolution annexing Texas, which had provided that the boundary difficulties between the two Republics be settled by negotiations, and had sent an emissary, Mr. Slidell, to Mexico with but one purpose in mind, the purchase of California and New Mexico. Secondly, when the Slidell mission failed and war came, Polk still attempted to find a way to achieve his goal, and the abortive scheme with Santa Anna, which brought that Mexican leader from exile in Cuba to control in Mexico, was entered into with the single purpose of securing California and New Mexico. Finally, when presented with a treaty which had been negotiated by the discredited and recalled envoy, Mr. Trist, Polk accepted it and sent it to the Senate, in spite of the opposition of members of his own Cabinet, including his Secretary of State. When the treaty ran into opposition in the Senate he stood firm and worked hard for its acceptance, and after it was ratified he used his persuasive powers to have both the chairman of the Senate's Committee of Foreign Relations and his own Attorney General resign their posts to take the treaty to Mexico so that they might insure that the treaty would be accepted by the Mexican Government. With the territory gained under this treaty and that already gained under the Oregon settlement, Polk had added to the United States territory out of which would be formed the states of Oregon, Washington, Idaho, California, New Mexico, Arizona, Nevada, Utah, and parts of Colorado, Montana, and Wyoming. "Who is James K. Polk?" He is the President who, except for Jefferson, brought more territory under our domain than any other President. When he left office, the United States was half again larger than it was when he became President.

The Words That Remade America: Lincoln at Gettysburg

by Garry Wills

Abraham Lincoln's (in office 1861–1865) short talk at the dedication of the Gettysburg battlefield cemetery has endured as one of the most important American speeches. Garry Wills (born 1934) sees the speech as a watershed in our history. He analyzed Lincoln's address in this article for the June, 1992 issue of The Atlantic Monthly.

In the aftermath of the battle of Gettysburg, both sides, leaving fifty thousand dead or wounded or missing behind them, had reason to maintain a large pattern of pretense—Lee pretending that he was not taking back to the South a broken cause, Meade that he would not let the broken pieces fall through his fingers. It would have been hard to predict that Gettysburg, out of all this muddle, these missed chances, all the senseless deaths, would become a symbol of national purpose, pride, and ideals. Abraham Lincoln transformed the ugly reality into something rich and strange—and he did it with 272 words. The power of words has rarely been given a more compelling demonstration.

The residents of Gettysburg had little reason to be satisfied with the war machine that had churned up their lives. General George Gordon Meade may have pursued General Robert E. Lee in slow motion, but he wired headquarters that "I cannot delay to pick up the debris of the battlefield." That debris was mainly a matter of rotting horseflesh and manflesh—thousands of fermenting bodies, with gas-distended bellies, deliquescing in the July heat. For hygienic reasons, the five thousand horses and mules had to be consumed by fire, trading the smell of decaying flesh for that of burning flesh. Human bodies were scattered over, or (barely) under, the ground. Suffocating teams of Union soldiers, Confederate prisoners, and dragooned civilians slid the bodies beneath a minimal covering as fast as possible—crudely posting the names of the Union dead with sketchy information on boards, not stopping to figure out what units the Confederate bodies had belonged to. It was work to be done hugger-mugger or not at all, fighting clustered bluebottle flies black on the earth, shoveling and retching by turns.

The whole area of Gettysburg—a town of only twenty-five hundred inhabitants—was one makeshift burial ground, fetid and steaming. Andrew Curtin, the Republican governor of Pennsylvania, was facing a difficult reelection campaign. He must placate local feeling, deal with other states diplomatically, and raise the funds to cope with corpses that could go on killing by means of fouled streams or contaminating exhumations.

Curtin made the thirty-two-year-old David Wills, a Gettysburg lawyer, his agent on the scene. Wills (who is no relation to the author) had studied law with Gettysburg's most prominent former citizen, Thaddeus Stevens, the radical Republican now representing Lancaster in Congress. Wills was a civic leader, and he owned the largest house on the town square. He put an end to land speculation for the burial ground and formed an interstate commission to collect funds for the cleansing of Gettysburg's bloodied fields. The states were to be assessed according to their representation in Congress. To charge them by the actual number of each state's dead would have been a time-consuming and complicated process, waiting on identification of each corpse, on the division of costs for those who could not be identified, and on the fixing of per-body rates for exhumation, identification, and reinterment.

Wills put up for bids the contract to rebury the bodies; out of thirty-four bids, the high one was eight dollars per corpse and the winning one was $1.59. The federal government was asked to ship in the thousands of caskets needed, courtesy of the War Department. All other costs were handled by the interstate commission. Wills took title to seventeen acres for the new cemetery in the name of Pennsylvania.

Wills meant to dedicate the ground that would hold the corpses even before they were moved. He felt the need for artful words to sweeten the poisoned air of Gettysburg. He asked the principal wordsmiths of his time to join this effort—Longfellow, Whittier, Bryant. All three poets, each for his own reason, found their muse unbiddable. But Wills was not terribly disappointed. The normal purgative for such occasions was a large-scale, solemn act of oratory, a kind of performance art that had great power over audiences in the middle of the nineteenth century. Some later accounts would emphasize the length of the main speech at the Gettysburg dedication, as if that were an ordeal or an imposition on the audience. But a talk of several hours was customary and expected then—much like the length and pacing of a modern rock concert. The crowds that heard Lincoln debate Stephen Douglas in 1858, through three-hour engagements, were delighted to hear Daniel Webster and other orators of the day recite carefully composed paragraphs for two hours at the least.

The champion at such declamatory occasions, after the death of Daniel Webster, was Webster's friend Edward Everett. Everett was that rare thing, a scholar and an Ivy League diplomat who could hold mass audiences in thrall. His voice, diction, and gestures were successfully dramatic, and he habitually performed his well-crafted text, no matter how long, from memory. Everett was the inevitable choice for Wills, the indispensable component in the scheme for the cemetery's consecration. Battlefields were something of a specialty with Everett—he had augmented the fame of Lexington and Concord and Bunker Hill by his oratory at those Revolutionary sites. Simply to have him speak at Gettysburg would add this field to the sacred roll of names from the Founders' battles.

Everett was invited, on September 23, to appear October 23. That would leave all of November for filling the graves. But a month was not sufficient time for Everett to make his customary preparation for a major speech. He did careful research on the battles he was commemorating—a task made difficult in this case by the fact that official accounts of the engagement were just appearing. Everett would have to make his own inquiries. He could not be ready before November 19. Wills seized on that earliest moment, though it broke with the reburial schedule that had been laid out to follow on the October dedication. He decided to move up the reburial, beginning it in October and hoping to finish by November 19.

The careful negotiations with Everett form a contrast, more surprising to us than to contemporaries, with the casual invitation to President Lincoln, issued some time later as part of a general call for the federal Cabinet and other celebrities to join in what was essentially a ceremony of the participating states.

No insult was intended. Federal responsibility for or participation in state activities was not assumed then. And Lincoln took no offense. Though specifically invited to deliver only "a few appropriate remarks" to open the cemetery, he meant to use this opportunity. The partly mythical victory of Gettysburg was an element of his Administration's war propaganda. (There were, even then, few enough victories to boast of.) Beyond that, he was working to unite the rival Republican factions of Governor Curtin and Simon Cameron, Edwin Stanton's predecessor as Secretary of War. He knew that most of the state governors would be attending or sending important aides—his own bodyguard, Ward Lamon, who was acting as chief marshal organizing the affair, would have alerted him to the scale the event had assumed, with a tremendous crowd expected. This was a classic situation for political fence-mending and intelligence-gathering. Lincoln would take with him aides who would circulate and bring back their findings. Lamon himself had a cluster of friends in Pennsylvania politics, including some close to Curtin, who had been infuriated when Lincoln overrode his opposition to Cameron's Cabinet appointment.

Lincoln also knew the power of his rhetoric to define war aims. He was seeking occasions to use his words outside the normal round of proclamations and reports to Congress. His determination not only to be present but to speak is seen in the way he overrode staff scheduling for the trip to Gettysburg. Stanton had arranged for a 6:00 a.m. train to take him the hundred and twenty rail miles to the noontime affair. But Lincoln was familiar enough by now with military movement to appreciate what Clausewitz called "friction" in the disposal of forces—the margin for error that must always be built into planning. Lamon would have informed Lincoln about the potential for muddle on the nineteenth. State delegations, civic organizations, military bands and units, were planning to come by train and road, bringing at least ten thousand people to a town with poor resources for feeding and sheltering crowds (especially if the weather turned bad). So Lincoln countermanded Stanton's plan:

> I do not like this arrangement. I do not wish to so go that by the slightest accident we fail entirely, and, at the best, the whole to be a mere breathless running of the gauntlet. . . .

If Lincoln had not changed the schedule, he would very likely not have given his talk. Even on the day before, his trip to Gettysburg took six hours, with transfers in Baltimore and at Hanover Junction. Governor Curtin, starting from Harrisburg (thirty miles away) with six other governors as his guests, was embarrassed by breakdowns and delays that made them miss dinner at David Wills's house. They had gathered at 2:00 p.m., started at five, and arrived at eleven. Senator Alexander Ramsey, of Minnesota, was stranded, at 4:00 a.m. on the day of delivery, in Hanover Junction, with "no means of getting up to Gettysburg." Lincoln kept his resolution to leave a day early even when he realized that his wife was hysterical over one son's illness soon after the death of another son. The President had important business in Gettysburg.

For a man so determined to get there, Lincoln seems—in familiar accounts—to have been rather cavalier about preparing what he would say in Gettysburg. The silly but persistent myth is that he jotted his brief remarks on the back of an envelope. (Many details of the day are in fact still disputed, and no definitive account exists.) Better-attested reports have him considering them on the way to a photographer's shop in Washington, writing them on a piece of cardboard as the train took him on the hundred-and-twenty-mile trip, penciling them in David Wills's house on the night before the dedication, writing them in that house on the morning of the day he had to deliver them, and even composing them in his head as Everett spoke, before Lincoln rose to follow him.

These recollections, recorded at various times after the speech had been given and won fame, reflect two concerns on the part of those speaking them. They reveal an understandable pride in participation at the historic occasion. It was not enough for those who treasured their day at Gettysburg to have heard Lincoln speak—a privilege they shared with ten to twenty thousand other people, and an experience that lasted no more than three minutes. They wanted to be intimate with the gestation of that extraordinary speech, watching the pen or pencil move under the inspiration of the moment.

That is the other emphasis in these accounts—that it *was* a product of the moment, struck off as Lincoln moved under destiny's guidance. Inspiration was shed on him in the presence of others. The contrast with Everett's long labors of preparation is always implied. Research, learning, the student's lamp—none of these were needed by Lincoln, whose unsummoned muse was prompting him, a democratic muse unacquainted with the library. Lightning struck, and each of our informants (or their sources) was there when it struck.

The trouble with these accounts is that the lightning strikes too often, as if it could not get the work done on its first attempt. It hits Lincoln on the train, in his room, at night, in the morning. If inspiration was treating him this way, he should have been short-circuited, not inspired, by the time he spoke.

These mythical accounts are badly out of character for Lincoln, who composed his speeches thoughtfully. His law partner, William

Herndon, having observed Lincoln's careful preparation of cases, recorded that he was a slow writer, who liked to sort out his points and tighten his logic and his phrasing. That is the process vouched for in every other case of Lincoln's memorable public statements. It is impossible to imagine him leaving his Gettysburg speech to the last moment. He knew he would be busy on the train and at the site—important political guests were with him from his departure, and more joined him at Baltimore, full of talk about the war, elections, and policy. In Gettysburg he would be entertained at David Wills's house, with Everett and other important guests. State delegations would want a word with him. He hoped for a quick tour of the battle site (a hope fulfilled early on the nineteenth). He could not count on any time for the concentration he required when weighing his words.

In fact, at least two people testified that the speech was mainly composed in Washington, before Lincoln left for Gettysburg—though these reports, like all later ones describing this speech's composition, are themselves suspect. Lamon claimed that a day or two before the dedication Lincoln read him substantially the text that was delivered. But Lamon's remarks are notoriously imaginative, and he was busy in Gettysburg from November 13 to 16. He made a swift trip back to Washington on the sixteenth to collect his marshals and instruct them before departing again the next morning. His testimony here, as elsewhere, does not have much weight.

Noah Brooks, Lincoln's journalist friend, claimed that he talked with Lincoln on November 15, when Lincoln told him he had written his speech "over, two or three times"—but Brooks also said that Lincoln had with him galleys of Everett's speech, which had been set in type for later printing by the Boston *Journal.* In fact the Everett speech was not set until November 14, and then by the Boston *Daily Advertiser*. It is unlikely that a copy could have reached Lincoln so early.

Lincoln's train arrived toward dusk in Gettysburg. There were still coffins stacked at the station for completing the reburials. Lamon,

Wills, and Everett met Lincoln and escorted him the two blocks to the Wills home, where dinner was waiting, along with almost two dozen other distinguished guests. Lincoln's black servant, William Slade, took his luggage to the second-story room where he would stay that night, which looked out on the square.

Everett was already in residence at the Wills house, and Governor Curtin's late arrival led Wills to suggest that the two men share a bed. The governor thought he could find another house to receive him, though lodgings were so overcrowded that Everett said in his diary that "the fear of having the Executive of Pennsylvania tumbled in upon me kept me awake until one." Everett's daughter was sleeping with two other women, and the bed broke under their weight. William Saunders, the cemetery's designer, who would have an honored place on the platform the next day, could find no bed and had to sleep sitting up in a crowded parlor.

It is likely that Everett, who had the galleys of his speech with him, showed them to Lincoln that night. Noah Brooks, who mistook the *time* when Everett showed Lincoln his speech, probably gave the right *reason*—so that Lincoln would not be embarrassed by any inadvertent correspondences or unintended differences.

Lincoln greeted Curtin after his late arrival, and was otherwise interrupted during the night. Bands and serenades were going through the crowded square under his window. One group asked him to speak, and the newspaper reported his words:

> I appear before you, fellow-citizens, merely to thank you for this compliment. The inference is a very fair one that you would hear me for a little while at least, were I to commence to make a speech. I do not appear before you for the purpose of doing so, and for several substantial reasons. The most substantial of these is that I have no speech to make. [Laughter.] In my position it is somewhat important that I should not say any foolish things. [A voice: If you can help it.] It very often happens that the only way to help it is to say nothing at all. [Laughter.]

> Believing that is my present condition this evening, I must beg of you to excuse me from addressing you further.

This displays Lincoln's normal reluctance to improvise words as President. Lincoln's secretary John Hay, watching the scene from the crowd, noted in his diary: "The President appeared at the door and said half a dozen words meaning nothing & went in."

Early in the morning Lincoln took a carriage ride to the battle sites. Later, Ward Lamon and his specially uniformed marshals assigned horses to the various dignitaries (carriages would have clogged the site too much). Although the march was less than a mile, Lamon had brought thirty horses into town, and Wills had supplied a hundred, to honor the officials present.

Lincoln sat his horse gracefully (to the surprise of some), and looked meditative during the long wait while marshals tried to coax into line important people more concerned about their dignity than the President was about his. Lincoln was wearing a mourning band on his hat for his dead son. He also wore white gauntlets, which made his large hands on the reins dramatic by contrast with his otherwise black attire.

Everett had gone out earlier, by carriage, to prepare himself in the special tent he had asked for near the platform. At sixty-nine, he had kidney trouble and needed to relieve himself just before and after the three-hour ceremony. (He had put his problem so delicately that his hosts did not realize that he meant to be left alone in the tent; but he finally coaxed them out.) Everett mounted the platform at the last moment, after most of the others had arrived.

Those on the raised platform were hemmed in close by standing crowds. When it had become clear that the numbers might approach twenty thousand, the platform had been set at some distance from the burial operations. Only a third of the expected bodies had been buried, and those under fresh mounds. Other graves had been readied for the bodies, which arrived in irregular order (some from this state, some from that), making it impossible to complete one section at a time. The whole burial site was incomplete. Marshals tried to keep the milling thousands out of the work in progress.

Everett, as usual, had neatly placed his thick text on a little table before hlm—and then ostentatiously refused to look at it. He was able to indicate with gestures the sites of the battle's progress, visible from where he stood. He excoriated the rebels for their atrocities, implicitly justifying the fact that some Confederate skeletons were still unburied, lying in the clefts of Devil's Den under rocks and autumn leaves. Two days earlier Everett had been shown around the field, and places were pointed out where the bodies lay. His speech, for good or ill, would pick its way through the carnage.

As a former Secretary of State, Everett had many sources, in and outside government, for the information he had gathered so diligently. Lincoln no doubt watched closely how the audience responded to passages that absolved Meade of blame for letting Lee escape. The setting of the battle in a larger logic of campaigns had an immediacy for those on the scene which we cannot recover. Everett's familiarity with the details was flattering to the local audience, which nonetheless had things to learn from this shapely presentation of the whole three days' action. This was like a modern "docudrama" on television, telling the story of recent events on the basis of investigative reporting. We badly misread the evidence if we think Everett failed to work his customary magic. The best witnesses on the scene—Lincoln's personal secretaries, John Hay and John Nicolay, with their professional interest in good prose and good theater—praised Everett at the time and ever after. He received more attention in their biography's chapter on Gettysburg than did their own boss.

When Lincoln rose, it was with a sheet or two, from which he read. Lincoln's three minutes would ever after be obsessively contrasted with Everett's two hours in accounts of this day. It is even claimed that Lincoln disconcerted the crowd with his abrupt performance, so that people did not know how to respond ("Was that *all?*"). Myth tells of a poor photographer making leisurely arrangements to take Lincoln's picture, expecting him to be standing for some time. But it is useful to look at the relevant part of the program:

> Music. *by Birgfield's Band.*
> Prayer. *by Rev. T.H. Stockton, D.D.*
> Music. *by the Marine Band.*
> ORATION. *by Hon. Edward Everett.*
> Music. *Hymn composed by B. B. French.*
> DEDICATORY REMARKS BY THE PRESIDENT OF THE UNITED STATES.
> Dirge. *sung by Choir selected for the occasion.*
> Benediction. *by Rev. H.L. Baugher, D.D.*

There was only one "oration" announced or desired here. Though we call Lincoln's text *the* Gettysburg Address, that title clearly belongs to Everett. Lincoln's contribution, labeled "remarks," was intended to make the dedication formal (somewhat like ribbon-cutting at modern openings). Lincoln was not expected to speak at length, any more than Rev. T. H. Stockton was (though Stockton's prayer *is* four times the length of the President's remarks). A contrast of length with Everett's talk raises a false issue. Lincoln's text *is* startlingly brief for what it accomplished, but that would be equally true if Everett had spoken for a shorter time or had not spoken at all.

Nonetheless, the contrast was strong. Everett's voice was sweet and expertly modulated; Lincoln's was high to the point of shrillness, and his Kentucky accent offended some eastern sensibilities. But Lincoln derived an advantage from his high tenor voice—carrying power. If there is agreement on any one aspect of Lincoln's delivery, at Gettysburg or elsewhere, it is on his audibility. Modern impersonators of Lincoln, such as Walter Huston, Raymond Massey, Henry Fonda, and the various actors who give voice to Disneyland animations of the President, bring him before us as a baritone, which is considered a more manly or heroic voice—though both the Roosevelt Presidents of our century were tenors. What should not be forgotten is that Lincoln was himself an actor, an expert raconteur and mimic, and one who spent hours reading speeches out of Shakespeare to any willing (or sometimes unwilling) audience. He knew a good deal about rhythmic delivery and meaningful inflection. John Hay, who had submitted to many of those Shakespeare readings, gave high marks to his boss's performance at Gettysburg. He put in his diary at the time that "the President, in a fine, free way, with more grace than is his wont, said his half dozen words of consecration." Lincoln's text was polished, his delivery emphatic; he was interrupted by applause five times. Read in a slow, clear way to the farthest listeners, the speech would take about three minutes. It is quite true the audience did not take in all that happened in that short time—we are still trying to weigh the consequences of Lincoln's amazing performance. But the myth that Lincoln was disappointed in the result—that he told the unreliable Lamon that his speech, like a bad plow, "won't scour"—has no basis. He had done what he wanted to do, and Hay shared the pride his superior took in an important occasion put to good use.

At the least, Lincoln had far surpassed David Wills's hope for words to disinfect the air of Gettysburg. His speech hovers far above the carnage. He lifts the battle to a level of abstraction that purges it of grosser matter—even "earth" is mentioned only as the thing from which the tested form of government shall not perish. The nightmare realities have been etherealized in the crucible of his language.

Lincoln was here to clear the infected atmosphere of American history itself, tainted with official sins and inherited guilt. He would cleanse the Constitution—not as William Lloyd Garrison had, by burning an instrument that countenanced slavery. He altered the document from within, by appeal from its letter to the spirit, subtly changing the recalcitrant stuff of that legal compromise, bringing it to its own indictment. By implicitly doing this, he performed one of the most daring acts of open-air sleight of hand ever witnessed by the unsuspecting. Everyone in that vast throng of thousands was having his or her intellectual pocket picked. The crowd departed with a new thing in its ideological luggage, the new Constitution Lincoln had substituted for the one they had brought there with them. They walked off from those curving graves on the hillside, under a changed sky, into a different America. Lincoln had revolutionized the Revolution, giving people a new past to live with that would change their future indefinitely.

Some people, looking on from a distance, saw that a giant (if benign) swindle had been performed. The Chicago *Times* quoted the letter of the Constitution to Lincoln—noting its lack of reference to equality, its tolerance of slavery—and said that Lincoln was betraying the instrument he was on oath to defend, traducing the men who died for the letter of that fundamental law:

> It was to uphold this constitution, and the Union created by it, that our officers and soldiers gave their lives at Gettysburg. How dared he, then, standing on their graves, misstate the cause for which they died, and libel the statesmen who founded the government? They were men possessing too much self-respect to declare that negroes were their equals, or were entitled to equal privileges.

Heirs to this outrage still attack Lincoln for subverting the Constitution at Gettysburg—suicidally frank conservatives like M. E. Bradford and the late Willmoore Kendall. But most conservatives are understandably unwilling to challenge a statement now so hallowed, so literally sacrosanct, as Lincoln's clever assault on the constitutional past. They would rather hope or pretend, with some literary critics, that Lincoln's emotionally moving address had no discernible intellectual content, that, in the words of the literary critic James Hurt, "the sequence of ideas is commonplace to the point of banality, the ordinary coin of funereal oratory."

People like Kendall and the Chicago *Times* editors might have wished this were true, but they knew better. They recognized the audacity of Lincoln's undertaking. Kendall rightly says that Lincoln undertook a new founding of the nation, to correct things felt to be imperfect in the Founders' own achievement:

> Abraham Lincoln and, in considerable degree, the authors of the post-civil-war amendments, attempted a new act of founding, involving concretely a startling new interpretation of that principle of the founders which declares that "All men are created equal."

Edwin Meese and other "original intent" conservatives also want to go back before the Civil War amendments (particularly the Fourteenth) to the original Founders. Their job would be comparatively easy if they did not have to work against the values created by the Gettysburg Address. Its deceptively simple-sounding phrases appeal to Americans in ways that Lincoln had perfected in his debates over the Constitution during the 1850s. During that time Lincoln found the language, the imagery, the myths, that are given their best and briefest embodiment at Gettysburg. In order to penetrate the mystery of his "refounding," we must study all the elements of that stunning verbal coup. Without Lincoln's knowing it himself, all his prior literary, intellectual, and political labors had prepared him for the intellectual revolution contained in those 272 words.

Lincoln's speech is brief, one might argue, because it is silent on so much that one would expect to hear about. The Gettysburg Address does not mention Gettysburg. Or slavery. Or—more surprising—the Union. (Certainly not the South.) The other major message of 1863, the Emancipation Proclamation, is not mentioned, much less defended or vindicated. The "great task" mentioned in the address is not emancipation but the preservation of self-government. We assume today that self-government includes self-rule by blacks as well as whites; but at the time of his appearance at Gettysburg, Lincoln was not advocating even eventual suffrage for African-Americans. The

Gettysburg Address, for all its artistry and eloquence, does not directly address the prickliest issues of its historical moment.

Lincoln was accused during his lifetime of clever evasions and key silences. He was especially indirect and hard to interpret on the subject of slavery. That puzzled his contemporaries, and has infuriated some later students of his attitude. Theodore Parker, the Boston preacher who was the idol of Lincoln's law partner, William Herndon, found Lincoln more clever than principled in his 1858 Senate race, when he debated Stephen Douglas. Parker initially supported William Seward for President in 1860, because he found Seward more forthright than Lincoln in his opposition to slavery. But Seward probably lost the Republican nomination *because* of that forthrightness. Lincoln was more cautious and circuitous. The reasons for his reserve before his nomination are clear enough—though that still leaves the omissions of the Gettysburg Address to be explained.

Lincoln's political base, the state of Illinois, runs down to a point (Cairo) farther south than all of what became West Virginia, and farther south than most of Kentucky and Virginia. The "Negrophobia" of Illinois led it to vote overwhelmingly in 1848, just ten years before the Lincoln-Douglas debates, to amend the state constitution so as to deny freed blacks all right of entry to the state. The average vote of the state was 79 percent for exclusion, though southern and some central counties were probably more than 90 percent for it. Lincoln knew the racial geography of his own state well, and calibrated what he had to say about slavery according to his audience.

Lincoln knew it was useless to promote the abolitionist position in Illinois. He wanted to establish some common ground to hold together the elements of his fledgling Republican Party. Even as a lawyer, Herndon said, he concentrated so fiercely on the main point to be established ("the nub") that he would concede almost any ancillary matter. Lincoln's accommodation to the prejudice of his time did not imply any agreement with the points he found it useless to dispute. One sees his attitude in the disarming concession he made to Horace Greeley, in order to get to the nub of their disagreement:

• • •

> I have just read yours of the 19th addressed to myself through the New-York Tribune. If there be in it any statements, or assumptions of fact, which I may know to be erroneous, I do not, now and here, controvert them. If there be in it any inferences which I may believe to be falsely drawn, I do not now and here, argue against them. If there be perceptable in it an impatient and dictatorial tone, I waive it in deference to an old friend, whose heart I have always supposed to be right.

Obviously, Lincoln did not agree with the aspersions that Greeley had cast, but this was not a matter he could usefully pursue "now and here." In the same way, Lincoln preferred agnosticism about blacks' intellectual inferiority to whites, and went along with the desire to keep them socially inferior. As George Fredrickson points out, agnosticism rather than *certainty* about blacks' intellectual disability was the liberal position of that time, and there was nothing Lincoln or anyone else could do about social mixing. Lincoln refused to let the matter of political equality get tangled up with such emotional and (for the time) unresolvable issues. What, for him, was the nub, the realizable minimum—which would be hard enough to establish in the first place?

At the very least, it was wrong to treat human beings as property. Lincoln reduced the slaveholders' position to absurdity by spelling out its consequences:

> If it is a sacred right for the people of Nebraska to take and hold slaves there, it is equally their sacred right to buy them where they can buy them cheapest; and that undoubtedly will be on the coast of Africa . . . [where a slavetrader] buys them at the rate of about a red cotton handkerchief a head. This is very cheap.

Why do people not take advantage of this bargain? Because they will be hanged like pirates if they try. Yet if slaves are just one form of property like any other,

> it is a great abridgement of the sacred right of self-government to hang men for engaging in this profitable trade!

Not only had the federal government, following international sentiment, outlawed the slave trade, but the domestic slave barterer was held in low esteem, even in the South:

> You do not recognize him as a friend, or even as an honest man. Your children must not play with his. . . . Now why is this? You do not so treat the man who deals in corn, cattle or tobacco.

And what kind of *property* is "set free"? People do not "free" houses or their manufactures to fend for themselves. But there were almost half a million freed blacks in Lincoln's America:

> How comes this vast amount of property to be running about without owners? We do not see free horses or free cattle running at large.

Lincoln said that in 1854, three years before Chief Justice Roger Taney declared, in the Dred Scott case, that slaves were movable property like any other chattel goods. The absurd had become law. No wonder Lincoln felt he had to fight for even minimal recognition of human rights.

If the black man owns himself and is not another person's property, then he has rights in the product of his labor:

> I agree with Judge Douglas [the Negro] is not my equal in many respects—certainly not in color, perhaps not in moral or intellectual endowment. But in the right to eat the bread, without leave of anybody else, which his own hand earns,

> he is my equal and the equal of Judge Douglas, and the equal of every living man.

Lincoln, as often, was using a Bible text, and one with a sting in it. The *curse* of mankind in general, that "in the sweat of thy face shalt thou eat bread" (Genesis 3:19), is, at the least, a *right* for blacks.

Lincoln tried to use one prejudice against another. There was in Americans a prejudgment in favor of anything biblical. There was also antimonarchical bias. Lincoln put the text about eating the bread of one's own sweat in an American context of antimonarchism.

> That is the issue that will continue in this country when these poor tongues of Judge Douglas and myself shall be silent. It is the eternal struggle between these two principles—right and wrong—throughout the world. They are the two principles that have stood face to face from the beginning of time; and will ever continue to struggle. The one is the common right of humanity and the other the divine right of kings. It is the same principle in whatever shape it develops itself. It is the same spirit that says, "You work and toil and earn bread, and I'll eat it." [Loud applause.] No matter in what shape it comes, whether from the mouth of a king who seeks to bestride the people of his own nation and live by the fruit of their labor, or from one race of men as an apology for enslaving another race, it is the same tyrannical principle.

In at least these two ways, then, slavery is wrong. One cannot own human beings, and one should not be in the position of a king over human beings.

Lincoln knew how to sneak around the frontal defenses of prejudice and find a back way into agreement with bigots. This explains, at the level of tactics, the usefulness to Lincoln of the Declaration of Independence. That revered document was antimonarchical in the common perception, and on that score unchallengeable. But because it indicted

King George III in terms of the equality of men, the Declaration committed Americans to claims even more at odds with slavery than with kingship—since kings do not necessarily claim to own their subjects. Put the claims of the Declaration as mildly as possible, and they still cannot be reconciled with slavery:

> I, as well as Judge Douglas, am in favor of the race to which I belong having the [politically and socially] superior position. I have never said anything to the contrary, but I hold that notwithstanding all this, there is no reason in the world why the negro is not entitled to all the natural rights enumerated in the Declaration of Independence, the right to life, liberty and the pursuit of happiness. [Loud cheers.] I hold that he is as much entitled to these as the white man.

Lincoln's speech at Gettysburg worked several revolutions, beginning with one in literary style. Everett's talk was given at the last point in history when such a performance could be appreciated without reservation. It was made obsolete within a half hour of the time when it was spoken. Lincoln's remarks anticipated the shift to vernacular rhythms which Mark Twain would complete twenty years later. Hemingway claimed that all modern American novels are the offspring of *Huckleberry Finn.* It is no greater exaggeration to say that all modern political prose descends from the Gettysburg Address.

The address looks less mysterious than it should to those who believe there is such a thing as "natural speech." All speech is unnatural. It is artificial. Believers in "artless" or "plain" speech think that rhetoric is added to some prior natural thing, like cosmetics added to the unadorned face. But human faces are born, like kitten faces. Words are not born in that way. Human babies, unlike kittens, later produce an artifact called language, and they largely speak in jingles, symbols, tales, and myths during the early stages of their talk. Plain speech is a later development, in whole cultures as in individuals. Simple prose depends on a complex epistemology—it depends on concepts like "objective fact." Language reverses the logic of horticulture: here the blossoms come first, and *they* produce the branches.

Lincoln, like most writers of great prose, began by writing bad poetry. Early experiments with words are almost always stilted, formal, tentative. Economy of words, grip, precision, come later (if at all). A Gettysburg Address does not precede rhetoric but burns its way through the lesser toward the greater eloquence, by long discipline. Lincoln not only exemplifies this process but studied it, in himself and others. He was a student of the word.

Lincoln's early experiments with language have an exuberance that is almost comic in its playing with contrivances. His showy 1838 speech to the Young Men's Lyceum is now usually studied to support or refute Edmund Wilson's claim that it contains oedipal feelings. But its most obvious feature is the attempt to describe a complex situation in neatly balanced structures (emphasized here by division into rhetorical units).

Theirs was the task
(and nobly they performed it)
to possess themselves,
and through themselves, us,
of this goodly land;
and to uprear upon its hills
and its valleys,
a political edifice of liberty
and equal rights;
'tis ours only,
to transmit these,
the former, unprofaned by the foot of an invader;
the latter, undecayed by the lapse of time,
and untorn by usurpation—
to the latest generation that fate shall permit
the world to know.

• • •

This is too labored to be clear. One has to look a second time to be sure that "the former" refers to "this goodly land" and "the latter" to "a political edifice." But the exercise is limbering Lincoln up for subtler uses of such balance and antithesis. The parenthetic enriching of a first phrase is something he would use in his later prose to give it depth (I have added all but the first set of parentheses):

Theirs was the task
(and nobly they performed it)
to possess themselves
(and through themselves, us)
of this goodly land

It is the pattern of

The world will little note
(nor long remember)
what we say here

And, from the Second Inaugural Address, of

Fondly do we hope
(fervently do we pray)
that this mighty scourge of war
may speedily pass away

And, also from the Second Inaugural,

. . . *with firmness in the right*
(as God gives us to see the right)
let us strive on to finish
the work we are in

To end after complex melodic pairings with a strong row of monosyllables was an effect he especially liked. Not only "the world to know" and "what we say here" and "the work we are in" in the examples above but also, from the 1861 Farewell Address at Springfield, Illinois, in

Trusting in Him,
who can go with me,
and remain with you
and be every where for good,
let us confidently hope
that all will yet be well.

And in this, from the Second Inaugural,

Both parties deprecated war;
but one of them would make *war*
rather than let the nation survive;
and the other would accept *war*
rather than let it perish.
And the war came.

And, in the 1862 message to Congress,

In giving *freedom to the* slave,
we assure *freedom to the* free—
honorable alike in what we give,
and what we preserve.
We shall nobly save,
or meanly lose,
the last best, hope of earth.

The closing of the sentence above from Lincoln's early Lyceum speech ("to the latest generation") gives a premonition of famous statements to come.

• • •

The fiery trial through which we pass,
will light us down,
(in honor or dishonor)
to the latest generation.

Those words to Congress in 1862 were themselves forecast in Lincoln's Peoria address of 1854.

If we do this,
we shall not only have saved the Union;
but we shall have so saved it,
as to make, and to keep it,
forever worthy of the saving.
We shall have so saved it,
that the succeeding millions
of free happy people,
the world over,
shall rise up,
and call us blessed, to the latest generations.

It would be wrong to think that Lincoln moved toward the plain style of the Gettysburg Address just by writing shorter, simpler sentences. Actually, that address ends with a very long sencence—eighty-two words, almost a third of the whole talk's length. So does the Second Inaugural Address, Lincoln's second most famous piece of eloquence: its final sentence runs to seventy-five words. Because of his early experiments, Lincoln's prose acquired a flexibility of structure, a rhythmic pacing, a variation in length of words and phrases and clauses and sentences, that make his sentences move "naturally," for all their density and scope. We get inside his verbal workshop when we see how he recast the suggested conclusion to his First Inaugural given him by William Seward. Every sentence is improved, in rhythm, emphasis, or clarity:

Seward	Lincoln
I close.	I am loth to close.
We are not, we must not be aliens or enemies, but fellow-countrymen and brethren.	We are not enemies, but friends. We must not be enemies.
Although passion has strained our bonds of affection too hardly, they must not, I am sure they will not, be broken.	Though passion may have strained, it must not break our bonds of affection.
The mystic chords which, proceeding from so many battle-fields and so many patriot graves, pass through all the hearts and all the hearths in this broad continent of ours, will yet harmonize in their ancient music when breathed upon by the guardian angel of the nation.	The mystic chords of memory, stretching from every battle-field, and patriot grave, to every living heart and hearthstone, all over this broad land, will yet swell the chorus of the Union, when again touched, as surely they will be, by the better angels of our nature.

Lincoln's lingering monosyllables in the first sentence seem to cling to the occasion, not wanting to break off the communication on which the last hopes of union depend. He simplified the next sentence using two terms ("enemies," "friends") where Seward had used two *pairs* ("aliens" and "enemies," "fellow-countrymen" and "brethren"), but Lincoln repeated "enemies" in the urgent words "We must not be enemies." The next sentence was also simplified, to play off against the long, complex image of the concluding sentence. The "chords of memory" are not musical sounds. Lincoln spelled "chord" and "cord" indiscriminately; they are the same etymologically. He used the geometric term "chord" for a line across a circle's arc. On the other hand, he spelled the word "cord" (in an 1858 speech) when calling the Declaration of Independence an electrical wire sending messages to American hearts: "the electric cord in that Declaration that links the hearts of patriotic and liberty-loving men together."

Seward knew that the chord to be breathed on was a string (of a harp or lute, though his "chords proceeding from graves" is grotesque). Lincoln stretched the cords between graves and living hearts, as in his earlier image of the Declaration. Seward also got ethereal when he talked of harmonies that come from breathing on the chords. Lincoln was more believable (and understandable) when he had the better angels of our nature touch the cords to swell the chorus of union. Finally, Seward made an odd picture to get his jingle of chords passing through "hearts and hearths." Lincoln stretched the chords from graves to hearts and hearthstones. He got rid of the crude rhyme by making a chiastic (a-b-b-a) cluster of "living heart and hearthstone"; the vital heart is contrasted with the inert hearth-stuff. Seward's clumsy image of stringing together these two different items has disappeared. Lincoln gave to Seward's fustian a pointedness of imagery, a euphony and interplay of short and long sentences and phrases, that lift the conclusion almost to the level of his own best prose.

The spare quality of Lincoln's prose did not come naturally but was worked at. Lincoln not only read aloud, to think his way into sounds, but also wrote as a way of ordering his thought. He had a keenness for analytical exercises. He was proud of the mastery he achieved over Euclid's Elements, which awed Herndon and others. He loved the study of grammar, which some think the most arid of subjects. Some claimed to remember his gift for spelling, a view that our manuscripts disprove. Spelling as he had to learn it (separate from etymology) is more arbitrary than logical. It was the logical side of language—the principles of order as these reflect patterns of thought or the external world—that appealed to him.

He was also, Herndon tells us, laboriously precise in his choice of words. He would have agreed with Mark Twain that the difference between the right word and the nearly right one is that between lightning and a lightning bug. He said, debating Douglas, that his foe confused a similarity of words with a similarity of things—as one might equate a horse chestnut with a chestnut horse.

As a speaker, Lincoln grasped Twain's later insight: "Few sinners are saved after the first twenty minutes of a sermon." The trick, of course, was not simply to be brief but to say a great deal in the fewest words. Lincoln justly boasted of his Second Inaugural's seven hundred words, "Lots of wisdom in that document, I suspect." The same is even truer of the Gettysburg Address, which uses fewer than half that number of words.

The unwillingness to waste words shows up in the address's telegraphic quality—the omission of coupling words, a technique rhetoricians call asyndeton. Triple phrases sound as to a drumbeat, with no "and" or "but" to slow their insistency:

we are engaged . . .
We are met . . .
We have come . . .

we can not dedicate . . .
we can not consecrate . . .
we can not hallow . . .

that from these honored dead . . .
that we here highly resolve . . .
that this nation, under God . . .

government of the people,
by the people,
for the people . . .

Despite the suggestive images of birth, testing, and rebirth, the speech is surprisingly bare of ornament. The language itself is made strenuous, its musculature easily traced, so that even the grammar becomes a form of rhetoric. By repeating the antecedent as often as possible, instead of referring to it indirectly by pronouns like "it" and "they," or by backward referential words like "former" and "latter," Lincoln interlocks his sentences, making of them a constantly self-referential system. This linking up by explicit repetition amounts to a kind of hook-and-eye method for joining the parts of his address. The rhetorical devices are almost invisible, since they use no figurative language. (I highlight them typographically here.)

> Four score and seven years ago our fathers brought forth on this continent, *a new nation, conceived* in Liberty, *and dedicated* to the proposition that all men are created equal.
>
> Now we are engaged in A GREAT CIVIL WAR, testing whether *that nation,* or any nation *so conceived and so dedicated,* can long endure.
>
> We are met on a great *BATTLE-FIELD* of THAT WAR.
>
> We have come to *dedicate* a portion of *THAT FIELD,* as a final resting place for those who here gave their lives that *that nation* might live. It is altogether fitting and proper that we should do this.
>
> But, in a larger sense, we can not *dedicate*—we can not *consecrate*—we can not hallow—this ground.
>
> The brave men, living and dead, who struggled here, have *consecrated* it, far above our poor power to add or detract. The world will little note, nor long remember what we say here, but it can never forget what they did here.
>
> It is for us the living, rather, to be *dedicated* here to the unfinished work which they who fought here have thus far so nobly advanced. It is rather for us to be here *dedicated* to the great task remaining before us—that from THESE HONORED DEAD we take increased devotion to that cause for which they gave the last full measure of devotion—

> that we here highly resolve that THESE DEAD shall not have died in vain—that this nation, under God, shall have a new birth of freedom—and that government of the people, by the people, for the people, shall not perish from the earth.

Each of the paragraphs printed separately here is bound to the preceding and the following by some resumptive element. Only the first and last paragraphs do not (because they cannot) have this two-way connection to their setting. Not all of the "pointer" phrases replace grammatical antecedents in the technical sense. But Lincoln makes them perform analogous work. The nation is declared to be "dedicated" before the term is given further uses for individuals present at the ceremony, who repeat (as it were) the national consecration. The compactness of the themes is emphasized by this reliance on a few words in different contexts.

A similar linking process is performed, almost subliminally, by the repeated pinning of statements to *this* field, *these* dead, who died *here*, for *that* kind of nation. The reverential touching, over and over, of the charged moment and place leads Lincoln to use "here" eight times in the short text, the adjectival "that" five times, and "this" four times. The spare vocabulary is not impoverishing, because of the subtly interfused constructions, in which the classicist Charles Smiley identified "two antitheses, five cases of anaphora, eight instances of balanced phrases and clauses, thirteen alliterations." "Plain speech" was never less artless. Lincoln forged a new lean language to humanize and redeem the first modern war.

This was the perfect medium for changing the way most Americans thought about the nation's founding. Lincoln did not argue law or history, as Daniel Webster had. He *made* history. He came not to present a theory but to impose a symbol, one tested in experience and appealing to national values, expressing emotional urgency in calm abstractions. He came to change the world, to effect an intellectual revolution. No other words could have done it. The miracle is that these words did. In his brief time before the crowd at Gettysburg he wove a spell that has not yet been broken—he called up a new nation out of the blood and trauma.

James McPherson has described Lincoln as a revolutionary in terms of the economic and other physical changes he effected, whether intentionally or not—a valid point that McPherson discusses sensibly. But Lincoln was a revolutionary in another sense as well—the one Willmoore Kendall denounced him for: he not only presented the Declaration of Independence in a new light, as a matter of founding law, but put its central proposition, equality, in a newly favored position as a principle of the Constitution (whereas, as the Chicago *Times* noticed, the Constitution never uses the word). What had been mere theory in the writings of James Wilson, Joseph Story, and Daniel Webster—that the nation preceded the states, in time and importance—now became a lived reality of the American tradition. The results of this were seen almost at once. Up to the Civil War "the United States" was invariably a plural noun: "The United States are a free country." After Gettysburg it became a singular: "The United States is a free country." This was a result of the whole mode of thinking that Lincoln expressed in his acts as well as his words, making union not a mystical hope but a constitutional reality. When, at the end of the address, he referred to government "of the people, by the people, for the people," he was not, like Theodore Parker, just praising popular government as a Transcendentalist's ideal. Rather, like Webster, he was saying that America was *a* people accepting as its great assignment what was addressed in the Declaration. This people was "conceived" in 1776, was "brought forth" as an entity whose birth was datable ("four score and seven years" before) and placeable ("on this continent"), and was capable of receiving a "new birth of freedom."

Thus Abraham Lincoln changed the way people thought about the Constitution. For a states'-rights advocate like Willmoore Kendall, for an "original intent" advocate like Edwin Meese, the politics of the United States has all been misdirected since that time. The Fourteenth Amendment was, in their view, ultimately bootlegged into the Bill of

Rights. But as soon as it was ratified, the Amendment began doing harm, in the eyes of strict constructionists.

As Robert Bork put it:

> Unlike the [Fourteenth Amendment's] other two clauses, [the due-process clause] quickly displayed the same capacity to accommodate judicial constitution-making which Taney had found in the fifth amendment's version.

Bork, too, thinks that equality as a national commitment has been sneaked into the Constitution. There can be little doubt about the principal culprit. As Kendall put it, Lincoln's use of the phrase from the Declaration about all men being equal is an attempt "to wrench from it a single proposition and make that our supreme commitment."

> We should not allow [Lincoln]—not at least without some probing inquiry—to "steal" the game, that is, to accept his interpretation of the Declaration, its place in our history, and its meaning as "true," "correct," and "binding."

But, as Kendall himself admitted, the professors, the textbooks, the politicians, the press, *have* overwhelmingly accepted Lincoln's vision. The Gettysburg Address has become an authoritative expression of the American spirit—as authoritative as the Declaration itself, and perhaps even more influential, since it determines how we read the Declaration. For most people now, the Declaration means what Lincoln told us it means, as he did to correct the Constitution without overthrowing it. It is this correction of the spirit, this intellectual revolution, that makes attempts to go back beyond Lincoln to some earlier version so feckless. The proponents of states' rights may have arguments to advance, but they have lost their force, in the courts as well as in the popular mind. By accepting the Gettysburg Address, and its concept of a single people dedicated to a proposition, we have been changed. Because of it, we live in a different America.

from Theodore Rex

by Edmund Morris

Five months into a strike of 140,000 coal miners, Theodore Roosevelt (in office 1901–1909) held a summit meeting with the opposing parties. Roosevelt was recovering from a car accident. George F. Baer, president of Reading Railroad, represented the mine owners. John Mitchell, president of the United Mine Workers, represented labor. This excerpt from Edmund Morris's (born 1940) three-volume life of Roosevelt describes how the 26th president handled the crisis.

Curious onlookers began congregating outside number 22 Jackson Place early on Friday, 3 October 1902. Their ranks were swelled by the largest contingent of reporters and photographers seen in Washington since the beginning of the Spanish-American War. It was an exquisite fall morning. Sun slanted through the open windows of the President's second-floor parlor, at such an angle that people across the street could make out several yards of silk wall-covering, and the tops of fourteen empty chairs. Roosevelt himself was nowhere to be seen.

Just before ten o'clock, the Attorney General, natty in white vest and bowler, skipped up the front steps with his hands in his pockets. Moments later, he reappeared above, suddenly bald. From within came a piping shout, "Hello, Knox!" Roosevelt rolled into view in a blue-striped robe, a bowl of asters in his lap. He placed the flowers on a sunny sill, then, to general disappointment, moved out of sight.

Actually, he had only wheeled himself into a corner between two windows. Flanked thus, he sat in inscrutable shadow, facing a semicircle of seats bathed in light. For once he was not performer, but audience. He could not direct the players who would soon appear before him, yet without him they could not interact: they must throw their speeches his way.

For almost an hour he conferred quietly with Knox and another early arrival, Commissioner of Labor Carroll D. Wright. Outside, police tried to contain the thickening crowd. John Mitchell and his three aides came across the square at six minutes before eleven. Kodaks clicked—probably in vain, because with his swarthy face and dark gray eyes under a black fedora, the union leader was dark enough to defeat any exposure. A black frock coat ballooned slightly behind him as he walked. Such saturninity was to be expected, perhaps, of a former coal miner. But Mitchell's white starched collar, dazzling in the sun, made him also look clean and handsome enough to thrill any woman in the crowd. Only the scarred hands betrayed the years he had spent underground.

While George Cortelyou was receiving the UMW delegation, a plush landau drew up. George F. Baer sat alone opposite two colleagues, his isolation proclaiming him their leader. He had breakfasted in his private railroad car, enjoyed a cigar, and taken a walk, yet his face was drawn and droopy-eyed. With his ascetic features and narrow beard (which he fingered nervously at the sight of the crowd), Baer looked almost French. But from behind, as he stepped down onto the sidewalk, he revealed a fat Teutonic neck, close-cropped and obstinate.

Eben B. Thomas, chairman of the Erie Railroad, and William H. Truesdale, president of the Delaware & Hudson, followed Baer into the house, doffing glossy hats, their silver whiskers flashing. Behind, in another landau, came David Willcox, waspishly elegant in a flowered silk vest. He was accompanied by Thomas P. Fowler of the New York, Ontario, & Western, all clenched mouth and crinkly hair, and John Markle, an independent mine owner, whose jowls and choleric complexion advertised him as the most dangerous man of the six.

"Gentlemen," said Cortelyou, "if you are ready, we will go to the President."

• • •

Roosevelt received his guests apologetically. "You will have to excuse me, gentlemen, I can't get up to greet you."

Commissioner Wright performed the introductions.

"Dee-*lighted,*" Roosevelt kept saying, snapping the syllables off with his teeth. He indicated the empty chairs. Watchers outside were amused to see fourteen heads dropping simultaneously, like cherries in a slot machine. The President reached for a typescript.

"Gentlemen, the matter about which I have called you here is of such extreme importance that I have thought it best to reduce what I have to say into writing." He began to read with great emphasis, pausing after each sentence to check reactions around the room.

> I wish to call your attention to the fact that there are three parties affected by the situation in the anthracite trade—the operators, the miners, and the general public. I speak for neither the operators nor the miners, but for the general public.

A yard or two beyond the President's propped-up leg, George Baer listened intently. Roosevelt admitted he had no "right or duty to intervene in this way upon legal grounds." He was bound, however, to use what influence he could to end an "intolerable" situation. His guests must consider the consequences of further disagreement.

> We are upon the threshold of winter, with an already existing coal famine, the future terrors of which we can hardly yet appreciate. The evil possibilities are so far-reaching, so appalling, that it seems to me that you [are] required to sink for the time being any tenacity as to your respective claims in the matter at issue between you. In my judgment the situation imperatively requires that you meet upon the common plane of the necessities of the public. With all the earnestness there is in me I ask that there be an immediate

> resumption of operations in the coal mines in some such way as will without a day's unnecessary delay meet the crying needs of the people.

Laying down his typescript, Roosevelt added, "I do not invite a discussion of your respective claims and positions." John Mitchell stood up in polite disobedience.

> Mr. President, I am much impressed with what you say. We are willing to meet the gentlemen representing the coal operators to try to adjust our differences among ourselves. If we cannot adjust them that way, Mr. President, we are willing that you shall name a tribunal who shall determine the issues that have resulted in this strike. And if the gentlemen representing the operators will accept the award or decision of such a tribunal, the miners will willingly accept it—even if it is against their claims.

Roosevelt moved quickly to forestall any response from Baer. "Before considering what ought to be done, I think it only just . . . that you should have time to consider what I have stated as to the reasons for my getting you together." He distributed copies of his opening declaration. "Give it careful thought and come back at three o'clock."

The operators returned in frustration to their private train. They had expected a formal hearing, at which they could argue that John Mitchell did not represent the peculiar interests of anthracite labor. He was, in fact, president of a union whose membership was predominantly bituminous. Since soft coal was to a certain extent competitive with hard (and might become more so, with emergency conversion of home heating appliances), Mitchell was a walking conflict of interest.

Roosevelt had discouraged them from expressing this reasonable scruple, while weakly—or deliberately?—allowing Mitchell to pontificate in time for the evening papers. Then, adding insult to injury, he had announced a long recess, which meant *they* would be unable to make any headlines before the next morning.

A typist awaited Baer in his mobile office. Her fingers began to fly as he told her exactly what he thought of the whole proceeding.

A bowl of white roses replaced the asters in Roosevelt's window that afternoon, but it stimulated no feelings of truce. The operators were in a mood of heavy, postprandial truculence. "Do we understand you correctly," Baer asked over the President's foot, "that we will be expected to answer the proposition submitted by Mr. Mitchell this morning?"

Roosevelt would have preferred a reply to his own statement. "It would be a pleasure to me," he said, "to hear any answer that you are willing to make.

"You asked us to consider the offer of Mr. Mitchell . . . to go back to work if you will appoint a commission to determine the questions at issue."

"I did not say that!"

"But you did, Mr. President. Or so we understood you."

"I did not say it!" Momentarily forgetting himself, Roosevelt leaned forward. Onlookers below saw his blue-sleeved arm punching the air. "And nothing that I did say could possibly bear that construction."

Cortelyou read back the stenographic record. Baer proceeded in tones of cool insolence.

"We assume that a statement of what is going on in the coal regions will not be irrelevant." Roosevelt, perhaps realizing that he had been unfair during the morning, made no protest.

Some fifteen to twenty thousand nonunion miners, Baer informed him, stood ready to provide the public with anthracite coal. But they had been terrorized by Mitchell and his goons. Free men were unable to trade their labor on the open market without being "abused, assaulted, injured, and maltreated." Operators needed armed guards and police to protect private property—all for fear of a bituminous upstart "whom," Baer scolded the President, "you invited to meet you."

Roosevelt stared out of the window, tapping his fingers.

For five months, Baer complained, there had been rampant violence in eastern Pennsylvania, "anarchy too great to be suppressed by the civil power." Governor Stone's shoot-to-kill order had had a salutary effect. However, anarchy would return if Mitchell's men got any "false hopes."

By now Baer's German blood was up, and he treated Roosevelt to a political lecture. "The Constitution of the United States requires the President, when requested by the Governor, to suppress domestic violence." Brushing aside the fact that Stone had not yet asked for help, he guaranteed that he and his colleagues would produce all the anthracite America needed, if they could be assured of federal protection. "The duty of the hour is not to waste time [but] to reestablish order and peace at any cost. Free government is a contemptible failure—"

The phrase *free government* sounded like a euphemism for *your government.*

"—is a contemptible failure if it can only protect the lives and property, and secure the comfort of the people, by compromising with the violators of the law and the instigators of violence and crime."

Baer concluded with a sarcastic rejection of "Mr. Mitchell's considerate offer to let our men work on terms that he makes." His tone was so bitter that neither Roosevelt nor the UMW men caught the significance of a last-minute counterproposal: that anthracite labor disputes be referred to local courts "for final determination."

Obliquely, Baer was accepting Mitchell's key demand: that the operators submit to the authority of a third power. The line between adjudication and arbitration was thin, and Baer had been forced to choose one side against the other. Contrary to popular impression, he was telling the truth when he said that a 10-percent wage hike would threaten industry profitability. Anthracite mining was a rich but moribund business, vulnerable to extinction if it allowed cheaper, more plentiful bituminous coal to become the Northeast's fuel of choice. By next spring, if the strike lasted through winter or was too expensively settled, Shenandoah could be on its way to ghosthood, and the Philadelphia & Reading's freight cars filled with nothing but air.

Roosevelt felt a twinge of sympathy. Baer was a self-made man who had begun work at thirteen. He rightly believed in capital as "the legitimate accumulations of the frugal and the industrious." Behind his bluster, he could not long deny the necessities of life—work and wages and warmth—to people as desperate as he once had been.

Mitchell, rising to reply, repeated his call for arbitration by a presidential board. He spoke with deliberate softness, looking earnestly into Roosevelt's eyes. Courteous, flattering phrases floated in the air: *much impressed with the views you expressed . . . deferring to your wishes . . . accept your award . . . respectfully yours*. He managed to use the second-person singular eleven times in six sentences.

Roosevelt asked the views of the other operators. E. B. Thomas specifically blamed the UMW for twenty deaths, plus "constant and increasing destruction of dwellings, works, machinery, and railroads." He echoed Baer's adjudication offer. Again it was ignored.

John Markle stood up next, and angrily loomed over Roosevelt's wheelchair. "This, Mr. President, is Exhibit A of the operators." He brandished a newspaper cartoon of the goddess Labor being pursued by hoodlums, while the goddess Justice sat blind and helpless, bound by political cords. "Are you asking us to deal with a set of outlaws?"

Roosevelt was fortunate in being confined to his wheelchair, for he confessed afterward that he would have liked to have taken Markle "by the seat of the breeches and nape of the neck" and thrown him out the window. He stoically endured a further indictment of UMW propaganda by Truesdale, and demands by Willcox for antitrust proceedings against the union. When silence fell at last, he asked Mitchell if he had anything more to say.

It was a crucial moment for the labor leader. Thomas had made serious accusations of homicide, which he must answer for the record. Roosevelt's eye calmed him.

"The truth of the matter," Mitchell said, "is, as far as I know, there have been seven deaths. No one regrets them more than I do." However, three of these deaths were caused by management's private police forces, and no charges had been leveled in the other four cases. "I want to say, Mr. President, that I feel very keenly the attacks made upon me and my people, but I came here with the intention of doing nothing and saying nothing that would affect reconciliation."

The air in the room was chill with failure. Roosevelt formally asked if Mitchell's arbitration proposal was acceptable. To a man, the operators replied, "No."

Outside in Lafayette Square, shadows were lengthening to dusk. The onlookers, especially those up telephone poles and trees, knew things were not going well. They had seen angry gestures, heard once the crash of a fist—Baer's?—on wood. Now the door of number 22 flew open, and the operators came out grimly en masse. They refused to take press questions. "You may as well talk to that wall," one of them said, "as to us." Upstairs, Mitchell and his deputies remained closeted with Roosevelt. Reporters guessed, correctly, that the most urgent colloquy of the day was taking place.

While doctors hovered to check his blood pressure, the President warned Mitchell that any more atrocities, as detailed in the afternoon's complaints, would warrant federal intervention. In that case he, as Commander-in-Chief of the United States Army, "would interfere in a way which would put an absolute stop to mob violence within twenty-four hours, and put a stop to it for good and all, too."

The bells of Washington struck five as Mitchell went down into the street, his face blank with despair.

"There is no settlement," he announced.

"Well, I have tried and failed," Roosevelt wrote Mark Hanna after the doctors had gone. "I feel downhearted over the result because of the great misery ahead for the mass of our people." Aides were surprised to find the President not angry. He even tried to find excuses for Baer. As for Mitchell, "I felt he did very well to keep his temper." Roosevelt agreed with Carroll Wright that the strike reflected injustice on both sides. "What my next move will be I cannot yet say."

He wanted to see how the American people would react to the official report of the day's proceedings, which was even now thumping through Government Printing Office presses. It was made available just before midnight. The next morning, Roosevelt sensed such a rush of popular approval as to sweep away any feelings of personal failure.

The national newspapers congratulated him almost unanimously for his courage in calling the conference. Never before, the New York *Sun* remarked, had a President of the United States mediated the contentions of capital and labor. The New York *Mail & Express* said his "happily worded" address was one "that any President might have been proud to utter." John Mitchell won praise for his firmness and good manners, and blame for "lack of patriotism" in bargaining with a vital resource. Most negative comments focused on the "insolent," "audacious," "sordid" behavior of the operators.

Roosevelt tended to agree with the Brooklyn *Eagle* that the fundamental issue now was "coal and not controversy." He was inundated with mail demanding a military invasion of the anthracite fields. Some letters, on heavy corporate stationery, reminded him that President Cleveland had not hesitated to break up the 1894 Pullman railroad strike, in the name of free enterprise and private property. Others, misspelled and querulous, besought him to seize the mines "for the people," under law of eminent domain.

Roosevelt began to empathize with Lincoln at the onset of the Civil War. For the first time in his Presidency, he breathed the alpine air of a great decision. He could not retreat from the height he had assumed on 3 October—not unless he wanted to risk "the most awful riots this country has ever seen." Only one other living American knew what it was like to be so alone at the peak of power. Or was that man too old and fat to remember, much less care?

As if to reassure him, Grover Cleveland wrote from Princeton, New Jersey. "My dear Mr. President, I read in the paper this morning on my way home from Buzzard's Bay, the newspaper accounts of what took place yesterday between you and the parties directly concerned in the coal strike." The patient, spiky, sloping script was the same as it had been when Cleveland had been in the White House, benignly tolerating Roosevelt's activism as Civil Service Commissioner. "I am so surprised and 'stirred up' by the position taken by the contestants that I cannot refrain from making a suggestion."

This was that Baer and Mitchell would welcome a "temporary escape" from their deadlock, if appealed to in such a way as to make them both look humane. They should be asked to postpone their quarrel long enough to allow the production of anthracite for the winter. Then they could "take up the fight again where they left off."

Roosevelt, of course, had already suggested much the same thing. Cleveland had always been a bit slow. Nevertheless, his counsel represented eight years of presidential experience. Here was the brute disciplinarian of 1894 recommending reason over force.

"Your letter was a real help and comfort to me," Roosevelt replied. He declined, however, to issue another appeal, feeling that Baer's attitude precluded it. "I think I shall now tell Mitchell that if the miners will go back to work I will appoint a commission to investigate the whole situation and will do whatever in my power lies to have the findings of such a commission favorably acted upon."

Roosevelt did not say which distinguished private citizen he hoped might chair this commission. He merely ended his letter with a reminder that he had been "very glad" to make one of Cleveland's friends Surgeon General.

John Mitchell received the President's new proposal doubtfully. He said he would consider it. Roosevelt, meanwhile, was put under medical orders to refrain from further work. He expressed his frustration to the Librarian of Congress:

> *Dear Mr. Putnam*: As I lead, to put it mildly, a sedentary life for the moment I would greatly like some books that would appeal to my queer taste. I do not suppose there are any histories or any articles upon the early Mediterranean races. That man Lindsay who wrote about prehistoric Greece has not put out a second volume, has he? Has a second volume

> of Oman's Art of War appeared? If so, send me either or both; if not, then a good translation of Niebuhr and Momsen [*sic*] or the best modern history of Mesopotamia. Is there a good history of Poland?

Putnam obliged, only to receive a presidential reprimand. "I do not like the Poland. It is too short."

While Roosevelt read and Mitchell pondered, violence continued to roar in the anthracite valleys. At night, military searchlights played nervously around Shenandoah. "Things are steadily growing worse," a state trooper reported, "and the future of this region is dark indeed." A Justice Department spy in Wilkes-Barre reported that he had lost sympathy for the miners. UMW executives were openly inciting mobs to riot. The New York *Sun* demanded that labor thugs be treated like Filipino guerrillas: "without parley and without terms." Governor Stone called out Pennsylvania's entire ten-thousand-man National Guard.

The weather turned cold and wet. Inch by inch, seepage mounted in empty mine shafts. Hills of unsold anthracite lay under the beating rain. Public pressure built on George Baer, who seemed at the point of a nervous breakdown before meeting with J. P. Morgan in New York. "He literally ran to the elevator making frantic motions with his right arm, to ward off the reporters," a UMW observer wrote Mitchell. "He almost hysterically repeated over and over, nothing to say, nothing to say. . . . He shook and trembled and his face was livid."

Mitchell, sensing weakness, turned Roosevelt down. "We believe that we went more than half way in our proposal at Washington, and we do not feel that we should be asked to make further sacrifice." His statement was published on 9 October. Within hours, a striker was shot dead at Shenandoah. Panicking, the mayors of more than one hundred of America's largest cities called for the nationalization of the anthracite industry.

Roosevelt noted that Poland's ancient kings had also been hampered by irresponsible subjects. "I must not be drawn into any violent step which would bring reaction and disaster afterward." He decided to appoint his commission of inquiry, whether Mitchell liked it or not. Congress was entitled to a full report on the situation before he took the law into his own hands. A follow-up letter reached Grover Cleveland on 11 October:

> In all the country there is no man whose name would add such weight to this enquiry as would yours. I earnestly beg you to say that you will accept. I am well aware of the great strain I put upon you by making such a request. I would not make it if I did not feel that the calamity now impending over our people may have consequences which without exaggeration are to be called terrible.

Cleveland was sixty-five years old, retired, and chronically short of money. His only substantial investment was in—of all things—the anthracite industry. If he accepted Roosevelt's invitation, he would be obliged to sell these stocks at current, depressed prices. "You rightly appreciate my reluctance to assume any public service," he wrote back. However, "I feel so deeply the gravity of the situation, and I so fully sympathize with you in your efforts to remedy present sad conditions, that I believe it is my duty to undertake the service."

Anticipating an early call, Cleveland sold his coal shares and waited for the President to tell him when he should report for work. But the call never came. Roosevelt's attention had been diverted by the magic name of J. P. Morgan.

It was Elihu Root who suggested that "Pierpontifex Maximus" might be able to succeed where reason had failed. Morgan was, after all, the financial gray eminence behind the mine operators. Their coal roads; slotted into his greater northeastern railway combination, and he had a seat on several of their boards.

Root told the President that he had "some ideas" that Morgan might persuade the operators to accept. Without saying what they were, he requested a temporary leave of absence, so that he could visit New York unofficially. "I don't want to represent you; I want entire freedom to say whatever I please."

One of the things Roosevelt liked about Root was his utter self-confidence. He granted leave, but first summoned Philander Knox and made his own attitude clear to both men: as soon as it became necessary for him to send the Army into Pennsylvania, he would do so without consulting them. He would use full force to reopen the mines, so that "the people on the eastern seaboard would have coal and have it right away." Root and Knox were welcome to submit formal, written protests, but he intended to act as if the nation were in a state of siege.

Far from dissenting, the Secretary of War put a force of ten thousand Army regulars on instant alert. Then Elihu Root, private citizen, took the midnight sleeper to New York.

While Root and Morgan conferred aboard the yacht *Corsair*, anchored off Manhattan, John Mitchell sat in his Wilkes-Barre digs, chewing on a cigar and snipping at the Sunday paper. A visitor saw that he was sinking into one of his frequent attacks of depression. All around him lay trashy piles of newsprint and dime novels; on his knees, a child's magazine cutout was gradually forming.

When Mitchell finished his scissor-work, he propped it on the mantelpiece. It depicted Abraham Lincoln and two unshackled black slaves, with a caption reading: "A Race Set Free, And The Country At Peace."

The weather turned dry and mild, but Roosevelt (semimobile now, on crutches) felt no release of tension. On the contrary, he began to hear rumors of a general strike. That, combined with a sudden frost, would certainly deliver him the greatest crisis faced by any President since April 1861.

Like Lincoln before him, he chose his military commander with care. General John M. Schofield, a veteran of the Pullman strike, was secretly summoned to 22 Jackson Place, and put in charge of Root's reserves. The President did not mince words. "I bid you pay no heed to any other authority, no heed to a writ from a judge, or anything else excepting my commands." Schofield must be ready to move at a half hour's notice, invade Pennsylvania, dispossess the operators, end the strike, and run the mines as receiver for the government.

The old soldier received these orders with equanimity. But Congressman James E. Watson, the House Republican Whip, was aghast when Roosevelt confided the details of his plan. "What about the Constitution of the United States? What about seizing private property without due process of law?" Exasperated, Roosevelt grabbed Watson by the shoulder and shouted, "The Constitution was made for the people and not the people for the Constitution."

Then, late on the evening of 13 October, Elihu Root and J. Pierpont Morgan crossed Lafayette Square and knocked on Roosevelt's door.

Walter Wellman, as usual the only journalist in town who knew what was going on, watched the door close behind Morgan. He knew the financier was carrying a document capable of ending the strike overnight—a document Root could have proclaimed from the deck of the *Corsair*. Yet here was the great J.P. coming south "to place the fruit of his power and labor before the young President." Capital, it would seem, was tacitly acknowledging the supremacy of Government.

At first, Roosevelt was disappointed with Morgan's "agreement," which was addressed to the American people and bore the signatures of all the operators. It began with several pages of familiar complaints, followed by an arbitration offer not much different from the one George Baer had floated at the conference. There was a stated willingness to accept, alternatively, Roosevelt's commission. But the operators sounded as arrogant as ever in dictating what kind of commissioners he should choose:

1. An officer of the Engineer Corps of either military or naval service of the United States.
2. An expert mining engineer, experienced in the mining

of coal and other minerals, and not in any way [still] connected with coal mining properties either anthracite or bituminous.

3. One of the judges of the United States court of the eastern district of Pennsylvania.
4. A man of prominence, eminent as a sociologist.
5. A man, who by active participation in mining and selling coal is familiar with the physical and commercial features of the business.

Anyone could see there was no place for labor here. The word sociologist introduced a note of jargon, yet signaled a clear preference: Carroll D. Wright was the author of *Outline of Practical Sociology*. Morgan added verbally that Judge George Gray, of the Third Judicial Circuit, and Thomas H. Watkins, a retired anthracite executive, would be acceptable candidates for slots 3 and 5. Three places on the proposed commission were thus earmarked for conservatives, and union sympathizers were unlikely to qualify for the first two.

Nevertheless, Roosevelt began to see a legal beauty in the document he held in his hands—beauty perfected by Elihu Root via many scratched-out sheets of *Corsair* stationery. Alone among his advisers, Root understood that the coal-strike conference had foundered not on the shoals of arbitration, but on the rock of recognition. The main element in Baer's and Markle's tirades had been their refusal to accredit a union, three fourths of whose members worked outside the anthracite field.

Thus, the language of the agreement pretended that the operators had never been against arbitration per se, only arbitration with the UMW. Their list of desirable commissioners took advantage of Mitchell's willingness to accept any board the President chose. It was also calculated to make Roosevelt seem to be taking their advice, whereas in fact Root's syntax left him plenty of room to negotiate each candidate. Ultimately, the operators hoped to boast that *they* had proposed arbitration, and were making the commission's decision *their* victory. A Pyrrhic one, perhaps—but Mitchell would surely concede it.

As Grover Cleveland remarked, "When quarreling parties are both in the wrong, and are assailed with blame . . . they will do strange things to save their faces."

Root and Morgan remained closeted with Roosevelt for one and a half hours. At last, the financier came down alone, and emerged into the night. Reporters surged around him. Usually, when confronted by the press, Morgan flinched, or cursed. Sometimes he even struck out with his cane. But now he smiled. A voice called, "Has the strike been settled?"

He stopped under a tree and relit his half-burned cigar, as if pondering an answer. Then, still smiling, he walked wordlessly off.

The "Corsair agreement" was announced on 14 October. Roosevelt invited John Mitchell to discuss it with him the following day. As he feared, the labor leader objected on the ground that it constrained free power of presidential appointment. Roosevelt asked if, "in view of the very great urgency of the case," the miners would perhaps "defer to the operators' views."

Mitchell was sure they would not—unless the commission was expanded to seven members, with at least two chosen freely. He would "do his best" to sell that notion to the UMW. Roosevelt said that if so, he would push for former President Cleveland in slot 1, instead of the Army engineer. The next four commissioners could be typecast as per the Agreement, while the last two would be selected by Mitchell and himself: a high Catholic ecclesiastic and a representative of labor.

Temptingly, he dropped the names of Bishop L. Spalding, a Baltimore patrician and industrial scholar, and Edgar E. Clark, chief of the Railway Conductors Union. Mitchell showed interest, and allowed that the latter would make an "excellent" commissioner. The first whiff of settlement gathered in the air.

Roosevelt cautioned that he could only "try" to get management to agree to all this. After Mitchell left, he ordered Root to get somebody from the House of Morgan to come south as quickly as possible. Then, feeling a need for fresh air, he laid aside his crutches and went for a long drive out of town.

George Perkins and Robert Bacon reached 22 Jackson Place at seven o'clock, as the President was dressing for dinner with John Hay. They said they had "full power" to represent both Morgan and the operators. He showed them his expanded list of commissioners, then limped the hundred yards to Hay's house. Perkins and Bacon remained behind to huddle on the telephone with Morgan and Baer.

While they conferred, Roosevelt celebrated. He obviously believed the strike was over. Pride in his skills as mediator, and joy in his returning health, bubbled up inside him. "He began talking at the oysters, and the *pousse-café* found him still at it," Hay reported to Henry Adams. "When he was one of us, we could sit on him—but who except you, can sit on a Kaiser?"

The strike, however, was not over, as Roosevelt found to his chagrin when he got back to Jackson Place at 10:00. Perkins and Bacon said they personally approved the idea of a seven-man commission, but that Baer was driving them mad with objections to the inclusion of Edgar Clark. Under no circumstances would the operators allow "a labor man" power over their future.

Roosevelt privately looked on the next three hours as a "screaming comedy." Yet the evening could well have disintegrated into tragedy. Perkins and Bacon predicted civil warfare if the President did not yield to Baer's objections. Roosevelt saw revolution if he did. Root and Wright joined in the debate, to a jangling counterpoint of long-distance telephone calls. Midnight struck. In two more hours, the morning newspapers would go to press. Roosevelt redoubled his pressure on Perkins and Bacon. Suddenly, the latter said there could be some "latitude" in choosing commissioners, as long as they were put under the right "headings." Roosevelt pounced.

I found that they did not mind my appointing any man,

> whether he was a labor man or not, so long as he was not appointed *as a labor man*. . . . I shall never forget the mixture of relief and amusement I felt when I thoroughly grasped the fact that while they would heroically submit to anarchy rather than have Tweedledum, yet if I would call it Tweedledee they would accept it with rapture; it gave me an illuminating glimpse into one corner of the mighty brains of these "captains of industry."

With a straight face, he proposed that Edgar E. Clark be moved to the "eminent sociologist" slot. After all, Mr. Clark must have "thought and studied deeply on social questions" as a union executive. Perkins and Bacon agreed at once. They also said yes to the selection of Bishop Spalding, while Roosevelt approved E. W. Parker of the United States Geological Survey as the scientist.

The President now had five commissioners acceptable to both sides, with one more slot—that of the Army engineer—not yet negotiated. For the seventh, he still hoped to appoint Grover Cleveland. If Clark qualified as a "sociologist," a former Commander-in-Chief could be described as having some military experience.

Suspecting, perhaps, that even mighty brains might jib at this, he said casually that he would like Carroll Wright to serve "as recorder." Perkins and Bacon again agreed, not realizing that the President now had, in effect, a reserve board member, whom he could promote at leisure if any of the seven proved problematic.

Morgan's men adjourned once more to the telephone. Back over the line came consent to the "eminent sociologist" and to the Catholic prelate. But Baer had the satisfaction of rejecting a former President of the United States. This permitted the instant elevation of Wright. And so, as Roosevelt put it, the thing was done. "Heavens and earth, it has been a struggle!"

Some weeks after the Coal Strike Commission had begun its work, and anthracite fires were glowing in forty million grates, George Baer encountered Owen Wister and roared at him, "Does your friend ever think?" The railroad executive was still furious over Roosevelt's "impetuous" intervention between free-market forces. Even the most conservative economic experts were predicting that United Mine Workers would win at least a 10 percent wage increase, plus fairer and safer working conditions and the right to arbitrate all disputes.

"He certainly seems to act," Wister replied.

The rest of the world seemed to agree. Theodore Roosevelt's mediation between capital and labor earned him fame as the first head of state to confront the largest problem of the twentieth century. He was cheered in the French Chamber of Deputies, and hailed by *The Times* of London as a political original. "In a most quiet and unobtrusive manner the President has done a very big and entirely new thing. We are witnessing not merely the ending of the coal strike, but the definite entry of a powerful government upon a novel sphere of operation."

At home, Roosevelt basked in a popular outpouring of admiration and affection that boded well for 1904. And far beyond that, to the end of his days, he could rejoice with falsetto giggles at "the eminent sociologist."

Honolulu Star-Bulletin 1st EXTRA

8 PAGES—HONOLULU, TERRITORY OF HAWAII, U. S. A., SUNDAY, DECEMBER 7, 1941—8 PAGES — PRICE FIVE CENTS

WAR!

(Associated Press by Transpacific Telephone)

SAN FRANCISCO, Dec. 7.—President Roosevelt announced this morning that Japanese planes had attacked Manila and Pearl Harbor.

OAHU BOMBED BY JAPANESE PLANES

SIX KNOWN DEAD, 21 INJURED, AT EMERGENCY HOSPITAL

Attack Made On Island's Defense Areas

By UNITED PRESS

WASHINGTON, Dec. 7.—Text of a White House announcement detailing the attack on the Hawaiian islands is:

"The Japanese attacked Pearl Harbor from the air and all naval and military activities on the island of Oahu, principal American base in the Hawaiian islands."

Oahu was attacked at 7:55 this morning by Japanese planes.

The Rising Sun, emblem of Japan, was seen on plane wing tips.

Wave after wave of bombers streamed through the clouded morning sky from the southwest and flung their missiles on a city resting in peaceful Sabbath calm.

According to an unconfirmed report received at the governor's office, the Japanese force that attacked Oahu reached island waters aboard two small airplane carriers.

It was also reported that at the governor's office either an attempt had been made to bomb the USS Lexington, or that it had been bombed.

CITY IN UPROAR

Within 10 minutes the city was in an uproar. As bombs fell in many parts of the city, and in defense areas the defenders of the islands went into quick action.

Army intelligence officers at Ft. Shafter announced officially shortly after 9 a. m. the fact of the bombardment by an enemy but long previous army and navy had taken immediate measures in defense.

"Oahu is under a sporadic air raid," the announcement said.

"Civilians are ordered to stay off the streets until further notice."

CIVILIANS ORDERED OFF STREETS

The army has ordered that all civilians stay off the streets and highways and not use telephones.

Evidence that the Japanese attack has registered some hits was shown by three billowing pillars of smoke in the Pearl Harbor and Hickam field area.

All navy personnel and civilian defense workers, with the exception of women, have been ordered to duty at Pearl Harbor.

The Pearl Harbor highway was immediately a mass of racing cars.

A trickling stream of injured people began pouring into the city emergency hospital a few minutes after the bombardment started.

Thousands of telephone calls almost swamped the Mutual Telephone Co., which put extra operators on duty.

At The Star-Bulletin office the phone calls deluged the single operator and it was impossible for this newspaper, for sometime, to handle the flood of calls. Here also an emergency operator was called.

HOUR OF ATTACK—7:55 A. M.

An official army report from department headquarters, made public shortly before 11, is that the first attack was at 7:55 a. m.

Witnesses said they saw at least 50 airplanes over Pearl Harbor.

The attack centered in the Pearl Harbor. Army authorities said:

"The rising sun was seen on the wing tips of the airplanes."

Although martial law has not been declared officially, the city of Honolulu was operating under M-Day conditions.

It is reliably reported that enemy objectives under attack were Wheeler field, Hickam field, Kaneohe bay and naval air station and Pearl Harbor.

Some enemy planes were reported shot down.

The body of the pilot was seen in a plane burning at Wahiawa.

Oahu appeared to be taking calmly after the first uproar of queries.

ANTIAIRCRAFT GUNS IN ACTION

First indication of the raid came shortly before 8 this morning when antiaircraft guns around Pearl Habor began sending up a thunderous barrage.

At the same time a vast cloud of black smoke arose from the naval base and also from Hickam field where flames could be seen.

BOMB NEAR GOVERNOR'S MANSION

Shortly before 9:30 a bomb fell near Washington Place, the residence of the governor. Governor Poindexter and Secretary Charles M. Hite were there.

It was reported that the bomb killed an unidentified Chinese man across the street in front of the Schuman Carriage Co. where windows were broken.

C. E. Daniels, a welder, found a fragment of shell or bomb at South and Queen Sts. which he brought into the City Hall. This fragment weighed about a pound.

At 10:05 a. m. today Governor Poindexter telephoned to The Star-Bulletin announcing he has declared a state of emergency for the entire territory.

He announced that Edouard L. Doty, executive secretary of the major disaster council, has been appointed director under the M-Day law's provisions.

Governor Poindexter urged all residents of Honolulu to remain off the street, and the people of the territory to remain calm.

Mr. Doty reported that all major disaster council wardens and medical units were on duty within a half hour of the time the alarm was given.

Workers employed at Pearl Harbor were ordered at 10:30 a. m. not to report at Pearl Harbor.

The mayor's major disaster council was to meet at the city hall at about 10:30 this morning.

At least two Japanese planes were reported at Hawaiian department headquarters to have been shot down.

One of the planes was shot down at Ft. Kamehameha and the other back of the Wa-

[illegible]

Hundreds See City Bombed

[illegible]

Names of Dead and Injured

[illegible]

Schools Closed

[illegible]

Editorial

HAWAII MEETS THE CRISIS

[illegible]

BULLETIN

Additional Star-Bulletin extras today will cover the latest developments in this war move.

from Roosevelt: The Soldier of Freedom

by James MacGregor Burns

The Japanese attack on Pearl Harbor on December 7, 1941 dealt a shocking blow to Americans' sense of security. Franklin D. Roosevelt (in office 1933–1945) provided exceptional leadership for the country and for the allied powers as well. James MacGregor Burns (born 1918) in his two-volume biography of Roosevelt offers this account of the 32nd president's response to the attack.

The war news from the Pacific was almost all bad. The Japanese were following their Pearl Harbor strike with lightning thrusts in the Philippines, Guam, Midway, Wake Island, in Kota Bahru, Singapore, Thailand, Hong Kong. The small, almost defenseless garrison on Guam faced impossible odds. Marines on Wake beat off the first Japanese landing, but the Pacific fleet was too crippled to send help, and it was clear that the Japanese would return. After smashing Clark Field, near Manila, enemy planes were striking at Cavite naval base. The Japanese, with nearly absolute freedom of naval and air movement, were rushing troops and arms west, south, and east.

The most crushing news of all arrived in Washington on the tenth. Japanese bombers from Saigon, catcing the *Prince of Wales* and the *Repulse* at sea without air cover, had bombed and torpedoed the great ships to the bottom. In London, Churchill twisted and writhed in bed as the import of the news sank in on him: the Japanese Navy was supreme from the Indian Ocean to the eastern Pacific.

For Roosevelt and his military chiefs the long-dreaded predicament was now fact: cut to the bone to help its allies, the nation's Army and Navy suddenly had to guard dozens of vital sectors. Rumors spread that Japanese warships were headed back to Hawaii, to Panama, even to California. Frantic calls for protection came in from coastal cities. The Army and Navy dared not be caught napping a second time. For a while all was improvisation and inadequacy. Antiaircraft regiments had to be sent to the West Coast without most of their guns. Aviation schools were stripped to fill out combat groups. A convoy of five ships, halfway to the Philippines with infantry, artillery, munitions, and seventy dive bombers and pursuit planes, was ordered back to Hawaii. But Stimson and Marshall, anxious to buck up MacArthur in his travail, appealed to the President, who asked the Navy chiefs to reconsider their decision. The convoy was rerouted to Brisbane.

During these days Roosevelt was never seen to lose his air of grave imperturbability, punctuated by moments of relief and laughter. He not only kept cool; he watched himself keep cool. He took the time to write to Early a curious memo noting the many comments that "the President seems to be taking the situation of extreme emergency in his stride, that he is looking well and that he does not seem to have any nerves." People tended to forget, the memo went on, that the President had been through this kind of thing in World War I, that he had personally visited practically all defense activities throughout the United States and many abroad, that he had gone to Europe in the spring of 1918 on a destroyer and "probably saw a greater part of the war area than any other American." Roosevelt had long been defensive about his failure to don uniform in World War I; now he was in psychological uniform as Commander in Chief.

In this, the biggest crisis of his life, Roosevelt's first instinct was to unify the nation, his next to unify the anti-Axis world. Churchill had asked if he could come over to Washington at once, for military conferences, and Roosevelt gladly agreed. While Churchill sailed westward on his new battleship the *Duke of York*, Roosevelt took steps to solidify the spirit of unity that had swept the country after Pearl Harbor.

Party harmony was no problem; the President accepted pledges from the Democratic and Republican National Chairmen of cooperation during the war and suggested that the two party organizations could help civil defense. Nor did the Great Debate have to be adjourned; former isolationists were tumbling over themselves with promises of support. The most worrisome continuing division was between management and labor. The National Defense Mediation Board had been devastated by the resignation of the CIO representatives. Clearly new machinery was necessary for industrial peace. Shortly after Pearl Harbor the President asked union chiefs and the Business Advisory Council of the Commerce Department to designate representatives for a conference to draft a basic wartime labor policy. The first and essential objective of the conference, the President made clear, would be to reach a unanimous agreement to prevent strikes during the war period.

The President invited the conferees to the White House for a preliminary talk. In they came: industrialists who had hated Roosevelt; Lewis, who had broken with him in the 1940 election; Green, friendly but wary. The President greeted each delegate and then spoke to the group for almost half an hour—about the need to do "perfectly unheard of things" in war, about the need for a complete agreement quickly, for a time limit on conference speeches, for a self-imposed discipline. He had just been thinking of an old Chinese proverb, he said: "Lord, reform Thy world, beginning with me."

There was not much difference between labor and management, the President went on. "It's like the old Kipling saying about 'Judy O'Grady an' the Colonel's Lady.' They are both the same under the skin. That is true in this country, especially this country, and we want to keep it so." His manner, Frances Perkins noted, was both sober and buoyant, confident and serious, and even touched with humility. The shock of Pearl Harbor, she felt, the hazards ahead, had acted like a spiritual purge and left him simply stronger, more single-minded. The conferees went on to their labors moved by the President, if still unsure of finding common ground.

Christmas was nearing, but a strange Christmas for the nation and for the Roosevelts. Thousands of men were taking their last leaves before shipping out; other thousands had their Christmas furloughs canceled; whole outfits were pulled out of posts and bases overnight. The Roosevelts were not immune to the new anxieties of war. In New York a few days before Christmas Joseph Lash talked with Eleanor Roosevelt on the phone. He found her worried and despondent in her Sixty-fifth Street home; she mentioned having had a hard day and then burst into tears. Lash wondered if she was upset by some trouble in her work at the Office of Civilian Defense; but not so. She and the President, she told him, had said good-by to their son James, who was headed for Hawaii, and to Elliott. They had to go, of course, but it was hard; if only by the law of averages, not all her boys would return. She wept again, then steadied herself. No one saw the President weep. Probably he could not; on his desk awaiting his signature was a bill that could send seven million men, from twenty to forty-four years old, off to the battle fronts.

Only one sock—Fala's—would hang from the White House mantle, it was reported. But on December 22 Winston Churchill arrived in Washington, and life at the White House was instantly transformed.

Roosevelt was waiting, propped against his car, at the Washington airport as Churchill flew in from Hampton Roads, where he and his party had disembarked. With the usual plump cigar clamped in his teeth, the Prime Minister marched over to the President and "clasped his strong hand with comfort and pleasure," Churchill wrote later. After a semiformal dinner for seventeen the Prime Minister was installed in the big bedroom across from Hopkins's, with his cherished traveling map room nearby.

Suddenly the second floor of the White House was an imperial command post, with British officials hurrying in and out with their old red leather dispatch cases. The White House servants were soon agape at Churchill's drinking, eating, and sleeping habits. The President and the Prime Minister were together for several hours every day, with Hopkins often present. They worked together in the closest familiarity:

sometimes after cocktails Churchill would wheel Roosevelt in his chair from the drawing room to the elevator, as a token of respect, but also with his image of Raleigh spreading his cloak before Elizabeth. Eleanor soon discovered with concern that her guest took a long nap in the afternoon while her husband worked—but that the President hated to miss any of Churchill's and Hopkins's talk in the evening, and stayed up much later than usual.

The two leaders and their staffs at once plunged into the business of war. Roosevelt's first priority, however, was not military strategy, but a declaration of the "associated nations" to symbolize the unity and aspirations of the anti-Axis coalition. The President and the Prime Minister, using a State Department draft and working much as they had at Argentia, each wrote a separate statement and then blended them together. Since many governments had to be consulted, further drafting went on while the two leaders turned to immediate military problems.

Christmas Eve they stood side by side on the south portico for the traditional ceremony of lighting the tree. A great throng waited in the cold blackness below. Addressing his listeners as "fellow workers for freedom," Roosevelt said: "Our strongest weapon in this war is that conviction of the dignity and brotherhood of man which Christmas Day signifies. . . ." He presented Churchill, who matched him in eloquence: "I have the honor to add a pendant to the necklace of that Christmas good will and kindness with which our illustrious friend, the President, has encircled the homes and families of the United States." Christmas Day was observed without a single son or grandchild in the house. Roosevelt and Churchill attended an interdenominational service, dined with a company of sixty, listened to Christmas carols by visiting carolers—and then worked on the war until long after midnight.

One paramount question had occupied Churchill and his colleagues as they plotted strategy in the ordered calm of the *Duke of York*. Would an aroused American people, venting its wrath over Pearl Harbor, force the President to turn the main weight of the nation against Japan, leaving Britain to cope alone with the Axis in Western Europe, Africa, and the Middle East? Had the carefully fashioned Atlantic First strategy collapsed when the first bombs were dropped in the Pacific? This cardinal question embraced numerous secondary ones. If Roosevelt stuck to Atlantic First—and it was Churchill's supreme aim to induce him to do so—what would be the plan of attack against Hitler? How could Japan be contained or at least slowed in the Pacific while the Allies concentrated on Germany? How would the Allied command be organized in the vast Pacific and Atlantic theaters? And how would new plans affect demand, supply, and transportation of munitions?

Atlantic First was not left long in doubt. Roosevelt and his military chiefs quickly made clear that—even under the frightful pressure of Pacific defeats—the Americans still saw Germany as the main enemy and victory in Europe as crucial to the whole global effort. Indeed, little time was spent during these tumultuous days on any fundamental reconsideration of the long-planned priority. The old Plan Dog was almost taken for granted. Reassured, Churchill, in the first evening's discussion, plunged into the next question—strategy for Europe.

The Prime Minister had rarely been in better form. He had carefully worked out his plans for Europe and cleared them with his military men on the way across the ocean. Now, flanked by Beaverbrook and Halifax, he presented his case to Roosevelt, Hull, Hopkins, and Welles. If the Germans were held in Russia, he said, they would try something else—probably an attack through Spain and Portugal into North Africa. It was vital to forestall such a move. He than presented his plan—GYMNAST. He proposed that American forces invade Northwest Africa in the Casablanca area, and later hook up with British troops renewing their drive along the North African coast from the east into Tunisia.

The eager Prime Minister wanted to launch the attack quickly—in three weeks, he hoped. He had 55,000 troops ready to load onto ships at short notice. The actual plan of operation would depend largely on whether the French authorities in Northwest Africa cooperated or not. It seemed to Churchill—and so he reported confidently to his War Cabinet—that Roosevelt favored the plan "with or without invitation" from the French.

Perhaps Roosevelt was merely being the polite host this first evening; perhaps, as the absent Stimson and Marshall feared, he tended to be vulnerable to Churchill's eloquence and zeal when his military staff was not with him. In any event, Roosevelt's enthusiasm for a North African invasion had cooled markedly by next day, when the two leaders presided over a meeting of their staffs. The President now spoke on the basis of a War Department memorandum that stressed the safety of the British Isles as the central "fortress" and of Atlantic communications, but played down the value of American action anywhere in the Mediterranean. Stimson and Marshall had won the President's endorsement of this approach at a war conference the day before the British arrived; but the Secretary was as surprised as he was delighted when his chief now used the memorandum to brief Churchill and his party.

While Churchill's hopes for GYMNAST sank, the President posed other major possibilities. He was willing to take over the defense of Northern Ireland, thus freeing British troops for use elsewhere. He granted the importance of the islands in the eastern Atlantic, but inclined toward the Cape Verde Islands, rather than the Azores. He acclaimed the British successes in Libya but doubted the value of placing American troops there. He then moved across the globe to the Pacific. It was vital, he said, that Singapore be held; the United States would do its utmost to save the Philippines, or at least to help the defense of the Dutch East Indies.

By the time Churchill took over, the initiative had been gained by the President. The Prime Minister still clung to GYMNAST, emphasizing that British advances into Tunisia might arouse French support, or precipitate a showdown between Berlin and Vichy—and in either case Africa would be a fine opportunity. But Marshall remained cool to GYMNAST if it required a large American force.

The emergent difference between the Allies cast a long shadow on future strategy. In proposing GYMNAST Churchill had challenged the strategic assumptions and professional bias of Marshall and his fellow soldiers, and especially Stimson. The Americans were inclining toward a long build-up and then a massive, concentrated thrust toward the enemy center—Germany. Any other move was a dispersion of effort unless it directly supported this central thrust. The American mind in war planning, as well as in commerce and production, Churchill felt, ran to "broad, sweeping, logical conclusions on the largest scale," while the British allowed more for the role of opportunism and improvisation, trying to adjust to unfolding events rather than to dominate them. To the American military such strategic assumptions led to expediency, dispersion of effort, to that "peripheralism" that had marked so much of Churchill's thinking beginning with the Dardanelles in World War I. To the British, with their limited resources and perhaps more patient view of history, this kind of strategy was more supple, flexible, sophisticated. Churchill also feared that a long preparation for the final assault by the Americans would mean their hoarding the munitions and supplies that he had been planning on for the months directly ahead.

GYMNAST was also being strangled by the rush of events. While the planners talked in Washington, the Japanese hurricane was sweeping south and west. Some in the White House feared that the Japanese might bombard the West Coast, lay mines in the ports, or even land troops from the sea or air. Roosevelt and his staff still did not flinch from their strategic commitment to Atlantic First, but the crisis in the Pacific could demand day-to-day commitments that might erode that strategy. Even to slow up the Japanese, Washington had to support and strengthen its outposts, and the shipping requirements were appalling. The Japanese were carving an enormous salient into the direct route between the West Coast and Tokyo, which ordinarily would run just south of Alaska. The turnaround time between the East Coast and Australia was three months. Shipping had been short all along; now it would clog Allied strategy in both oceans.

The Pacific crisis also precipitated the whole problem of unified command. On Christmas afternoon, at a meeting of the American and British military chiefs in the Federal Reserve Building, across Constitution Avenue from the War and Navy buildings, Marshall seized the initiative. The Japanese could not be stopped, he said, unless there was complete unity of command over naval, land, and air forces. "With differences between groups and between services, the situation is impossible unless we operate on a frank and direct basis." He was no orator, but he was so earnest that his words became eloquent. "I am convinced that there must be one man in command of the entire theatre—air, ground, and ships." Cooperation was not enough; human frailties were such that local commanders would not put their troops under another service. He was ready to go the limit.

Marshall had a special reason to speak feelingly; at this point he was still smarting from a brief skirmish with the President. That morning he had heard that on Christmas Eve his Commander in Chief had blithely discussed with Churchill the possibility that if American forces assigned to MacArthur were not able to get to the Pacific, they be turned over to the British. When Marshall and his colleagues took this report to Stimson, the Secretary became so heated over this threat to his precious reserves for MacArthur that he telephoned Hopkins that he would resign if the President persisted in this kind of thing. Hopkins raised this matter with Roosevelt and Churchill, who both denied that they had reached such an agreement—but Stimson cited the minutes that a British secretary had made of the evening meeting. The episode bolstered Marshall's view that only a unified Pacific Theater command would permit orderly planning and decision making.

That way of running things was not much to Roosevelt's taste. Typically he had not made basic changes in his own command arrangements. He had put the old Army-Navy Joint Board under the White House in 1939, but he preferred to deal informally and often separately with his military chiefs. His British guests were agog at the American command setup. "There are no regular meetings of their Chiefs of Staff," Dill wrote home to Brooke, "and if they do meet there is no secretariat to record their proceedings. They have no joint planners and executive planning staff. . . ." Simply informing the President was a problem. "He just sees the Chiefs of Staff at odd times, and again no record. There is no such thing as a Cabinet meeting. . . . The whole organization belongs to the days of George Washington. . . ."

In the press of crisis, though, Roosevelt was willing to change his ways—at least for a theater 8,000 miles away. He supported Marshall's specific proposal that the combined American, British, Dutch, and Australian—ABDA—sea, land, and air forces in the Southwest Pacific be placed at once under a single top commander with an inter-Allied staff. The huge theater would embrace not only the East Indies, Malaya, the Philippines, New Guinea, and Burma, but would also stretch limitlessly to New Britain, the Solomons, the Fijis, Samoa. Marshall won the grudging backing of Knox and some of the admirals. The main obstacle would be the British—and here Roosevelt tried some reverse English. "Don't be in a hurry to turn down the proposal the President is going to make to you," Hopkins said to Churchill, "before you know who is the man we have in mind." It was Wavell. Churchill was dubious about unity of command over such a vast expanse; some of his staff wondered whether Wavell was slated to be a British scapegoat who would preside over a rapidly disappearing command. But in the face of Roosevelt's and Marshall's persuasiveness, backed by Beaverbrook at a timely moment, Churchill agreed to the new command and commander.

This step in turn forced a far bigger decision on the structure of the top command. To whom was the ABDA commander to report? The British proposed a divided chiefs of staff committee, operating in both Washington and London and clearing with the Dutch, Australians, and New Zealanders. After some hesitation Roosevelt rejected this cumbersome arrangement and substituted a simple meeting in Washington between the American and British staffs, in turn reporting to the President and the Prime Minister, with the other nations consulted "if advisable." It was no embarrassment to Roosevelt that he had no joint chiefs in the British sense, and that he had no air chief as a counterpart to the head of Britain's RAF. He simply created, as the American component of the Combined Chiefs of Staff, a Joint Chiefs of Staff composed of Marshall, King, a hard-bitten old salt slated to replace Stark as Chief of Naval Operations, and General Henry H. ("Hap") Arnold, whose genial manner masked a flair for organization and management. In this rather backward fashion were the Allied and American command structures established.

"The Americans have got their way and the war will be run from Washington," wrote Churchill's observant personal physician, Sir Charles Wilson (later Lord Moran), doubtless reflecting feeling among the British chiefs, "but they will not be wise to push us so unceremoniously in the future." Churchill accepted the decision with good grace, largely because of his profound confidence in Roosevelt, Marshall, and Hopkins.

from Truman

by David McCullough

David McCullough's (born 1933) biography of Harry Truman (in office 1945–1953) includes this account of the weeks leading up to the detonation of an atomic bomb over Hiroshima. Truman's advisors included Secretary of War Henry Stimson and newly appointed Secretary of State Jimmy Byrnes.

With the start of his second week at Potsdam, Truman knew that decisions on the bomb could wait no longer.

At 10:00 Sunday morning, July 22, he attended Protestant services led by a chaplain from the 2nd Armored Division. Then later in the morning he went to a Catholic mass conducted by his old friend Father Curtis Tiernan, the chaplain of Battery D, who was serving as Chief of Army Chaplains in Europe and had been flown to Berlin at Truman's request.

"I'm going to mass at 11:30 presided over by him," Truman wrote to Bess at mid-morning. "I've already been to a Protestant service so I guess I should stand in good with the Almighty for the coming week—and my how I'll need it."

Stimson had appeared at Number 2 Kaiserstrasse shortly after breakfast, with messages from Washington saying all was about ready for the "final operation" and that a decision on the target cities was needed. Stimson wanted Kyoto removed from the list, and having heard the reasons, Truman agreed. Kyoto would be spared. "Although it was a target of considerable military importance," Stimson would write, "it had been the capital of Japan and was a shrine of Japanese art and culture. . . . " First on the list of approved targets was Hiroshima, southern headquarters and depot for Japan's homeland army.

Early on Monday, Stimson came again to Truman's second-floor office. A warning message to Japan, an ultimatum, was nearly ready, the document to be known as the Potsdam Declaration. Stimson thought it unwise at this point to insist on unconditional surrender, a term the Japanese would take to mean they could not keep their Emperor. He urged a revision to read that the Allies would "prosecute the war against Japan until she ceases to resist." But Byrnes had vehemently opposed any such change. Unconditional surrender was an objective too long established, too often proclaimed; it had been too great a rallying cry from the time of Pearl Harbor to abandon now, Byrnes insisted. Truman had reaffirmed it as policy in his first speech to Congress on April 16. It was what the Nazis had been made to accept, and its renunciation with the Japanese at this late date, after so much bloodshed, the acceptance of anything less with victory so near, would seem like appeasement. Politically it would be disastrous, Byrnes was also sure. To most Americans, Hirohito was the villainous symbol of Japan's fanatical military clique. A Gallup Poll in June had shown that a mere fraction of Americans, only 7 percent, thought he should be retained after the war, even as a puppet, while a full third of the people thought he should be executed as a war criminal. Like others who had been advising Truman, Byrnes considered any negotiations with Japan over terms a waste of time and felt that if Hirohito were to remain in place, then the war had been pointless. Though Truman listened carefully, Stimson failed to convince him otherwise.

Tuesday, July 24, was almost certainly the fateful day.

At 9:20 a.m. Stimson again climbed the stairs to Truman's office, where he found the President seated behind the heavy carved desk, "alone with his work." Stimson had brought another message:

Washington, July 23, 1945

> Top Secret
> Operational Priority
> War 36792 Secretary of War Eyes Only top secret from Harrison.
> Operation may be possible any time from August 1 depending on state of preparation of patient and condition of atmosphere. From point of view of patient only, some chance August 1 to 3, good chance August 4 to 5 and barring unexpected relapse almost certain before August 10.

Truman "said that was just what he wanted," Stimson wrote in his diary, "that he was highly delighted. . . . "

Later, Truman wrote of a consensus at Potsdam, among Byrnes, Stimson, Leahy, Marshall, and General Arnold, that the bomb should be used. He recalled that Marshall again stressed the number of lives that would be saved. "I asked General Marshall what it would cost in lives to land on the Tokyo plain and other places in Japan. It was his opinion that such an invasion would cost at a minimum a quarter of a million American casualties. . . ." He himself reached his own conclusion only "after long and careful thought," he wrote, adding, "I did not like the weapon."

Very possibly there was no one, clearcut moment when he made up his mind, or announced that he had. Most likely, he never seriously considered not using the bomb. Indeed, to have said no at this point and called everything off would have been so drastic a break with the whole history of the project, not to say the terrific momentum of events that summer, as to have been almost inconceivable.

Some critics and historians in years to come would argue that Japan was already finished by this time, just as Eisenhower had said and as several intelligence reports indicated. Japan's defeat, however, was not the issue. It was Japan's surrender that was so desperately wanted, since every day Japan did not surrender meant the killing continued. In theory, Japan had been defeated well before Truman became President. (Studies by the Japanese themselves had determined a year and a half before, by January 1944, that Japan had lost the war.) Yet in the three months since

Truman took office, American battle casualties in the Pacific were nearly half the total from three years of war in the Pacific. The nearer victory came, the heavier the price in blood. And whatever the projected toll in American lives in an invasion, it was too high if it could be avoided.

"We had only too abundant evidence in those days that surrender was excluded from the Japanese ethos," remembered a captain in Military Intelligence, Charlton Ogburn, Jr. "Thousands of our Marines and soldiers had died rooting Japanese from their foxholes and bunkers when they were perfectly aware that their situation was hopeless." During the whole war, not a single Japanese unit had surrendered.

While intelligence reports indicated that Japan was beaten, they also forecast that the Japanese would hold out for months longer, meanwhile issuing intermittent peace feelers, both to bring the war to what they would regard as an acceptable conclusion, and "to weaken the determination of the United States to fight to the bitter end. . . ."

> The basic policy of the present [Japanese] government [said a combined Intelligence Committee report of July 8, 1945] is to fight as long and as desperately as possible in the hope of avoiding complete defeat and of acquiring a better bargaining position in a negotiated peace. Japanese leaders are now playing for time in the hope that Allied war weariness, Allied disunity, or some "miracle" will present an opportunity to arrange a compromise peace.

Nor, it must be stressed, was there ever anything hypothetical about preparations for the invasion—on both sides—a point sometimes overlooked in later years.

Truman had earlier authorized the Chiefs of Staff to move more than 1 million troops for a final attack on Japan. Thirty divisions were on the way to the Pacific from the European theater, from one end of the world to the other, something never done before. Supplies in tremendous quantity were piling up on Saipan. Japan had some 2.5 million regular troops on the home islands, but every male between the ages of fifteen and sixty, every female from seventeen to forty-five, was being conscripted and armed with everything from ancient brass cannon to bamboo spears, taught to strap explosives to their bodies and throw themselves under advancing tanks. One woman would remember being given a carpenter's awl and instructed that killing just one American would do. "You must aim at the abdomen," she was told. "Understand? The abdomen." The general in charge of defense plans told other senior officers, "By pouring 20 divisions into the battle within two weeks of the enemy's landing, we will annihilate him entirely and insure a Japanese victory." Thousands of planes were ready to serve as *kamikazes*.

To no one with the American and Allied forces in the Pacific did it look as though the Japanese were about to quit. On July 15, *The New York Times* reported that twenty-five war-front correspondents from the United States and Australia had compared notes and their guess was the war would not end for nearly a year, not until June 1946. At the Pentagon, a long-remembered poster in the halls showed the face of a combat-hardened infantryman looking with grim determination at a map of the Japanese home islands, while across the top in bold letters was slashed the single word "Next!" There was no talk at the Pentagon of an early end to the war. The great concern was the likelihood of huge Japanese forces in China and Southeast Asia fighting on even if the government in Tokyo were to give up.

Truman foresaw unprecedented carnage in any attempted invasion. "It occurred to me," he would remark a few months later, "that a quarter of a million of the flower of our young manhood were worth a couple of Japanese cities, and I still think they were and are." But whether 250,000 or 20,000 casualties would result was not the issue at the moment, not if the shock effect of a single devastating blow, or two, could stop the war—and particularly when devastating blows, in the form of B-29 raids, had become the standard, almost daily routine.

"Today's prime fact is war," Henry Stimson had said at the start of one Interim Committee meeting. The Japanese were the despised enemy, perpetrators of the treacherous attack on Pearl Harbor (and then in the midst of peace talks), perpetrators of the bombing of Manila and the Bataan death march. They were the murderers of American prisoners of war, the fanatics who ordered the seemingly insane *kamikaze* attacks. The details of the Bataan death march had become known only in February and enraged the country. Other atrocities included the Palawan Massacre, during which Japanese soldiers on the Philippine island of Palawan lured 140 American prisoners of war into air-raid trenches, then doused them with gasoline and burned them alive. A few days after the German surrender in May, the papers had carried a photograph of a blindfolded prisoner of war, an American flyer down on his knees, his hands tied behind his back, about to be beheaded by a Japanese officer swinging a sword.

At Potsdam, as Bohlen was to write, "the spirit of mercy was not throbbing in the breast of any Allied official," either for the Germans or the Japanese.

And how could a President, or the others charged with responsibility for the decision, answer to the American people if when the war was over, after the bloodbath of an invasion of Japan, it became known that a weapon sufficient to end the war had been available by midsummer and was not used?

Had the bomb been ready in March and deployed by Roosevelt, had it shocked Japan into surrender then, it would have already saved nearly fifty thousand American lives lost in the Pacific in the time since, not to say a vastly larger number of Japanese lives.

Nor had anyone ever doubted that Roosevelt would use it. "At no time, from 1941 to 1945, did I ever hear it suggested by the President, or by any other responsible member of the government, that atomic energy should not be used in the war," wrote Stimson. "All of us of course understood the terrible responsibility involved . . . President Roosevelt particularly spoke to me many times of his own awareness of the catastrophic potentialities of our work. But we were at war. . . ."

Leahy later said, "I know FDR would have used it in a minute to prove that he hadn't wasted two billion dollars."

"I'll say that we'll end the war a year sooner now," Truman had told Bess in a letter the week before, speaking of Stalin's agreement to come in against Japan, "and think of the kids who won't be killed! That's the important thing." To him it was always the important thing. An invasion of Japan would be work for ground troops, dirty, God-awful business for infantry and artillery, as he knew from experience. For unlike Roosevelt or Woodrow Wilson, or any Commander in Chief since the advent of modern war, Truman had been in combat with ground troops. At the Argonne, seeing a German battery pull into position on the left flank, beyond his assigned sector, he had ordered his battery to open fire, because his action would save lives, even though he could face a court-martial. "It is just the same as artillery on our side," he would say later of the bomb, which would strike many people as appallingly insensitive and simplistic, but he was speaking from the experience of war.

Once, when presiding judge of Jackson County, he had, by his own private confession, allowed a crooked contractor to steal $10,000 in order to forestall the stealing of ten times the amount. He had permitted evil in order to prevent a larger evil and saw no other choice. Had he done right, had he done wrong, he had asked, writing alone late at night in the Pickwick Hotel. "You judge it, I can't."

Conceivably, as many would later argue, the Japanese might have surrendered before November and the scheduled invasion. Conceivably, they could have been strangled by naval blockade, forced to surrender by continued fire bombing, with its dreadful toll, as some strategists were saying at the time. Possibly the single sticking point was, after all, the Allied demand for unconditional surrender. But no one close to Truman was telling him not to use the new weapon. General Marshall fully expected the Japanese to fight on even if the bomb were dropped and proved as effective as the scientists predicted. Marshall saw the bomb more as a way to make the invasion less costly. That it might make the invasion unnecessary was too much to expect. "We knew the Japanese were determined and fanatical . . . and we would have to exterminate them man by man," he would later tell David Lilienthal. "So we thought the bomb would be a wonderful weapon as a protection and preparation for landings." Marshall had been so appalled by American casualties at Iwo Jima that he had favored using poison gas at Okinawa.

A petition drawn up by Leo Szilard, urging on grounds of morality that Japan be warned in advance, had been signed by seventy scientists but was not delivered to Washington until after Truman had left for

Potsdam. Truman never saw it. But neither did he see the counter opinions voiced by those scientists urging that the bomb be used, and on grounds of morality. "Are not the men of the fighting forces . . . who are risking their lives for the nation, entitled to the weapons which have been designed," said one petition. "In short, are we to go on shedding American blood when we have available means to a steady victory? No! If we can save even a handful of American lives, then let us use this weapon—now!"

> It is hard to imagine anything more conclusive than the devastation of all the eastern coastal cities of Japan by fire bombs [wrote another scientist]; a more fiendish hell than the inferno of blazing Tokyo is beyond the pale of conception. Then why do we attempt to draw the line of morality here, when it is a question of degree, not a question of kind?

In a poll of 150 scientists at the Metallurgical Laboratory at Chicago, 87 percent voted for military use of the weapon, if other means failed to bring surrender. Arthur Compton was asked for his opinion:

> What a question to answer [he later wrote]! Having been in the very midst of these discussions, it seemed to me that a firm negative stand on my part might still prevent an atomic attack on Japan. Thoughts of my pacifist Mennonite ancestors flashed through my mind. I knew all too well the destruction and human agony the bombs would cause. I knew the danger they held in the hands of some future tyrant. These facts I had been living with for four years. But I wanted the war to end. I wanted life to become normal again. . . . I hoped that by use of the bombs many fine young men I knew might be released at once from the demands of war and thus be given a chance to live and not to die.

Churchill was to write of the decision that was no decision, and in retrospect this seems to have been the case. "The historic fact remains, and must be judged in the after-time," Churchill wrote, "that the decision whether or not to use the atomic bomb to compel the surrender of Japan was never an issue. There was unanimous, automatic, unquestioned agreement around our table; nor did I ever hear the slightest suggestion that we should do otherwise."

"Truman made no decision because there was no decision to be made," recalled George Elsey, remembering the atmosphere of the moment. "He could no more have stopped it than a train moving down a track. . . . It's all well and good to come along later and say the bomb was a horrible thing. The whole goddamn war was a horrible thing."

For his part, Truman stated later:

> The final decision of where and when to use the atomic bomb was up to me. Let there be no mistake about it. I regarded the bomb as a military weapon and never had any doubt that it should be used. The top military advisers to the President recommended its use, and when I talked to Churchill he unhesitatingly told me that he favored the use of the atomic bomb if it might aid to end the war.

Though nothing was recorded on paper, the critical moment appears to have occurred at Number 2 Kaiserstrasse later in the morning of Tuesday, July 24, when, at 11:30, the combined American and British Chiefs of Staff convened with Truman and Churchill in the dining room. This was the one time when Truman, Churchill, and their military advisers were all around a table, in Churchill's phrase. From this point it was settled: barring some unforeseen development, the bomb would be used within a few weeks. Truman later told Arthur Compton that the day of the decision was the same day he informed Stalin, and that occurred late the afternoon of the 24th.

It happened at the end of a particularly contentious session at the Cecilienhof Palace. The meeting was just breaking up when Truman rose from his chair and alone walked slowly around the table to where Stalin stood with his interpreter.

"I casually mentioned to Stalin that we had a new weapon of

unusual destructive force," Truman remembered. "All he said was that he was glad to hear it and hoped we would make 'good use of it against the Japanese.' "

Truman did not specify what kind of weapon it was—he did not use the words "atomic bomb"—or say anything about sharing scientific secrets. Stalin seemed neither surprised nor the least curious. He did not ask the nature of the weapon, or how it was made, or why he hadn't been told before this. He did not suggest that Soviet scientists be informed or permitted to examine it. He did not, in fact, appear at all interested.

To Bohlen, who was watching closely from across the room, Stalin's response seemed so altogether offhand that Bohlen wondered whether the President had made himself clear. "If he had had the slightest idea of the revolution in world affairs which was in progress his reactions would have been obvious," wrote Churchill, who had kept his eye on Stalin's face. Byrnes, too, was certain Stalin had "not grasped the importance of the discovery," and would soon be asking for more details. But this Stalin never did. He never mentioned the subject again for the remainder of the conference.

The fact was Stalin already knew more than any of the Americans or British imagined. Soviet nuclear research had begun in 1942, and as would be learned later, a German-born physicist at Los Alamos, a naturalized British citizen named Klaus Fuchs, had been supplying the Russians with atomic secrets for some time, information that in Moscow was judged "extremely excellent and very valuable." Stalin had understood perfectly what Truman said. Later, in the privacy of their Babelsberg quarters, according to Marshal Georgi Zhukov, Stalin instructed Molotov to "tell Kurchatov [of the Soviet atomic project] to hurry up the work." (Also, according to the Russian historian Dmitri Volkogonov, Stalin went even further that evening when he cabled Lavrenti Beria, who had overall supervision of the project, to put on the pressure.)

In years to come Truman often said that having made his decision about the bomb, he went to bed and slept soundly. He would be pictured retiring for the night at the White House, his mind clear that he had done the right thing. But in the strange "nightmare" house at

Babelsberg, in the unremitting heat of the German summer, he was sleeping rather poorly and in considerably more turmoil than his later claims ever suggested.

"No one who played a part in the development of the bomb or in our decision to use it felt happy about it," recalled Jimmy Byrnes, who was quartered downstairs.

"We have discovered the most terrible bomb in the history of the world," Truman wrote in his diary on Wednesday, July 25, the day the general military order was issued to the Air Force to proceed with the plan, and "terrible" was the word he would keep coming back to. He wondered if the bomb might be "the fire of destruction" prophesied in the Bible. As if to convince himself, he wrote of how it would be used on military targets only, which he knew to be only partly true.

> This weapon is to be used against Japan between now and August 10th. I have told the Sec of War, Mr. Stimson, to use it so that military objectives and soldiers and sailors are the target and not women and children. Even if the Japs are savages, ruthless, merciless and fanatic, we as the leader of the world for the common welfare cannot drop this terrible bomb on the old capital [Kyoto] or the new [Tokyo, where the Imperial Palace had been spared thus far].
>
> He and I are in accord. The target will be a purely military one and we will issue a warning statement asking the Japs to surrender and save lives. I'm sure they will not do that, but we will have given them a chance. It is certainly a good thing for the world that Hitler's crowd or Stalin's did not discover this atomic bomb. It seems to be the most terrible thing ever discovered, but it can be made useful.

Whether this final thought—that it could be made useful—was his irrepressible, native optimism and faith in progress coming to the fore, or yet another way of trying to convince himself, or both of these, or merely means useful to end the war, is open to question.

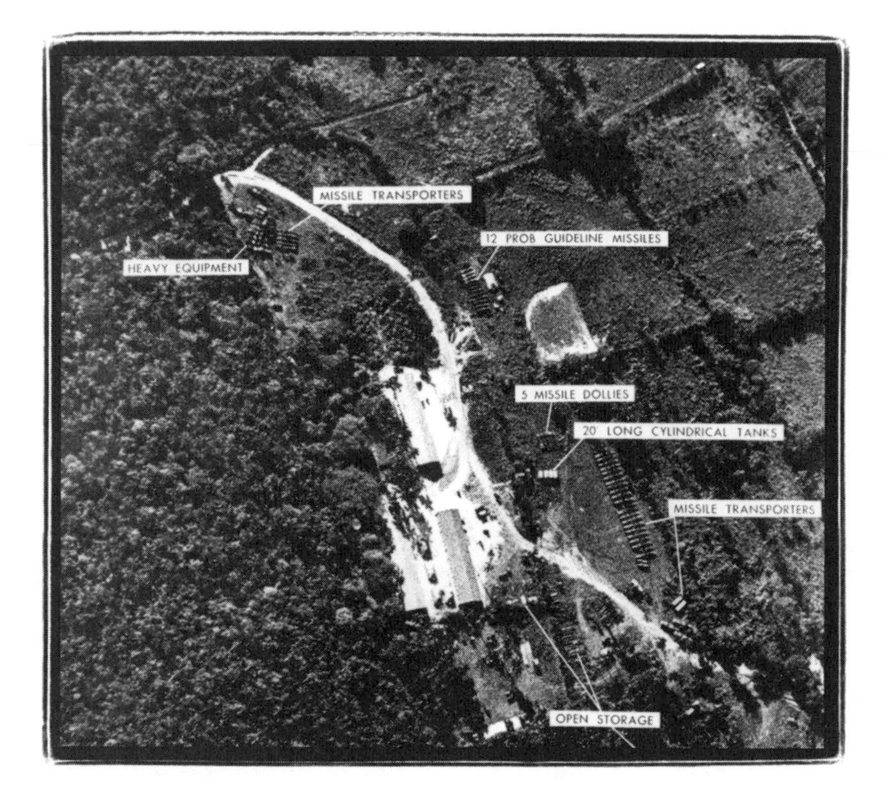

from The Crisis Years

by Michael R. Beschloss

John F. Kennedy (in office 1961–1963) in October, 1962, learned that the Russians were installing nuclear missiles in Cuba. Historian Michael R. Beschloss (born 1955) chronicles the president's advisory meetings during the early stages of the crisis.

Around the Cabinet table, Tuesday, October 16, at noon, with the reels of the President's secret tape recorder turning and microphones hidden in the curtains, Kennedy and his advisers stared at the two-day-old aerial pictures of MRBM sites in Cuba.

The enlargements were propped up on an easel in front of the fireplace, above which loomed a Stuart portrait of George Washington. The President summoned his photographer, Captain Cecil Stoughton, to capture the meeting for history. Roswell Gilpatric noted that Kennedy was "very clipped, very tense. I don't recall a time when I saw him more preoccupied and less given to any light touch at all."

Just before this meeting, Kennedy had called Bohlen to his office and told him the secret that Bundy had confided to him in his bedroom after breakfast. Bohlen thought it "almost purely a Khrushchev venture." He found the President "absolutely determined" that the missiles would leave Cuba.

Dean Rusk had learned of the missiles on Monday night. Now he told the men in the Cabinet Room, "We, all of us, had not really believed the Soviets could carry this far. . . . Now I do think we have to set in motion a chain of events that will eliminate this base. I don't think we can sit still. The questioning becomes whether we do it by sudden, unannounced strike of some sort—or we build up the crisis to the point where the other side has to consider very seriously about giving in, or even the Cubans themselves take some . . . action on this."

Throughout the secret meetings on Mongoose, Rusk had asked for covert action to promote a split between the Russians and Cubans. Now he suggested using some channel to tell Castro privately "that Cuba is being victimized here, and that the Soviets are preparing Cuba for destruction or betrayal."

The Secretary noted that on Monday the *New York Times* had reported that the Russians might wish to trade Cuba for Berlin: "This ought to be brought to Castro's attention. It ought to be said to Castro that . . . the time has now come when he must take the interests of the Cuban people—must now break clearly with the Soviet Union, prevent this missile base from becoming operational."

Rusk said he was "very conscious" that "there is no such thing . . . as unilateral action by the United States. It's so heavily involved with forty-two allies and confrontation in many places that any action that we take will greatly increase the risks of direct action involving our other alliances and our other forces in other parts of the world."

Aside from notifying Castro, they had two broad alternatives: "One, the quick strike. The other, to alert our allies *and* Mr. Khrushchev that there is an utterly serious crisis in the making here. . . . Mr. Khrushchev may not himself really understand that or believe that at this point." The situation "could well lead to general war." They must "do what has to be done" in light of the President's September warning against offensive weapons in Cuba. But they must try to settle the problem "before it gets too hard."

McNamara said that any air strike against the missiles had to be scheduled before they became operational. If the missiles were launched, "there is almost certain to be chaos in part of the East Coast or the area in a radius of six hundred to a thousand miles from Cuba."

Such an air strike would have to include not only the missile sites but airfields, hidden aircraft, and possible nuclear storage sites. They must assume that the planes had nuclear warheads or at least "high explosive potential." This kind of broad air strike would mean perhaps two or three thousand Cuban casualties.

McNamara reported that the Joint Chiefs would prefer to have several days to prepare such an assault. But if "absolutely essential, it could be done almost literally within a matter of hours. . . . The air strike could continue for a matter of days following the initial day, if necessary. Presumably there would be some political discussions taking place either just before the air strike or both before and during. In any event, we would be prepared, following the air strike, for an . . . invasion both by air and by sea."

The air strike option must involve mobilization of American forces "either concurrently with or somewhat following, say, possibly five days afterwards, depending upon the possible invasion requirements." The first phase could be carried out under the congressional resolution on Cuba signed by the President just a week ago. The second would require declaration of a national emergency, as Kennedy had considered doing in 1961 over Berlin.

Newly sworn as Chairman of the Joint Chiefs, Maxwell Taylor said, "Once we have destroyed as many of these offensive weapons as possible, we should . . . prevent any more coming in, which means a naval blockade. . . . At the same time, reinforce Guantanamo and evacuate the dependents." Then, "continuous reconnaissance." The results of the air strike would help them decide "whether we invade or not. I think that's the hardest question militarily in the whole business—one which we should look at very closely before we get our feet in that deep mud in Cuba."

Rusk: "I don't believe myself that the critical question is whether you get a particular missile before *it* goes off because if they shoot *those* missiles, we are in general nuclear war." If Khrushchev wanted nuclear war, he did not need to launch MRBMs from Cuba.

With his abiding worry about nuclear war by accident, McNamara noted that someone might somehow get his thumb on the nuclear trigger against the wish of the Kremlin: "We don't know what kinds of communications the Soviets have with those sites. We don't know what kinds of control they have over the warheads."

The President broke his silence: "What is the advent—must be some major reason for the Russians to set this up as a—must be that they're not satisfied with their ICBMs. What'd be the reason that they would—"

Taylor argued that missiles in Cuba would supplement the Soviet Union's "rather defective ICBM system."

Kennedy: "Of course, I don't see how we could prevent further ones from coming in by submarine. I mean, if we let 'em blockade the thing, they come in by submarine."

McNamara: "I think the only way to prevent them coming in, quite frankly, is to say you'll take them out the moment they come in. You'll take them out and you'll carry on open surveillance and you'll have a policy to take them out if they come in."

Rusk: "About why the Soviets are doing this. Mr. McCone suggested some weeks ago that one thing Mr. Khrushchev may have in mind is that he knows that we have a substantial nuclear superiority, but he also knows that we don't really live under fear of his nuclear weapons to the extent that he has to live under fear of ours. Also, we have nuclear weapons nearby—in Turkey and places like that."

The President asked how many missiles the United States had in Turkey. The reply: about fifteen Jupiter IRBMs.

Rusk said McCone believed "that Khrushchev may feel that it's important for us to learn about living under medium-range missiles, and he's doing that to sort of balance that . . . political, psychological fact. I think also that Berlin is very much involved in this. For the first time, I'm beginning really to wonder whether maybe Mr. Khrushchev is entirely rational about Berlin."

Perhaps the Russians thought they could "bargain Berlin and Cuba against each other or . . . provoke us into a kind of action in Cuba which would give an umbrella for them to take action with respect to Berlin" just as Khrushchev had exploited Suez in 1956 to deflect world attention and scorn from his invasion of Hungary. "But I must say I don't really see the rationality of the Soviets pushing it this far unless they grossly misunderstand the importance of Cuba to this country."

With the benefit of his eight years of diplomacy under Eisenhower, Douglas Dillon warned that "OAS action and telling people in NATO" in advance of an air strike on Cuba had the danger of forcing the Russians "to take a position that if anything was done, they would have to retaliate. Whereas a quick action, with a statement at the same time saying this is all there is to it, might give them a chance to back off and not do anything."

Bundy worried about the "noise we would get from our allies saying that they can live with Soviet MRBMs, why can't we?" and the "certainty that the Germans would feel that we were jeopardizing Berlin because of our concern over Cuba."

Rusk: "And if we go with the quick strike, then . . . you've exposed all of your allies . . . to all these great dangers . . . without the slightest consultation or warning or preparation."

Kennedy: "But, of course, warning them, it seems to me, is warning everybody. And I, I—obviously you can't sort of announce that in four days from now you're going to take them out. They may announce within three days they're going to have warheads on 'em: if we come and attack, they're going to fire them. Then what'll—what'll we do? Then we don't take 'em out. Of course, we then announce, well, if they do that, then we're going to attack with nuclear weapons."

Adamant about telling only "the minimum number of people that we really have to tell," the President asked how long they could expect to keep the secret before it became known beyond the highest levels of the government.

McNamara said, "I think, to be realistic, we should assume that this will become fairly widely known, if not in the newspapers, at least by political representatives of both parties within . . . I'd say a week. . . . I doubt very much that we can keep this out of the hands of members of Congress, for example, for more than a week." Rusk said, "Not later than Thursday or Friday of this week."

Kennedy warned the group that whatever course of action they ultimately chose must be the "tightest" secret of all: "Because otherwise we bitch it up."

Listening to the discussion of an air strike, Robert Kennedy had passed a note to Sorensen: "I now know how Tojo felt when he was planning Pearl Harbor." This comment was an abuse of history: there was only the most surperficial comparison between Japan's unprovoked surprise attack and a surprise assault against an offensive base in Cuba against whose construction the United States had warned the Soviet Union, however belatedly.

The Attorney General warned the group that with a full-fledged air strike, "you're going to kill an awful lot of people and we're going to take an awful lot of heat on it. . . . You're going to announce the reason that you're doing it is because they're sending in this kind of missiles. Well, I would think it's almost incumbent upon the Russians then to say, 'Well, we're going to send them in again, and if you do it again . . . we're going to do the same thing to Turkey, or . . . Iran.' "

The President asked how the Cuban people would react to an air strike. Taylor said, "Great confusion and panic." McNamara said, "There's a real possibility you'd *have* to invade. If you carried out an air strike, this might lead to an uprising such that in order to prevent the slaughter of—of—of the free Cubans, we would have to invade to—to reintroduce order into the country. . . . It's not probable, but it's conceivable that the air strike would trigger a nationwide uprising."

Bundy argued that there should be an "enormous premium" on making the air strike as "small and clear-cut" as possible.

Kennedy said, "The advantage of taking out these airplanes would be to protect us against a reprisal by them. I would think you'd have to . . . assume they'd be using iron bombs and not nuclear weapons, because obviously why would the Soviets permit nuclear war to begin under that sort of half-assed way?"

He returned to the heart of the matter: "I don't think we've got much time on these missiles. . . . It may be that we just have to—we can't wait two weeks while we're getting ready to—to roll. Maybe just have to take *them out,* and continue our other preparations if we decide to do that. That may be where we end up. . . . Because that's what we're going to do *anyway.*

"We're certainly going to do Number One—we're going to take out these missiles. The questions will be . . . what I describe as Number Two, which would be a general air strike. . . . The third is the—is the general invasion. At least we're going to do Number One, so it seems to me that we don't have to wait very long. We—we ought to be making *those* preparations."

Bundy worried that the President had seemed to leap so hastily to a decision in favor of an air strike. Gently he said, "You want to be clear, Mr. President, whether we have *definitely* decided *against* a political track."

Why had the revelation of the missiles caught Kennedy by such surprise? Khrushchev had publicly warned in the summer of 1960 and during the Bay of Pigs that missiles might be used to defend Cuba. In early 1961, Dean Rusk and Allen Dulles had privately raised the matter with the Senate Foreign Relations Committee. In August 1962, Walt Rostow had issued an alarm with his "Khrushchev at Bay" memo. John McCone repeatedly raised the possibility in August and September, saying that if he were Khrushchev he would send offensive missiles to Cuba.

Nevertheless until mid-October 1962, Kennedy accepted—oddly, with almost none of his usual skepticism—the consensus view of his Soviet experts that the Chairman would not violate his self-imposed ban against stationing nuclear missiles outside Soviet territory. As Bundy recalled, the President and his circle assumed that Khrushchev "was much too sensible to challenge us in the way that nuclear weapons in Cuba so obviously would."

Kennedy's partisans later lauded his detached ability to see things from his opponents' point of view and his care not to push them to the wall. This quality was not in consistent evidence in his relations with Khrushchev through 1961 and early 1962. The President had almost no understanding of the extent to which his allusions to American nuclear superiority and a possible first strike had made Khrushchev feel trapped and deeply insecure.

Bundy recalled how in 1962 Kennedy and his aides "believed that in the overall contest with the Soviet Union we were still on the defensive. It was not we who threatened destabilizing changes in Berlin or in Southeast Asia. . . . We did not suppose that nuclear superiority conferred on us the opportunity for political coercion that Khrushchev took for granted."

By the summer of 1962, the President had been persuaded by McNamara's insistence that nuclear superiority mattered little as long as a nation had sufficient warheads and delivery systems to inflict unacceptable damage on another. So captured was Kennedy by this reasoning that he did not pause to think that Khrushchev might not share it. He gave short shrift to McCone's arguments that Khrushchev had both the motive and the ability to quickly repair his missile gap by sending MRBMs and IRBMs to Cuba.

Kennedy's inclusion of ground-to-ground missiles in his September public warning reflected not that he had realized his mistake but instead that he still had no notion Khrushchev might need or want to send such weapons to Cuba. He issued the warning on the basis of Robert Kennedy's reminder that offensive missiles would "create a major political problem here." Its main purpose was to provide a showy demonstration to Republican critics that the President was capable of drawing the line on Cuba. He did not know that he was closing the barn door after the cows were out.

Kennedy gave only secondary thought to how the warning might influence the course of world history. He did not canvass a full range of advisers before making it. Despite the warnings of Allen Dulles, Rusk, McCone, and the Chairman himself, the President was still so certain Khrushchev would not dream of sending offensive missiles to Cuba that he assumed he was issuing a challenge he would never have to back up with force.

Had the President issued his warning in March 1962, it is not so likely that Khrushchev would have defied it, especially in his then-current gloom about American first-strike capability. By September, the Chairman could not have reversed course without becoming a laughingstock in the Kremlin and throughout the Communist bloc, when his ignominy became known. Castro might have cried out to the world about how the Soviets had failed to fulfill their treaty commitment to send him missiles.

Had Kennedy taken the time to convene a cross-section of his advisers and examine the dangers of issuing such a warning, they might have impressed on him that mid-range missiles might go to Cuba and counseled him to word the statement more ambiguously.

It can be argued that in the fall of 1962 and the hot political climate over Cuba, Americans would never have tolerated nuclear missiles in Cuba and that anyone who was President would have felt compelled to demand their removal. The problem with Kennedy's warning was that it locked him into a specific course of action. In his haste to remedy his domestic political worries and his excessive certainty about his judgment of Khrushchev and Soviet motives, Kennedy had issued a blanket warning that had the effect of foreclosing any presidential action if missiles were found in Cuba short of risking nuclear war.

On Tuesday afternoon in the Oval Office, Kennedy pored over Kohler's cables on his three-hour morning meeting with Khrushchev. The Chairman had assured him, "I am most anxious not to do anything that will embarrass the President during the campaign."

Khrushchev had told Kohler he would do nothing new about Germany and Berlin until after the American elections in November. But then a German solution must finally be found. He was still considering a visit to the UN and to President Kennedy in November.

Khrushchev's complaint about the Jupiter missiles in Turkey and Italy took Kohler by surprise. The State Department had not briefed him on how to respond to such a complaint because it considered the matter so extraneous. Not so Khrushchev. He almost certainly knew that in six days the Jupiters were scheduled to be turned over to Turkish command.

To help relieve post-Sputnik fears about a missile gap, NATO had decided in late 1957 to install IRBMs on European soil. Sixty Thors were earmarked for Britain, thirty Jupiter launchers for Italy, fifteen for Turkey.

In June 1959, after Khrushchev complained to Washington about the IRBMs, Eisenhower privately told his Defense Secretary, Neil McElroy, that he could see good reason for them to go into West Germany, France, and Britain, but that provoking the Russians by going so close to their border as Greece seemed "very questionable."

McElroy reminded the President that Khrushchev had threatened "to obliterate Western Europe" and the allies were "showing signs of being shaken by the threat." One day the IRBMs could be used as bargaining chips. Eisenhower rejoined that the missiles would hardly "reduce tensions between ourselves and the Soviets." He worried that the Soviets might equate the deployment of missiles on NATO's southern flank with the installation of Soviet missiles in "Cuba or Mexico."

The Jupiters went into Turkey at about the time of Khrushchev's first visit to the United States in 1959. Eisenhower's aide Karl Harr reminded the President that "in terms of public relations" the installation must be handled carefully in light of Khrushchev's "particular political sensitivity" about IRBMs along his border.

American ICBMs and missiles launchable from Polaris submarines soon made the Jupiters obsolete. Dean Rusk was told that Turkish motorists could strike the above-ground missiles with a BB-gun and that the Jupiters were so out of date that, if launched, the United States could not be certain which way they would fly.

Like the Russians, the Congressional Joint Committee on Atomic Energy worried that American control over the missiles in Turkey might be too lax. Kennedy had asked for a review of the matter in March 1961 but was advised in June that in light of Khrushchev's "hard posture" at Vienna, withdrawing the Jupiters "might seem a sign of weakness." General Norstad warned him that the Turks would feel insulted. The President gibed, "What the Turks want and need is the American payrolls these represent."

The British announced in August 1962 that the Thors were being phased out. (The job was completed by December.) Kennedy again pondered pulling out the Jupiters but knew this would require negotiation within NATO. As Rostow recalled, "Neither the Pentagon nor the State Department had gotten on with the diplomacy of getting them out of Turkey and Italy."

Were the President aware that the missiles in Turkey were being turned over on October 22 with ceremony to the command of Turkish armed forces, he would have seen the gesture as a sop to good alliance relations. He would have presumed that the question of ownership meant little as long as the United States controlled their nuclear warheads.

Khrushchev may not have known that their nuclear warheads were to remain under strict American control. He was always worried that some local commander in West Germany or elsewhere might be able to put his finger on the nuclear trigger. Misapprehension that the Turks might be about to gain the ability to launch nuclear warheads against the Soviet Union would have caused him to place high value on getting the Jupiters out of Turkey.

At six-thirty, Kennedy and his men returned to the Cabinet Room. McCone's deputy, General Carter, reported that the latest reconnaissance of Cuba showed "a capability of from sixteen or possibly twenty-four missiles." There was "no evidence whatsoever" of nuclear warheads, although this did not prove the absence of such weapons. The Soviet launchers in Cuba "could be operational within two weeks" or, in the case of one, "much sooner." Once operational, "they could fire on very little notice."

Rusk pursued his idea of persuading Castro to evict the Soviet missiles from Cuba. He thought that Castro might "break with Moscow if he knew that he were in deadly jeopardy. Now this is one chance in a hundred, possibly. But in any event, we're very much interested in the possibility of a direct message to Castro as well as Khrushchev."

If the United States took the air-strike route, "we would expect, I think, maximum Communist reaction in Latin America." About six Latin American governments "could easily be overthrown." After an air strike, "the Soviets would almost certainly take some kind of action somewhere." Could Washington take such an action "without letting our closer allies know of a matter which could subject them to very great danger?" The United States could find itself "isolated and the alliance crumbling."

McNamara opposed any discussion with Castro, Khrushchev, or NATO leaders before an air strike occurred: "It almost *stops* subsequent military action." He raised a new, middle option: "a blockade against offensive weapons entering Cuba in the future" and constant reconnaissance of the island.

He warned that any form of direct military action "will lead to a Soviet military response of some type someplace in the world." American military action could generate an anti-Castro uprising in Cuba: the United States might be forced to accept an "unsatisfactory uprising," like the Bay of Pigs, or else have to invade.

Now the President spoke: "I completely agree that there isn't any doubt that if we announced that there were MRBM sites going up . . . we would secure a good deal of political support after my statement. And the fact that we indicated our desire to restrain, this really would put the burden on the Soviet."

He agreed that if the United States revealed the missiles to the world before it used force against Cuba, "we lose all the advantages of our strike. Because if we announce that it's there, then it's quite obvious to them [the Soviet Union] that we're gonna probably do something about it—I would *assume*." He doubted that a message to Castro about the missiles would turn the dictator against Moscow: "I don't think he plays it that way."

Nor did he think a message to Khrushchev would work. He noted that the Chairman had obviously ignored his September warnings against missiles in Cuba: "It seems to me my press statement was so *clear* about how we *wouldn't* do anything under these conditions, and under the conditions that we *would*. He must know that we're going to find out [about the missiles], so it seems to me he just—"

Bundy: "That's, of course, why he's been very, very explicit with us in communications to us about how dangerous this is, and the [September 11] TASS statement and his other messages."

Kennedy: "That's right. But he's—he's initiated the danger really, hasn't he?"

As the President's tape machine churned on, he made a muffled comment on Khrushchev that could be interpreted as "He's the one playing his card"—"cahd" in the Boston accent—"not us." He may also have said, "He's the one playing God, not us."

Rusk: "And his statement to Kohler on the subject of his visit and so forth. *Completely hypocritical.*"

McNamara warned again that the Soviet missiles on Cuba could be placed "in operational condition quickly." Whether six hours or two weeks, "we don't know how much time has started."

Rusk: "We could be just utterly wrong, but we've never *really* believed that Khrushchev would take on a general nuclear war over Cuba."

Kennedy: "We certainly have been wrong about what he's trying to do in Cuba. There isn't any doubt about that. . . . [Not] many of us thought that he was going to put MRBMs on Cuba."

Bundy: "Yeah. Except John McCone."

Carter: "Mr. McCone."

Kennedy: "Yeah."

Now, for the first time in the Cabinet Room all day, Bundy finally raised the most fundamental issue: "Quite aside from what we've said—and we're very hard-locked onto it, I know—what is the strategic impact on the position of the United States of MRBMs in *Cuba*? How gravely does this change the strategic balance?"

McNamara: "Mac, I asked the Chiefs that this afternoon, in effect. And they said, 'Substantially.' My own personal view is, *not at all.*"

Defending the Joint Chiefs, Taylor said, "They *can* become a very"—he corrected himself—"a *rather* important adjunct and reinforcement to the strike capability of the Soviet Union. We have no idea how far they will go. But more than that . . . to our nation, it means, it means a good deal more—you all are aware of that—in Cuba and not over in the Soviet Union." By this he meant that Americans would feel more insecure when they learned that Soviet missiles had been placed in the Western Hemisphere, only ninety miles away.

Dillon did not speak, but he and Paul Nitze considered the missiles in Cuba "a major step toward nuclear parity" by the Soviet Union, as Nitze said years later: "Not in numbers but in military effectiveness, because their capability in an initial strike from those sites would be tremendous. . . . Between the MRBMs and the IRBMs there was hardly any part of the United States that wasn't vulnerable to these missiles."

Kennedy returned to the possibility that the missiles were already operational: "Then you don't want to knock 'em out. . . . There's too much of a gamble. Then they just begin to build up those air bases there and then put more and more. . . . Then they start getting ready to squeeze us in Berlin." He embraced McNamara's view that the Soviet nuclear danger was not now necessarily greater than it had been before the missiles were sent to Cuba: "You may say it doesn't make any difference if you get blown up by an ICBM flying from the Soviet Union or one that was ninety miles away. Geography doesn't mean that much."

Taylor: "We'd have to target them with our missiles and have the same kind of—of pistol-pointed-at-the-head situation as we have in the Soviet Union at the present time."

Kennedy noted that if he had pressed the April 1961 invasion of Cuba to the point of success, he would not be facing this monumental crisis: "That's why it shows that the Bay of Pigs was really right."

Robert Kennedy said, "The other problem is in South America a year from now. And the fact that you got *these* things in the hands of Cubans here and then you—say, your—some problem arises in Venezuela. You've got Castro saying, 'You move troops down into that part of Venezuela, we're going to fire these missiles.' "

Edwin Martin, Assistant Secretary of State for Latin America: "It's a psychological factor. It won't reach as far as Venezuela is concerned."

McNamara: "It'll reach the U.S. though. This is the *point.*"

Martin: "Well, it's a psychological factor that we have sat back and let 'em do it to us. That is more important than the direct threat."

The President agreed: "Last month I said we weren't going to." By this he meant allowing offensive weapons in Cuba. He laughed caustically: "Last month I *should* have said we're—that we don't care. But when we said we're *not* going to and then they go ahead and do it, and we do nothing, then our risks increase. . . . I think it's just a question of, after all, this is a political struggle as much as military."

He assessed the options: "Don't think the message to Castro's got much in it." He proposed that "twenty-four hours ahead of our doing something" with military force, the U.S. government should announce the presence of missiles in Cuba: "That would be notification in a sense that, of their existence, and everybody could draw whatever conclusion they wanted to."

McNamara disagreed: the missiles could be readied "between the time we in effect *say* we're going to come in and the time we *do* come in. This—this is a very, very great danger to this, this coast. . . . If you are going to strike, you shouldn't make an announcement."

Kennedy renewed discussion of how widespread the military attack against Cuba should be: "I don't think we ought to abandon just knocking out these missile bases. . . . That's much more defensible, explicable, politically or satisfactory-in-every-way action than the general strike which takes us—us into the city of Havana."

Bundy agreed: "It corresponds to the—the punishment fits the crime in political terms." They would be "doing only what we *warned* repeatedly and publicly we would *have* to do."

Kennedy: "Once you get into beginning to shoot up those airports, then you get in, you get a lot of antiaircraft. . . . I mean, you're running a much more major operation. Therefore the dangers of the worldwide effects are substantial to the United States, are increased. I quite agree that if we're just thinking about Cuba, the best thing to do is to be bold if you're thinking about trying to get this thing under some degree of control."

He asked why the Russians put in the missiles if they "did not increase very much their strategic strength." Hadn't Khrushchev been cautious throughout his dealings on Berlin?

George Ball called attention to the Chairman's trial balloon about a New York visit in November: perhaps he had intended to reveal that "here is Cuba armed against the United States, or possibly use it to try to trade something in Berlin, saying he'll disarm Cuba if we'll yield some of our interests in Berlin and some arrangement for it."

Bundy: "I would think one thing that I would still cling to is that he's not likely to give Fidel Castro nuclear warheads."

Kennedy: "That's right, but what is the advantage of that? It's just as if we suddenly began to put a major number of MRBMs in Turkey. Now that'd be goddamn dangerous, I would think."

Someone said, "Well, we *did*, Mr. President."

Kennedy: "Yeah, but that was five years ago. . . . That was during a different period then." The President betrayed no knowledge that the Jupiters were to be transferred to the Turks next week. No one else raised the subject.

Someone speculated that Khrushchev's generals "have been telling him for a year and a half that he had—was missing a golden opportunity to add to his strategic capability."

Robert Kennedy said, "One other thing is whether we should also think of whether there is some *other* way we can get involved in this through Guantanamo Bay or something, or whether there's some ship that—you know, sink the *Maine* again or something." This was a dangerous suggestion: using a transparent pretext to justify a military action against Cuba for which the United States had substantial reason would have undermined the American case in the court of world opinion.

The President remembered that he was scheduled to see Gromyko in the Oval Office two days hence. He asked for advice on "whether we ought to say anything to *him*, whether we ought to indirectly give him sort of a—give him an ultimatum on this matter, or whether we just ought to go ahead without him." Dobrynin had told the Attorney General and others "that they were not going to put these weapons there. Now either he's lying or doesn't know."

Bundy said he "wouldn't bet a *cookie*" that Dobrynin knew.

Kennedy suggested that Robert tell Dobrynin that if offensive missiles were found in Cuba, the United States "would have to take action." Perhaps this would make the Soviets "reconsider their decision. . . . I can't understand their viewpoint, if they're aware of what we said at the press conferences. . . . I don't think there's any record of the Soviets ever making this direct a challenge ever, really, since the Berlin Blockade."

Courageously Bundy told his boss what he could not have wanted to hear: "We have to be clear, Mr. President, that they made this decision, in all probability, *before* you made your statements."

McNamara: "Uh-huh."

Bundy read aloud from the September TASS statement that the Soviet Union had such powerful missiles that it had "no need" to place them outside of its own territory.

Kennedy: "Well, what date was that?"

Bundy: "September eleventh."

The President remained baffled by the Soviet boldness in Cuba: "We never really ever had a case where it's been quite this—after all, they backed down in—Chinese Communists in '58. They didn't go into Laos, agreed to a cease-fire there. . . . I don't know enough about the Soviet Union, but if anybody can tell me any other time since the Berlin Blockade where the Russians have given us so clear provocation, I don't know when it's been. Because they've been awfully cautious really. . . . Now maybe our mistake was in not saying sometime *before* this summer that if they do this, we're [bound] to act."

McNamara said, "I'll be quite frank. I don't think there *is* a military problem here. . . . This is a domestic political problem. The announcement—we didn't say we'd go in . . . and kill them. We said we'd *act*. Well, how will we act? . . . First place, we carry out open surveillance, so we know what they're doing. . . . Twenty-four hours a day from now and forever. . . . We prevent any further offensive weapons coming in. In other words, we blockade offensive weapons."

The United States should also make "a statement to the world, particularly to Khrushchev, that . . . if there is ever any indication that they're to be launched against this country, we will respond not only against Cuba, but we will respond directly against the Soviet Union with—with a full nuclear strike. Now this alternative doesn't seem to be a very acceptable one, but wait until you work on the others. . . . As I suggested, I don't believe it's primarily a military problem. It's primarily a domestic political problem."

Ball: "Yeah? Well, as far as the American people are concerned, action means military action. Period."

In his emphatic way, McNamara threw out more questions: "What do we expect *Castro* will be doing after you attack these missiles? Does he survive as a—as a political leader? Is he overthrown? . . . How could Khrushchev *afford* to accept this action without *some* kind of rebuttal? I don't think—he *can't* accept it without some rebuttal. . . . Where? How do *we* react in relation to it? What happens when we *do* mobilize? How does this affect our *allies'* support of us in relation to Berlin?"

Gilpatric suggested that they all study American "points of vulnerability around the world," especially Berlin, Iran, Turkey, Korea. McNamara warned the group that if Khrushchev struck back at Berlin, "the risk of disaster would go way up."

The record of Kennedy's Tuesday Cabinet Room meetings does not quite bear out the later claims made on his behalf that this was a President superbly in command of the crisis from the start. Even allowing for the fact that he may not have wished to inhibit the conversations by dominating them, he made little effort to provide discipline, other than by injecting questions and comments. Not until halfway through the evening session did the conversation, thanks to Bundy, meander to the central question of whether MRBMs in Cuba actually changed the American-Soviet balance of power.

The Tuesday meetings rested on Kennedy's immediate assumption that the United States was "certainly going to . . . take out these missiles"—by diplomacy or force, perhaps at risk of nuclear war. This was despite the fact that at a March 1962 press conference, he had said that there was not "a significant difference" between a nuclear warhead "stationed in this area" and one five thousand miles away.

McNamara was confident that while nuclear missiles in Cuba might increase the speed, power, and accuracy of a Soviet first strike, they could not remotely upset the vast American advantage. As he said years later, if Khrushchev in 1962 "thought he was numerically behind by seventeen to one or thereabouts, do you think an extra forty-two missiles in Cuba, each carrying one warhead, would have led him to think he could use his nuclear weapons? No way!"

The reason the President felt he had to take out the missiles was not because he felt they violated the Monroe Doctrine. He privately thought that the doctrine lacked meaning in international law. But he was unwilling to take the heat of being the first President to say in public that the doctrine had little value.

Asked in August 1962 what the doctrine meant to him, Kennedy replied that it "means what it has meant since President Monroe and John Quincy Adams enunciated it, and that is that we would oppose a foreign power extending its power to the Western Hemisphere. And that's why we oppose . . . what's happening in Cuba today." Two weeks later in private, told by a Justice Department official that the doctrine gave the United States special hemispheric rights, Kennedy snapped, "The Monroe Doctrine—what the hell is that?"

He was angry at the secrecy and deception by which Khrushchev had conducted his Cuba operation, in defiance of the assurances the Chairman had given him publicly and privately since early September. Otherwise it was not easy to argue that the Soviet missiles in Cuba could be any less acceptable to the United States than NATO's IRBMs along the Soviet border were to the Soviet Union.

Bundy had had to remind the President that he had issued his warning against missiles in Cuba considerably after the moment at which Khrushchev must have decided to send them. Kennedy now knew he had erred badly by brushing aside McCone's numerous warnings that Khrushchev might be taking such a gamble. Instead, in September he had issued the American people an unambiguous pledge to "do whatever must be done" if Khrushchev moved ground-to-ground missiles into Cuba.

How different these Cabinet Room conversations might have been had Kennedy phrased his September pledge more vaguely or not at all. Instead of discussing how to take the missiles out, he and his advisers would now be able to consider the option of explaining to Americans that they had little to fear from the missiles in Cuba.

As when Eisenhower reassured Americans during the Sputnik and missile gap hysteria, this approach might have forced Kennedy to brave charges that he was too sanguine about the Soviet threat, especially because Kennedy lacked Eisenhower's military prestige. It might have caused the Democrats to lose the 1962 elections.

Still, this would have been preferable to the Kafkaesque nightmare that now faced the President—risking nuclear war to eliminate missiles that, in his own opinion and that of his Secretary of Defense, did little to harm American security.

The clock could not be turned back now. Kennedy had issued his warning. Like Khrushchev's decision to install the missiles, he had made exactly the kind of fateful miscalculation he had cautioned the Chairman against at Vienna. He could not discard his September warning now without shattering his political career and the world's faith in American threats and promises. He later told his brother Robert that if he hadn't acted against the missiles, "I would have been impeached."

from Counsel to the President

by Clark Clifford

Clark Clifford (1906–1998) was a key foreign affairs advisor to Lyndon Johnson (in office 1963–1969). Clifford favored restricting U.S. involvement in Vietnam. His memoir includes this description of the 1965 meetings that led to Johnson's commitment to greatly increase the number of American troops in the region.

Bob McNamara returned from a visit to Vietnam with a recommendation for a huge increase in American ground troops. At 3 p.m. the next day, July 21, President Johnson's secretary, Juanita Roberts, called and said that the President wanted me to come to the White House immediately to join a meeting on Vietnam. It was particularly urgent, she said—the meeting was already in progress. I walked rapidly across Lafayette Park and into the most remarkable series of meetings that I had attended since the showdown with General Marshall over Israel in 1948. As an assistant to the President in 1948, I had known exactly what my role was; this time I had only a small sense of what was going on, and no idea at first of what role I should play.

As I entered the Cabinet Room, President Johnson waved me to an empty seat at the table. He was flanked by Secretary of State Rusk on one side and Secretary of Defense McNamara on the other. Next to McNamara sat the Chairman of the Joint Chiefs of Staff, General Earle Wheeler. Around the room were other senior members of the

Administration: National Security Assistant McGeorge Bundy, Undersecretary of State Ball, Assistant Secretary of State for Far Eastern Affairs William P. Bundy, CIA Director Raborn and Deputy CIA Director Helms, former Ambassador to South Vietnam Henry Cabot Lodge, U.S. Information Agency Director Carl Rowan, Deputy Secretary of Defense Cyrus Vance, and two White House aides, Press Secretary Bill Moyers and Special Assistant Jack Valenti.

These men had been deeply influenced by the lessons of the Cuban Missile Crisis, especially the value of "flexible response" and "controlled escalation." Their success in handling a nuclear showdown with Moscow had created a feeling that no nation as small and backward as North Vietnam could stand up to the power of the U.S. These men were not arrogant in the sense that Senator Fulbright and others later accused them of being, but they possessed a misplaced belief that American power could not be successfully challenged, no matter what the circumstances, anywhere in the world.

Still, everyone in the room seemed deeply aware that we were facing—belatedly, in my opinion—a momentous decision. Westmoreland had requested thirty-two additional American combat battalions—100,000 more men by the end of the year, *more* in 1966, plus an intensification of the bombing of the North and a partial mobilization of the National Guard and the Reserves. McNamara, once the advocate of bombing the North, in part to avoid deploying ground troops, supported this request. Taylor had also changed his position, and now supported Westmoreland, thinking it too late for the nation to turn back.

When I entered, George Ball was speaking. "We can't win," he said, his deep voice dominating the Cabinet Room. "The war will be long and protracted, with heavy casualties. The most we can hope for is a messy conclusion. We must measure this long-term price against the short-term loss that will result from a withdrawal."

Producing a chart that correlated public opinion with American casualties in Korea, Ball predicted that the American public would not support a long and inconclusive war. World opinion would also turn against us. Ball said he knew that withdrawal was difficult for a

President, "But almost every great captain in history at some time in his career has had to make a tactical withdrawal when conditions were unfavorable." He compared the situation to that of a cancer patient on chemotherapy: we might keep the patient alive longer, but he would be fatally weakened in the long run.

Looking straight at Ball, the President said—not harshly, but with deep concern bordering on anguish, I thought—"Wouldn't all these countries—Korea, Thailand, Western Europe—say Uncle Sam is a paper tiger? Would we lose credibility by breaking the word of three Presidents if we give up as you propose? It would seem to me to be an irreparable blow, but I gather that you don't think so."

"If we were actively helping a country with a stable, viable government, it would be a vastly different story," Ball replied.

One by one, the other senior members of the Administration lined up against Ball. McGeorge Bundy argued, in his usual crisp style, that Ball's views constituted "a radical switch in policy, without any evidence it should be done." Ball's arguments, he asserted, went "in the face of all that we have said and done."

"It will not be quick," he added. "No single action will bring victory, but I think it is essential to make clear that we are not going to be thrown out—"

Ball interrupted: "My problem is not that we will get thrown out, but that we will get bogged down and won't be able to win."

Since I had entered the room, Dean Rusk had been silent. I was curious to see where he would come out. Now he spoke, in the calm, lucid, methodical manner that gave his words such authority: "I am more optimistic about the situation in Vietnam than some of my colleagues. . . . We should not worry about massive American casualties when the military says, at the same time, that we cannot find the enemy. I don't see great American casualties unless the Chinese come in. Vietnam is a testing ground of us by the Russians and the Chinese. Certainly we have had setbacks in Vietnam, just as we had setbacks in Korea. We may have more. But Vietnam must be an example for the entire Free World."

Henry Cabot Lodge joined the discussion. This tall, slender, and attractive man with his curious upper-class Boston intonations and manners was not noted for his intellect, but his position would carry extra weight with President Johnson for two good reasons: he was a prominent Republican, and he had just agreed to return to the most difficult assignment in the American diplomatic service—the Ambassadorship in Vietnam—at an age when most men had already retired. "There is a greater threat of World War III if we don't go in than if we go in," he said. "I cannot be as pessimistic as George Ball about the situation in Vietnam."

Bob McNamara joined in, with his usual precision and air of certainty: "Our national honor is at stake. Our withdrawal would start further probing by the communists. We would lose all of Southeast Asia. I feel that the risks of following my program have been vastly overstated by George Ball."

I took careful notes, but said nothing. Shortly after 5 p.m., the meeting adjourned, and I returned to my office deeply troubled by the magnitude of the McNamara request.

We resumed the discussion at noon the next day, July 22, with the Joint Chiefs of Staff presenting their formal position on the need for the buildup. Although it had a slightly ritualistic air, this meeting was an essential part of the process. The President could not address an issue of such importance without giving the Chiefs a chance to present their views. In addition to the President and the Chiefs, the three service secretaries—Stanley Resor for the Army, Paul Nitze for the Navy, and Harold Brown for the Air Force—were also present. The only others there were McNamara, Vance, McGeorge Bundy, and me.

The President opened the meeting by listing three options: we could leave—an "elegant bug-out," as he put it; we could maintain our current force levels and lose slowly; or we could add 100,000 men to our force levels in Vietnam, recognizing that this may not be enough to achieve our objectives, and that we might have to add more next year.

One by one the Chiefs gave their views. Although they all favored escalation, none offered assurance of success. Admiral David

McDonald, the Chief of Naval Operations, said, "More troops are needed to turn the tide. Otherwise, we'll lose slowly." The President looked at him for a moment then asked, "But you say you don't know if a hundred thousand more men will be enough. What makes you conclude that, if you don't know where we are going, and what will happen, that we shouldn't pause to find out?"

McDonald replied, "I believe that sooner or later we'll force the enemy to the conference table. We can't win an all-out war."

"Is this a chance we want to take?"

"Yes, in my opinion," Admiral McDonald responded, "when we view the alternatives—get out now or pour in more men."

And so it went. Repeatedly, the President asked the military the same questions. The answers varied little. Nitze said that putting in more men would give us about a "sixty-forty chance to turn the tide." He suggested giving Westmoreland more troops than he had asked for in order to increase the chances of success. But McNamara, clearly annoyed at the questioning of his position by Nitze, disagreed; the levels he and Westmoreland had requested, he said, were the most that South Vietnam could absorb. McNamara estimated the cost of the buildup at $12 billion in 1966—a low estimate, as it turned out.

President Johnson showed pain at the choices he faced. Turning toward McNamara he said, "Westmoreland's request means that we are in a new war. This is going off the diving board."

McNamara replied with the most extreme version of the domino theory that I had ever heard: "Laos, Cambodia, Thailand, Burma, Malaysia are all at immediate risk. For two or three years, communist domination would stop there, but the ripple effect would be great—in Japan, and India. We would have to give up some of our bases. Ayub Khan [of Pakistan] would move closer to China. Greece and Turkey would move to neutralist positions. Communist agitation would increase in Africa."

Air Force Secretary Harold Brown agreed that all the alternatives are "dark," but said that "the chances of losing are less if we move in."

Someone mentioned a recent Gallup poll showing substantial

public support for a hard line with Hanoi. The President understood that the polls meant little so early in the war: "If you make a commitment to jump off a building and you find out that the building is too high, you may withdraw the commitment."

I had remained silent; as the sole private citizen in the room, present only as a personal friend and adviser to the President, I felt I should express my opinions privately to him before discussing them with anyone else. But near the end of the meeting, without commenting directly on McNamara's proposals, I asked General Wheeler a simple question: "If the military plan that you propose is carried out, what is its ultimate result if it is 'successful'?" Wheeler answered that, in all likelihood, we would be able to withdraw most of our forces, but there was a chance that we would have to stay for a long time with a smaller number of troops to help secure a stable government. Shortly after our exchange, the meeting adjourned and the Chiefs left.

When we resumed the meetings after luncheon, the President made an emotional statement, reflecting his growing frustration, I thought, with the State Department's failure to produce a peace plan. "This war is like a prizefight," he said. "Our right hand is our military power, but our left must be peace proposals. Every time you move troops forward, you should move diplomats forward too. I want this done. The Generals want more and more from me. They want to go farther and farther. But State has to supply me with something, too." There was no reply from Dean Rusk.

The meetings had depressed me. The pressure on the President for escalation was overwhelming. As we left the room, George Ball whispered that he wanted to speak with me privately. We walked down the hall a few yards to the Roosevelt Room. Once we were alone, Ball asked me if he was correct in assuming that I had deep doubts about the war and McNamara's proposals. I told him that not only did I have such doubts, but I had sent the President a letter stating my concerns in May.

"Then you and I are in total agreement," he said enthusiastically. "I have been looking for support for a long time. I think your influence with the President is tremendously important. I want to put into your hands a series of memoranda which I have sent to the President. Can you handle them? They are highly classified."

I reminded Ball that, as a member of the PFIAB, I had the necessary clearances and a safe at my house. "Have the memos hand-delivered to me," I said, "and I will see that they are properly cared for."

As I started to leave the White House, a guard said the President was looking for me. I returned to the small anteroom adjoining the Oval Office to find Johnson and McGeorge Bundy waiting for me. The President wanted to know my reactions to what I had heard over the past two days. I replied that I needed more time to reflect on what I had heard, but I had some preliminary reactions. "The way the military acted today reminded me of the way they dealt with President Truman during the Korean War," I said. "Some of what General Wheeler said today was ridiculous." I quoted from my notes. " 'The more men we have, the greater the likelihood of smaller losses. And if they infiltrate more men into the South, it will allow us to cream them.' These are disturbing statements. I don't believe they are being straight with us."

"I am bearish about this whole exercise," I continued. "I know what pressure you're under from McNamara and the military, but if you handle it carefully, you don't have to commit yourself and the nation. If you overplay the decisions now under consideration, the nation will be committed to win a ground war in Asia. I asked myself two questions today, as I listened to McNamara and the Chiefs. First, can a military victory be won? And second, what do we have if we do win? Based on what we have heard, I do not know the answer to either question."

The President listened in silence, and Bundy jotted down a few notes. When I finished, Johnson said he wanted to talk to me again in the next few days, when I had had time to reflect more on the meetings that I had attended.

Shortly after I returned to my office, an aide from Ball's office arrived with a thick bundle of documents, the memoranda that Ball had been writing since October of the previous year, arguing against each stage of the escalation. I took them home and stayed up until almost 2 a.m. reading them and taking careful notes. They were everything that I would have expected—forceful, fearless, and, to my mind, convincing. They amplified and gave historical context to the presentations that I had heard him make to the President. I realized as I read them that George had been fighting his lonely battle so long that, to a certain extent, the President was probably no longer paying Ball the close attention he deserved. Perhaps I had been brought into the discussions by the President in part because he wanted a new voice to argue against McNamara, Rusk, and the Chiefs.

On Friday, July 23, I called George and told him that the documents he had sent me were impressive and persuasive. He was, he said, "elated" to have me as an ally. He was going with Rusk to the White House for another meeting and would call me as soon as he got back.

Ball called again after the meeting. It had involved a much smaller group—Rusk, McNamara, Wheeler, Moyers, and McGeorge Bundy. George was convinced that my talk with Johnson the previous evening had had a "salutary effect."

I was less hopeful: I told him I had just finished talking on the telephone to "another source" and, based on that conversation, it appeared that President Johnson had virtually made up his mind to support McNamara and Westmoreland. My informant had been another participant in the meeting—Bill Moyers, who sympathized with Ball and me, but felt he could not play an open role in policy-making because his job as Press Secretary constrained him from active policy formulation. Moyers told me it would take a miraculous effort to change the President's course—requiring not only a change in Johnson's mind, but also Rusk's, McNamara's, and Bundy's.

Ball told me he understood the difficulties, but he felt I was the only person who had even the slightest chance to stem the rush toward disaster. I promised to have "a very hard and long talk" with the President, but I cautioned him against false hope. "Individuals sometimes become so bound up in a certain course," I said, "that it is difficult to know where objectivity stops and personal involvement begins."

According to Ball, the President was not much concerned with the opposition from students and the Left, and my presentation would have to deal primarily with his fear of a right-wing backlash. Ball repeated a comment that President Johnson had made to him: "George, don't pay any attention to what those little shits on the campuses do. The great beast is the reactionary elements in this country. Those are the people we have to fear."

Just before 7 p.m., the President called to invite Marny and me to come to Camp David on Saturday. Bob and Margie McNamara would be there, he said, along with a few other people. We would relax, and we would have a chance to talk privately about Vietnam. The stage was now set for the final argument. I knew Moyers was correct: it would be very difficult, perhaps impossible, to stop the rush toward escalation. Could the President reject the advice of his three top national security advisers—all inherited from Kennedy—as well as the unanimous advice of the Joint Chiefs of Staff and the Ambassador in Vietnam, himself a former Chairman of the Joint Chiefs of Staff? Could he change a policy that had the support of a substantial majority of the American public? Would he risk going down in history as the first American President to lose a foreign war? The answer seemed likely to be negative.

On the other hand, Lyndon Johnson had just won an overwhelming victory in a campaign built around the theme of his restraint versus Goldwater's extremism. The next election was as far away as could be, and if the economy did not deteriorate, there would be ample time to repair any political damage inflicted by the Right. The effect on our position in Asia of a withdrawal from Vietnam would be difficult to predict, but I believed it could be contained and minimized. And the support of the American public was clearly based on a belief that the conflict would be short in duration; if the war dragged on, we all agreed this support would erode.

In thinking about the meeting about to take place at Camp David, I thought particularly of Bob McNamara, who had been playing a dominant role in the government during an extraordinarily difficult period, and who was now leading the support for a policy that he would have opposed six months earlier. Although Rusk, Bundy, Taylor, Lodge, and the Chiefs all were important, McNamara held the key; his formidable intelligence and reputation were the critical variables in the process driving the President toward approval of Westmoreland's request. Bob's mastery of facts and his analytical skills had led him, I felt, into a logical fallacy, but his reputation for personal integrity and the force of his personality were carrying the case against those few voices calling for a different course.

I had liked and respected Bob McNamara from the moment we had first met in 1960, and it pained me that we would be cast into advocating opposing points of view. As in almost every such disagreement in my life, I determined to do my best to keep the argument totally impersonal. Bob had his views, I had mine—I thought he was wrong, but I did not question his motives or his professionalism. We would present our views to the President and let him decide.

Marny and I flew to Camp David Saturday afternoon, sharing a helicopter with Bob and Margie McNamara and their son Craig, the Johnsons' daughter Luci, and her husband Pat Nugent. On the beautiful twenty-five-minute flight from Washington to Camp David, we chatted in the most friendly fashion. Vietnam was never mentioned, and an observer would never have guessed that a major confrontation was about to take place between two of the passengers on the plane.

We spent the afternoon relaxing in the glorious surroundings of Camp David. Each guest or couple was assigned a separate cabin. The accommodations, contrary to public perception, were not opulent, but they were extremely relaxing. Because the cottages are dispersed, the guests could keep to themselves much of the time, play golf or tennis, or stroll around the Presidential retreat.

Supreme Court Justice Arthur Goldberg, who was going to be sworn in as the Ambassador to the U.N. the following day, was another guest at Camp David, as were Indiana Senator Birch Bayh and his wife, Marvella. Two important members of the White House staff—Horace

Busby and Jack Valenti—joined us, and we ate dinner with the Johnsons. Despite the informal and friendly environs, the President was more subdued than normal.

On Sunday morning, I went over my notes one last time. From Ball's memoranda and my own thoughts, I had assembled the strongest case that I could, against McNamara's proposals and had structured it as though I was arguing in a courtroom, with McNamara as the opposing attorney and the President as the judge. My case boiled down to a few fundamentals. I knew that the President had heard them before, but I hoped that, if properly assembled, they would shake McNamara's certitude, impose their own logic on the President, and lead to a new conclusion.

At 5 p.m. on Sunday, President Johnson asked me to join him and Bob McNamara at Aspen Lodge. From the large, glassed-in living-dining room looking out over a beautiful panoramic view, I could see, through the large windows to the right, the little golf course that Ike had installed, and straight ahead, the lovely green hills called the Catoctin Mountains. In sharp contrast to the subject we were about to discuss, the sylvan setting gave a seemingly relaxed air to the conversation; from a distance, one would not have imagined that the subject under discussion was a decision that would change American history.

Aspen Lodge was decorated as a hunting lodge, with unassuming furnishings surrounding a large fireplace on one side. On the left side of the living room was a rectangular dining-room table, around which President Johnson often held conferences and late-night meetings. It was here that we sat to discuss Vietnam.

The President sat at the head of the table with his back to the fireplace. I sat on his right, directly across from McNamara. To his left sat Arthur Goldberg, and to my right sat Jack Valenti, who took notes, and Horace Busby. As we talked, two Filipino stewards served drinks. The President drank Fresca, I sipped club soda.

The President began, primarily because of Goldberg's presence, by mentioning a proposal to take the Vietnam issue to the U.N. He asked for my views, and I quickly dismissed the idea, saying that the risks far outweighed the potential gains at the U.N.—then I moved into the broader discussion for which I had prepared myself.

"We must not create an impression that we have decided to replace the South Vietnamese and win a ground war in Vietnam," I began. "If the decisions about to be made are interpreted as the beginning of a permanent and long-range policy, it will severely limit the flexibility which the President must have."

"What happened in Vietnam is no one person's fault," I continued, trying to reduce President Johnson's overpersonalization of the situation. "The bombing might have worked, but it hasn't. A commitment like the one that we have made in Vietnam can change as conditions change. A failure to engage in an all-out war will not lower our international prestige. This is not the last inning in the struggle against communism. We must pick those spots where the stakes are highest for us and we have the greatest ability to prevail."

McNamara listened without showing the slightest emotion, but I put more passion into what I was saying than in any presentation I had ever made to a President:

> I hate this war. I do not believe we can win. If we send in 100,000 more men, the North Vietnamese will match us. If the North Vietnamese run out of men, the Chinese will send in "volunteers." Russia and China don't intend for us to win the war. If we "won," we would face a long occupation with constant trouble. And if we don't win after a big buildup, it will be a huge catastrophe. We could lose more than 50,000 men in Vietnam. It will ruin us. Five years, 50,000 men killed, hundreds of billions of dollars—it is just not for us.

I paused for a moment, then went on:

> For the time being, Mr. President, let us hold to our present course, without dramatic escalation. You will probably

> need to send some additional men now for this strategy, but not many. At the end of the year, after the monsoon season, let us probe, let us quietly search with other countries for an honorable way out. Let us moderate our position in order to do so, and lower our sights—lower the sights of the American people—right away. Let the best minds in your Administration look for a way out, not ways to win this unwinnable war. I can't see anything but catastrophe for my country.

I did not know, at the time, that Jack Valenti, the President's chief assistant, had kept a permanent record of my remarks. However, many years later, as we went through files at the Johnson Library, we came across the notes that he had written. It is interesting to see what impressed him the most. His entry reads as follows:

> CLIFFORD: "Don't believe we can win in South Vietnam. If we send in 100,000 more, the North Vietnamese will meet us. If the North Vietnamese run out of men the Chinese will send in volunteers. Russia and China don't intend for us to win this war. If we don't win, it is a catastrophe. If we lose 50,000 men it will ruin us. Five years, billions of dollars, 50,000 men, it is not for us. At end of monsoon, quietly probe and search out with other countries—by moderating our position—to allow us to get out. Can't see anything but catastrophe for my country."

After I had finished, President Johnson turned to McNamara, who replied forcefully that he did not agree with my premises or my assessment of the chances for success in Vietnam. He repeated arguments he had made earlier in the week, but added nothing new. Without more American troops, he said, South Vietnam would fall, and this would hurt the U.S. throughout the entire world. The buildup was essential if we wanted to avoid a rapid defeat.

I was prepared to debate McNamara on every point, but to my disappointment the President wanted to end the discussion. Perhaps he sensed the futility of further debate. The lines were drawn clearly; he had heard the arguments on both sides, and there was little else to say. He told us that no one wanted peace more than he, but he did not discuss the details of my position.

When the meeting ended, we returned to our respective cottages. While we waited for dinner or word that we were going home, the President did something quite unusual. He drove around the Camp David area alone for an hour; then, for another hour, he walked around the grounds, also alone. It had been a lovely day, and the soft summer light lasted late into the evening.

During his lonely drive and walk, I assume that he reviewed all that he had heard in the previous week and made up his mind. When he returned to the Aspen Lodge, we ate another family meal with some other friends whom he had invited to Camp David, but never once did he refer to the debate between McNamara and me. We returned to Washington with President and Mrs. Johnson shortly before midnight for a short night's sleep before the final meetings.

We resumed shortly after noon on Monday and continued, with a break in the afternoon, until 7 p.m., but the meetings had a different tone than those of the previous week. Johnson shifted the discussion toward important but secondary, matters—the exact number of men to be sent, the timing of the deployments, the public and Congressional aspects of the announcement, and so on.

The President asked me to repeat the presentation I had made the previous evening at Camp David. So, for the first time, I stated to a larger group my objections to the escalation and my dark fears for the future. After I had finished speaking, George Ball slipped me a note that I saved with pride:

> Clark-
>
> I'm glad to have such an eloquent and persuasive comrade

> bleeding on the same barricade. I thought your statement was great.

But both George and I sensed that the battle was over. I felt the President had asked me to repeat my arguments in the larger group only to show that he had listened to both sides before granting the massive troop increase.

In the evening on July 26, the same group—now in effect a war council—returned to the White House to discuss whether or not to attack the surface-to-air missiles recently installed in North Vietnam. Given the fact that American pilots were risking their lives daily in raids over the North, I argued strongly that we should take the SAMs out with whatever means were available. It was the first, but not the last time, I would argue for a tough position on a question of military tactics. Once the President had committed us in Vietnam, I would generally support actions that I hoped would shorten the war or minimize American losses.

Ironically, the one minor success Ball and I had during the debate actually worked *against* our larger purpose. We both had argued that we should "underplay" any public announcements so as to maintain maximum flexibility for future withdrawal, while arguing, of course, against any escalation at all. In the actual event, the President turned down our strategic objective, but handled the public announcement in a manner consistent with our suggestion. Instead of a nationally televised speech in prime time, the President simply disclosed the buildup during a midday press conference on July 28. Even though he had already secretly approved an increase of 100,000 men by year's end, with the possibility of another 100,000 in 1966, he referred only to an increase of 50,000 men, and told reporters that the additional troops did "not imply any change in policy whatsoever." Thus, in our last-ditch efforts to stop the escalation, Ball and I had unintentionally encouraged a major Presidential deception that added significantly to the emerging "credibility gap."

from The Great Coverup

by Barry Sussman

Richard Nixon (in office 1969–1974) in 1971 ordered the installation of a voice-activated taping system in the White House to preserve a record for historians. Barry Sussman (born 1934) describes the role those tapes played in the Watergate scandal that brought down Nixon's administration.

On Friday night, October 19, 1973, President Nixon began what many people have since come to regard as the most reckless step of his political career. Plagued by the Watergate and related scandals, and ordered by the courts to relinquish the tapes of nine of his private conversations, Nixon announced that he had effected a "compromise" that would both allow him to maintain the confidentiality his office required and give Special Prosecutor Archibald V. Cox the material he needed to conduct his investigation at the same time.

Under the plan, Nixon would submit summaries of the relevant portions of the tapes to Judge John J. Sirica, and an independent verifier, Senator John Stennis of Mississippi, would be allowed to listen to the tapes to authenticate the version given the judge. It would be Nixon's last bow to Cox—the Special Prosecutor would have to agree not to use the judicial process to seek further tapes or other records of Nixon's conversations in the future.

Because of this shortcoming and others in the plan, Nixon's aides knew that Cox would not accept it. On Saturday, as he refused, White House chief of staff Alexander Haig ordered Attorney General Richardson to fire Cox. Richardson resigned instead. Haig then ordered Deputy Attorney General William Ruckelshaus to fire him, and Ruckelshaus also resigned. Finally, the number-three man in the Justice Department, Solicitor General Robert Bork, was named acting attorney general, and he fired Cox. White House press secretary Ronald Ziegler announced that the Office of Special Prosecutor had been abolished, and FBI agents were dispatched to prevent Cox's staff members, whose status was in limbo, from taking their files out of their offices.

What came to be known as the "Saturday Night Massacre" then unleashed the torrent of public anger at Nixon that had been building across the nation. In a period of ten days, more than a million letters and telegrams descended on members of Congress, almost all of them demanding Nixon's impeachment. Before long, according to some, there were three million letters and telegrams, and an impeachment inquiry was begun.

All this was a result of what seemed at first to have been an impetuous action by the President. But Nixon's firing of Cox was by no means a rash, sudden action. The President, who knew how dangerous a special prosecutor could be, agreed to the appointment of one in the spring of 1973 only after severe pressure had been placed on him. By the middle of June, 1973, Nixon's aides were complaining about Cox. Nixon himself voiced extreme displeasure in the first days of July, and by early October—at least twelve days before the Saturday Night Massacre—he announced privately that Cox would be fired.

Early on and occasionally after that, the President broke through his own veil of insulation and revealed his thinking to his third attorney general, Elliot Richardson. Through subsequent testimony before the Senate and House judiciary committees and in statements to intimates, Richardson dispassionately put into the record strong evidence that Nixon's behavior during this period continued to be that of a man bent on using any and all means to block the pursuit of justice.

• • •

When Archibald Cox settled in as special prosecutor in May, 1973, he told friends he expected to be in Washington for three to possibly seven years. His assignment was monumental. He was given carte blanche to investigate as he saw fit in a public pledge by Elliot Richardson at the Attorney General's Senate confirmation hearings. Only the Attorney General could fire Cox, and then only for what Richardson said would be "extraordinary improprieties."

President Nixon, in his May 22, 1973, statement, had promised that "Executive privilege will not be invoked as to any testimony concerning possible criminal conduct, in the matters presently under investigation, including the Watergate affair and the alleged coverup." Cox had the authority and the blessing to seek and get any and all information, or so it appeared.

But on May 25, the day Richardson was sworn in, the President told the new Attorney General in a conversation in the Oval Office that he had used the word "testimony" advisedly, that he had meant it to apply only to oral testimony and not to documents.

Earlier, on April 30, when Nixon spoke to Richardson about the appointment of a special prosecutor, the President mentioned only Watergate and not related scandals. The statement was vague; Nixon didn't specifically rule out investigations of incidents other than the break-in and bugging. But it served to alert Richardson that there might be trouble on down the road, possible problems he should note and come back to at another time. Richardson didn't have to wait long before the problem came back to him. Almost immediately afterward, John Ehrlichman, although he resigned the morning of April 30, called to say that the Special Prosecutor had to be kept away from "national security" matters.

Nevertheless, as Cox began to settle in, there was an air of optimism at his office and at that of the Attorney General's as well. Richard Darman, who had followed Richardson as a close aide from the Office of Health, Education and Welfare to the Defense Department and then to the Justice Department, explained it to me in this manner: "Those first days at Justice were euphoric for anyone who could remember how hard it was to get anything from the White House while at HEW. Now there was cooperation."

It was a moment when the President was at his weakest—under pressure from every quarter in March and April, he had let go of Haldeman and Ehrlichman only to be smashed by the Ellsberg revelations and the CIA testimony and the opening of Senate Watergate hearings in May. For a period of about a month, Nixon and his new chief of staff, Alexander Haig, under constant battering, submitted to requests for materials by both the Senate Watergate Committee and the Special Prosecutor.

Cox also had the fruits of the work done by the original Watergate prosecutors, Silbert, Glanzer, and Campbell, who had broken the case by the time of his appointment. He was getting cooperation from at least four of the men who were conspirators in the bugging or the coverup and in other related scandals: John Dean, Jeb Magruder, Herbert Kalmbach, and Frederick C. LaRue.

With such a fast start and a $2.8 million annual budget that allowed him ninety employees, Cox immediately extended the Watergate inquiry so broadly that the term "Watergate" had little to do with much of his investigation; it was only a convenient label to attach to the many probes of the Executive branch under Nixon.

Cox was looking into the work of the White House plumbers, the early White House wiretaps, and illegal campaign contributions to Nixon, including those that allegedly had been a payoff to Nixon by the dairy industry for the promise to raise milk price supports. He was investigating the role of the White House in the ITT merger plans, and dirty tricks aside from Watergate in the 1972 campaign. Much of his inquiry paralleled that of the Senate Watergate Committee, with one crucial difference: Cox worked through the criminal justice system and had the power, therefore, to follow his investigation through with criminal prosecutions. So while the Ervin Committee gave public airing to the most sensational charges of corruption ever made about a presidential staff, Cox quietly began putting together material for indictments.

In the middle of June, Haig called Richardson to express displeasure at the scope of Cox's investigations. Then, on July 3, three and a half months before the Saturday Night Massacre, came the first warning that the President was considering firing Cox.

That morning, the *Los Angeles Times* reported that Cox's staff had begun a preliminary inquiry into the President's acquisition of his estate at San Clemente and improvements made on it. The report, according to Cox, who was forced to issue a denial later in the day, was incorrect. What had happened, he said, was that he had been questioned so frequently about San Clemente at press conferences that he asked an aide to get him newspaper articles on it to increase his understanding of the subject. The aide called the *Los Angeles Times* and asked for all their clips on San Clemente, which led to the writing of the July 3 article.

Nixon was in Key Biscayne when the story appeared. Haig, who was with him, telephoned Richardson, who was in the midst of a meeting with Baltimore U.S. attorney George Beall and three of his assistants. Richardson excused himself to take the call in another office. Haig said that Cox was overstepping his bounds enormously if he was looking into San Clemente, and that Cox would be fired if he didn't shape up.

As though the Haig warning were not serious enough business in itself, when Richardson returned to his visitors, Beall and his assistants began to spell out to the Attorney General, for the first time, the incriminating testimony they had been gathering against Vice-President Spiro T. Agnew in the course of an investigation of kickbacks and corruption in Maryland. As this new, terrifying scandal was being thrust in his lap, Richardson had to leave the room several more times to talk to Cox or Haig. Finally he was able to tell Haig that Cox was only asking for newspaper clippings to read, that he was not investigating San Clemente.

Nixon broke into the call himself, angrily demanding that the Attorney General have Cox issue an immediate denial of the *Los Angeles Times* story. Cox did, explaining, however, that he had ordered a review of "relevant public knowledge" of the purchase of and improvements on the property.

From then on, Nixon's aides—Haig and attorneys Leonard Garment and J. Fred Buzhardt—repeatedly complained to Richardson about Cox and his staff. Richardson was warned that Nixon would not tolerate a prosecution of Ehrlichman, Charles Colson, or plumber Egil Krogh because national security projects would be brought to light at a trial, and that was impermissible. The President had begun to rebound from his losses of the spring; the White House returned to its earlier hard-line stance, and cooperation with investigators came to a virtual halt.

By July 16, when Alexander Butterfield revealed the existence of the White House taping system, the early euphoria that Richardson's aide Darman had spoken of was gone. On July 18, Cox wrote Buzhardt asking for the tapes of nine conversations. Five were of talks between Nixon and Dean, the others between Nixon and Haldeman, Ehrlichman, or Mitchell in the thirteen days following the Watergate arrests of June 17, 1972. On July 20, having received no reply, Cox wrote again. This time he got an answer from Charles Alan Wright, the University of Texas law professor who was to serve as Nixon's principal attorney in the battle over the tapes.

Wright told Cox that Nixon would not surrender the tapes either to the Ervin Committee, which had requested five of them, or to the Special Prosecutor. Since Cox planned to use the tapes in the courts, a separate branch of government, Wright wrote, the principle of Executive privilege would be violated were Nixon to give Cox the tapes. "The successful prosecution of those who have broken the laws is a very important national interest, but it has long been recognized that there are other national interests that, in specific cases, may override this," he said. Nixon felt he had to maintain the confidentiality "that is imperative to the effective functioning of the presidency," Wright said; the President would stand by this decision even at the risk of having prosecutions arising from Watergate thrown out of court.

On July 23, realizing he was at an impasse, Cox served a subpoena on Nixon's attorneys. The President refused to obey it, throwing the battle of the tapes into the courts, before Judge John Sirica, for the first time. On August 29, Sirica, saying Nixon's arguments on the separation of powers were unpersuasive but that he wanted to "walk the middle ground," ruled that the tapes should be given to him, and he would decide what to forward to the Special Prosecutor and what would be kept secret on the basis of presidential confidentiality. Nixon was in San Clemente that day; the White House issued a statement saying the President "will not comply with this order."

Wright appealed to the U.S. Circuit Court of Appeals, whose judges urged that Cox and Wright seek a compromise and avoid the constitutional confrontation that would arise through pushing the argument to a conclusion in the courts. On September 20, both sides notified the Appeals Court that they could reach no agreement, and on Friday, October 12, the Appeals Court ruled that Nixon would have to turn the tapes over to Sirica.

Out of that ruling, Nixon forced the confrontation with Cox that led to the Saturday Night Massacre. The fact is, however, that in late September or early October—before the court ruling, some time prior to the forced resignation of Vice-President Agnew on October 10—Nixon told Richardson that he was going to fire Cox.

Agnew at the time was struggling to avoid a criminal prosecution, claiming that as Vice-President he could not be indicted. Richardson went to Nixon to seek approval for the final steps to be taken against Agnew. The President concurred, but he said, "After this, we're going to get rid of Cox."

On the weekend following the Appeals Court ruling on the tapes, Nixon's resolve hardened. He could have taken the tapes case to the Supreme Court, but he decided not to. He was insistent on firing Cox. On Sunday night, October 14, Haig called Richardson on the telephone and asked him to come to the White House the following morning. It was the beginning of seven days of negotiations, during which, at times, Haig warned Richardson that the United States was on the edge of a possible confrontation with the Soviet Union in the Middle East and that Richardson should weigh the possible international effect of any decision he made that went against the President's wishes.

From 9 to 11:30 a.m. on Monday, October 15, Richardson met at the White House with Haig and Buzhardt. He was told that despite the ruling that Nixon had to submit the tapes to Sirica, the President had his own plan: he would prepare an "authenticated version" of them, and he would fire Cox. Once Cox was gone, Nixon would not be in violation of a court order since the agent requesting the order—the Special Prosecutor—was no longer in existence.

Under the terms of Cox's appointment, however, only the Attorney General could fire him. Richardson reminded Haig and Buzhardt that he had pledged not to dismiss Cox except for "extraordinary improprieties" and said that if Nixon went ahead with his plan, he would resign.

During the day, Haig backed off on the necessity to fire Cox, and between Monday afternoon and Thursday evening, Richardson served as a middle man between the White House and Cox, trying to effect a compromise. Cox seemed receptive, but he objected to various aspects of the proposal given him. On Thursday evening, October 18, Richardson transmitted Cox's written response to Haig, Buzhardt, Garment, and Wright. The Nixon aides seized on Cox's objections, said he had rejected the plan, and that he should be fired. They suggested that Richardson and Assistant Attorney General Henry Petersen take charge of the investigation. Richardson was incredulous. He said the public would not have faith in such an investigation.

"I wondered whether I was the only sane man in the room or whether I was the one who was crazy," Richardson said later. He urged Wright to speak with Cox before any action was taken. Wright agreed—but Richardson was warned that if Cox could not be persuaded to accept the offer, he would be dismissed.

Richardson went home fully expecting the worst. He sat down and wrote out a letter titled "Why I Must Resign." He discussed the conversation at the White House with intimates, saying, "You won't believe what those guys think they're going to get away with." The question arose as to whether the President's assistants were serious in their hard-line position—Cox, after all, had the court ruling on his side—or whether they adopted such an extreme position in hopes of having Richardson help get Cox to capitulate.

Meanwhile, Wright called Cox and they failed to reach an agreement. After the conversation, Wright sent Cox a note, saying that "if you think there is any purpose in our talking further, my associates and I stand ready to do so. If not, we will have to follow the course of action that we think in the best interest of the country." The letter spelled out a requirement that Cox not pursue further requests for additional tapes or documents, where the earlier proposal had not.

Friday morning Cox wrote Wright to tell him exactly why it was wrong to call the Stennis plan a "very reasonable" proposal, as Wright had. After repeating objections he had given to Richardson earlier, Cox noted, in addition, that he simply could not promise there would be no "further legal challenges to claims of Executive privilege. I categorically assured the Senate Judiciary Committee that I would challenge such claims so far as the law permitted. The Attorney General was confirmed on the strength of that assurance. I cannot break my promise now."

Notified of the impasse, Richardson asked Haig if he could meet with the President to submit his resignation. Haig said Nixon could see him immediately. The Attorney General told his aides as he left that it looked like it was all over. Resignation in hand, he went to the White House, going directly to Haig, who occupied the grand Vice-Presidential ceremonial office that had been Haldeman's before him. But Haig took Richardson by surprise. He said the firing of Cox might not be necessary after all, and Richardson didn't go to the Oval Office.

Buzhardt, Garment, and Wright joined the conversation. Richardson was shown Cox's letter to Wright, and the reference Cox had made to further legal challenges confused him—he was not aware, he said later, of Wright's stipulation to Cox. But Richardson saw a glimmer of hope. Several new proposals were discussed, including one Richardson thought might have promise, calling for Judge Sirica to rule on the merits of the Stennis plan. The so-called "linked proposal"—

combining the Stennis verification plan and agreement by Cox that he not seek access to other tapes or documents—was also aired. Richardson said he felt Cox would resign before accepting it.

When Richardson returned to the Justice Department, it was his understanding that no decision on a final course had been made, and that he would be consulted before any was. He and his three closest aides went to his private dining room for lunch. They were joined by Deputy Attorney General Ruckelshaus, and they remained there for hours, trying to come up with an acceptable solution.

Three times during the afternoon, Richardson spoke on the telephone with Haig or Buzhardt. The Appeals Court had given Nixon until Friday to move the case before the Supreme Court; it was now late Friday afternoon and time was running out. Nixon could always ask for an extension and no doubt get it—but he had to do something.

During the day, Senator Ervin and Senator Baker were called to the White House separately and asked if they would consent to a plan in which Senator Stennis would authenticate a version of the tapes prepared by Nixon for use by their committee. The courts earlier had ruled that the Ervin Committee was not entitled to the five tapes it had sought, and both senators—who stood to gain no access to material from the tapes otherwise—agreed to the Stennis plan.

At 7 o'clock Friday, Haig called Richardson and read a letter to him from the President instructing the Attorney General to order Cox not to go to court to seek any further records of presidential conversations. Richardson, taken by surprise, realized he could not comply with such an order.

Expecting Nixon to make public the letter to him, Richardson prepared a press release in which he termed the Stennis authentication plan a reasonable compromise but objected to tying it to a promise by Cox not to seek further material through the courts. "I plan to seek an early opportunity to discuss this plan with the President," Richardson's statement said.

Richardson had no need to release his statement, however. At

8 o'clock, bypassing Richardson, the President announced that he was implementing the "linked proposal," calling it a compromise. It was Nixon's last, failing attempt to shake loose from Watergate.

Noting the strain that the scandal had imposed on the American people, Nixon said the possibility of a constitutional confrontation was especially damaging. At home, he said, Watergate "has taken on overtones of a partisan political contest," and such divisiveness could "tempt those in the international community . . . to misread America's unity and resolve in meeting the challenges we confront abroad."

For these reasons, the President said, "I have concluded that it is necessary to take decisive actions that will avoid any possibility of a constitutional crisis and that will lay the groundwork upon which we can assure unity of purpose at home and end the temptation abroad to test our resolve."

The President said he was confident that the Supreme Court would have reversed the Appeals Court ruling on the tapes, but "that it is not in the national interest to leave this matter unresolved for the period that might be required for a review by the highest court."

The President then announced the details of the Stennis plan, saying that Senator Ervin and Senator Baker had accepted it as a means of forwarding information from the tapes to the Senate Watergate Committee, but that the Special Prosecutor rejected the proposal. Nixon said he would go ahead with the plan anyway, that his aim was

> . . . to bring the issue of Watergate tapes to an end and assure our full attention to more pressing business affecting the very security of the nation. Accordingly, though I have not wished to intrude upon the independence of the Special Prosecutor, I have felt it necessary to direct him, as an employee of the Executive branch, to make no further attempts by judicial process to obtain tapes, notes, or memoranda of presidential conversations.

Every shibboleth that has come to be equated with Nixonism was contained in this statement. The President said he was seeking to assuage damages to the nation, making no mention of damages to himself. He invoked the threat of danger from foreign powers should an investigation of his own honesty be pursued. He charged that those seeking to find the truth about Watergate, or those disturbed by the crimes that had become so apparent, were motivated by partisan interest and not by a desire to clean up corruption. Throughout, he attempted to give the appearance of being above the fray, and he concluded with a statement that he was cooperating with the Watergate inquiry when, in fact, he was defying a court order.

Cox immediately issued a statement charging that the President had refused to abide by the court decrees and stating he would bring that to the attention of the court. "For me to comply with these instructions," he said, as he had written Wright earlier in the day, "would violate my solemn pledge to the Senate and the country to invoke judicial process to challenge exaggerated claims of Executive privilege. I shall not violate my promise. Acceptance of these directions would also defeat the fair administration of justice."

True to form, the first reaction from leadership on Capitol Hill was one of siding with Nixon. Senate Majority Leader Mansfield, while saying he thought Cox had been given independent powers, termed the President's Stennis plan "a move to avoid a constitutional confrontation." Minority Leader Hugh Scott said he felt "a very wise solution had been reached and a constitutional question avoided." Senator Baker, who reportedly was unaware that Cox had objected to the proposal, said through his press aide that it seemed "very good, totally in the best interests in the country."

On Saturday morning, Richardson still thought it possible that the firing of Cox could be avoided. In response to the directive Nixon had sent him the previous night, he sent word to the President that he hoped Nixon would allow the courts to decide on whether the Stennis plan was in compliance with court rulings.

By early afternoon he had not heard back. Any possibility that Nixon might reconsider vanished, as Special Prosecutor Cox called a press conference and spelled out, for the first time, the story of the months of resistance he had received from the White House. He complained that long before the tapes conflict arose, the White House had established a pattern of failing to turn over information necessary for his inquiry, that papers "of many White House aides—Haldeman, Ehrlichman, Krogh, Young, Dean, and others—were taken into custody and they're in a special room, and many of their papers were taken out of the usual files and put in something special called presidential files." He said the White House had refused his request for an inventory of those papers, and he suggested that the President's refusal to relinquish the tapes be seen in that light—the tapes were not the only information the President was withholding; this was only the most recent and sensational example of Nixon's failure to cooperate in the inquiry.

In answer to questions, Cox said he might seek an order to have the President placed in contempt of court.

"Mr. Cox, I think you believe that Attorney General Richardson will not fire you," one reporter said. Cox said that whether or not Richardson would dismiss him, the President could always find a way of forcing him out, citing a precedent in which Andrew Jackson fired a Secretary of the Treasury, named a new one, and had to fire him as well before a third appointee could be found who would follow a presidential order. "Eventually a President can always work his will," Cox said. Nixon was to work his sooner rather than later.

At 2:20 p.m., Haig called Richardson and told him to fire Cox. Richardson said he couldn't do that, that he would come to the White House at Nixon's convenience and resign. An hour later, Haig invited the Attorney General to see Nixon and, on his arrival, ushered him into the Oval Office. Richardson said he would have to resign. Nixon brought up the problems in the Middle East, Richardson said later, suggesting that resignation right then might have a bad effect. The President asked Richardson to think less of his pledge to the Senate—his personal commitment—and more in terms of the national interest. Richardson said that, in his view, he was thinking of the national interest.

"It is fair to say," Richardson said later, "that I have never had a harder moment than when the President put it on me in terms of the potential repercussion of my resignation on the Middle East situation. I remember a long moment when the President looked me in the eye and I said:

"'Mr. President, I feel that I have no choice but to go forward with this.' I had the feeling, God, maybe the bombs are going to drop."

Haig then called William Ruckelshaus and asked him to fire Cox, again issuing a warning that a decision not to could have bearing on the Middle East situation. Ruckelshaus, who had already told Richardson he would also resign rather than fire Cox, has been quoted as telling Haig that if the situation in the Middle East were that ticklish, "Why don't you put off firing Cox?"

Haig responded, "Your commander-in-chief has given you an order." Ruckelshaus then resigned.

Both Richardson and Ruckelshaus had spoken to the third in command at the Justice Department, Solicitor General Bork, who had told them that someone would certainly eventually be found to fire Cox, so he would do it and then resign. Richardson suggested that Bork fire Cox and stay on, as someone was needed to run the shop.

At 8:25 p.m., Ronald Ziegler announced the developments of the afternoon to the press, saying that the office of the special prosecutor had been abolished. "Its function to investigate and prosecute those involved in the Watergate matter will be transferred back into the institutional framework of the Department of Justice, where it will be carried out with thoroughness and vigor." From Ziegler's statement it was unclear whether Cox's staff would continue to exist at all. The possibility arose that Nixon had, in one daring maneuver, put an end to the entire investigation, placing responsibility in the Justice Department, which had been so maligned for submitting to White House control the first time around.

At least six FBI agents were sent by the White House to the office of the special prosecutor, where some twenty or more attorneys who worked under Cox were gathering in their moment of crisis. The agents refused to allow staff members to remove any files—"They won't even let me take a pencil out," one lawyer complained. FBI agents sealed off Richardson's and Ruckelshaus's offices at the Justice Department as well.

In a brief statement, Cox said, "Whether ours shall continue to be a government of laws and not of men is now for the Congress and ultimately the American people to decide."

Nixon had made a terrible miscalculation.

Contacted by reporters, members of both parties attacked the President. Democrat Jerome Waldie of California said he would immediately introduce an impeachment resolution, charging that Nixon "in one wild move, has removed the few remaining men of demonstrable integrity in the Administration." The action, he said, left no doubt that release of the tapes would prove the President's guilt in obstructing justice. A leading Republican congressman, John B. Anderson of Illinois, stated Nixon had "precipitated a constitutional crisis" and said he was certain impeachment resolutions would be immediately introduced.

Senator Edward Kennedy, in his most outspoken moment during the Watergate scandal, said the firing of Cox was "a reckless act of desperation by a President who is afraid of the Supreme Court, who has no respect for law and no regard for men of conscience." He said it was "obvious that Mr. Nixon is bent on maintaining the Watergate coverup at any cost. The burden is now on Congress and the courts to nullify this historic insult to the rule of law and to the nation's system of justice."

Republican Edward Brooke, Kennedy's colleague from Massachusetts, who had long been critical of Nixon, said the act was "sufficient evidence which the House of Representatives should consider to begin impeachment proceedings."

At least half a dozen other members of the House and Senate of both parties made similar remarks. Gerald Ford, Nixon's nominee as successor to Agnew, hollowly defended the President, saying Nixon "had no other choice after Cox, who was, after all, a subordinate, refused to accept the compromise solution to the tapes issue." But hardly any other voices were raised in support of Nixon.

The next day, Sunday, in the middle of the long Veterans Day holiday weekend, thousands of telegrams began to descend on empty offices on Capitol Hill, and motorists on Pennsylvania Avenue in front of the White House were exhorted by demonstrators holding signs to honk if they favored impeachment. The noise disturbed Nixon and his attorneys inside as they prepared to defend the President's action in court during the week.

His opinion solicited by a reporter, Senate Majority Whip Robert C. Byrd charged that the President had "defied the courts, defied Congress." Byrd said "this sounds like a brown shirt operation thirty years ago—gestapo tactics." Byrd said the President had left Congress no choice but to impeach him.

Others in the Senate saw a need to reestablish the special prosecutor's office, this time assuring through legislation that the prosecutor was not responsible to the President. The members of Cox's staff—their positions in limbo since Nixon had abolished their office—decided they would continue to investigate under the direction of the Justice Department if they were allowed to do so.

A press aide for the Cox staff, James Doyle, told a reporter, "It's really a very extraordinary situation for Washington, D.C. The White House said we were abolished, but if they say the sky is green and you look out and see it's blue, well . . ."

On Monday a few members of the House Democratic Party leadership met with Speaker Carl Albert and launched plans to begin a preliminary study on possible impeachment—a means of preventing the institution of immediate formal impeachment proceedings. Reaction from Republicans to Nixon's firing of Cox continued to be unfavorable. "I've carried Nixon's flag faithfully for five years," said Congressman William Whitehurst of Virginia, "and it's getting awfully heavy." California Republican Jerry Pettis said, "I'm bending over backwards to believe him. I'm bending over so far backwards my fifth vertebra is about to break."

Across the country, sentiment poured in from quarters that had been previously silent. Raoul Berger, a Harvard Law professor who had written what was considered the definitive work on impeachment, said, "I have hesitated to say it before, but after the events of the past few days, he must be impeached."

Berger said Nixon was in violation of a court order by offering to produce a summary of the tapes when he had been ordered to release the tapes themselves. "Disobedience of the law is a subversion of the Constitution, which is an impeachable offense," he said. Berger said that "obviously more serious than the Middle East War is the attempt of the President to set himself above the law. We just cannot permit that. It's the road to tyranny, dictatorship, and Hitlerism. Democracy cannot survive if a President is allowed to take the law into his own hands."

Other noted constitutional lawyers agreed, and the deans of fifteen major law schools, acting as a body, urged that Congress create a special committee "to consider the necessity of presidential impeachment."

Equally ominous for Nixon was the word on Monday that Judge Sirica, who had been out of town Saturday and Sunday, had been in touch with his own staff and was known to be considering holding the President in contempt of court for failure to comply with the court order. No President had ever been held in contempt of court. The force of such an order was undetermined—no one expected the President to pay fines or go to jail. But such an order would be one more item to add to an impeachment bill of particulars, and anger from Sirica would undoubtedly fan the enormous flames of public discontent.

On Tuesday morning, with Western Union officials saying their wires to Washington were running at triple their normal rate, Republican leaders warned the President through emissaries he sent to Capitol Hill that they could not defend him against an impeachment move unless he surrendered the tapes. Some demanded that he also appoint another special prosecutor, or run the risk of seeing the Senate appoint one.

Elliot Richardson, who was to become immensely popular for

having resigned rather than fire Cox, held a televised press conference in a large hall at the Justice Department and was greeted by a sustained ovation that lasted more than two minutes as about five hundred Justice employees expressed their appreciation for the man who had restored a semblance of honor to their agency. Richardson deplored the President's actions but stopped short of impugning his motives. He said, in answer to a question, that he would have done what Cox had done. He recommended that the President appoint another special prosecutor, and said that impeachment was a question not for him, but for the American people.

"Although I strongly believe in the general purposes and priorities of his Administration, I have been compelled to conclude that I could better serve my country by resigning from public office than by continuing in it," Richardson said.

No one asked, and Richardson had no reason to mention that he had seen the President since his resignation Saturday. He had been called to the White House after Nixon heard that he was to hold the press conference. The President urged Richardson to cast things in a favorable light for him.

In early November, 1973, Richard Nixon's attorneys said that two of the nine tapes Nixon had finally promised to relinquish never existed in the first place. Then it was revealed that the tape of a conversation with H. R. Haldeman only three days after the bugging arrests had a gap in it—a hum—of 18 ½ minutes duration.

If there were reasonable people who still felt the President wanted to bring out the facts of Watergate, surely many of them were convinced otherwise by that hum. No one could satisfactorily explain it, and a group of experts jointly chosen by the Court and the White House later concluded that it was the result of a segment of conversation being manually erased between five and nine times.

The erased part came near the start of the conversation on Nixon's and Haldeman's first day back at the White House after the Watergate arrests. Nixon had just spoken to John Ehrlichman, who was gathering information about the bugging and the inquiry into it, and Haldeman had spoken to Ehrlichman, John Mitchell, John Dean, and reportedly to Attorney General Richard Kleindienst as well. It would have been a perfect occasion for the President and his chief of staff, his most trusted aide, to make plans that they never would want to surface.

The hum was particularly damaging to Nixon in that it was difficult for people to understand why he would have allowed the tape to be erased if he were truly innocent in the coverup. With the vast resources of the White House at his disposal, it would have been the easiest thing in the world for Nixon to insure that the tape he turned over to a court of law would not be erased before it got there. One simple procedure would have been to have a copy made of each tape. Nixon's secretary, Rose Mary Woods, could transcribe from the copy, thus preventing each tape from being damaged.

The fact that any tape of such importance should be marred in any way, let alone be erased between five and nine times, seemed reason enough to conclude that the President wanted some of the conversation to be lost forever. There was another alarming aspect to the mysterious erasure as well. Could a President who couldn't protect a spool of tape really be trusted to safeguard the interest and security of two hundred million people?

The 18 ½-minute gap subjected Nixon to scorn and humiliation as well as suspicion; the President of the United States became the nightly butt of late-hour TV entertainment shows, and in Washington a prevailing joke was that a secretary could get a job at the White House if she could erase a hundred words a minute. The ridicule never ceased, and after April 30, 1974, when Nixon made public his own incomplete, embarrassing, and misleading version of the transcripts of the tapes of forty-three meetings and telephone conversations between himself and his associates, it got worse.

Long before then the President was simply a man trying to hold onto his office, capable of any effrontery but essentially powerless. He could compare himself to Lincoln, tell newspaper editors in Disney World that he was not a crook, travel the world over in hopes of persuading Americans that they needed him as President. But his fate was to be controlled by a forum outside his control, the Congress of the United States.

As impeachment resolutions were introduced in the House of Representatives in October and November, 1973, the House Speaker, Carl Albert, referred each of them to the Judiciary Committee for consideration. Impeachment was seen as a remedy that could work for the President as well as against him. According to the thinking of many people at the time, there was little sentiment in Congress for removing Nixon from office, and a verdict in his favor could help clear the air. The first serious public discussions of impeachment had, in fact, come from the Nixon side—from Richard Kleindienst in April, 1973, and then from the President's attorneys as they argued in court over the tapes that summer.

Many in Congress viewed impeachment as a cure that was worse than the disease. A devastating impeachment battle would further the divisiveness among an already unsettled populace, some said. It could be viewed as a partisan endeavor by the majority party, the Democrats, to revoke the enormous mandate Nixon had received from the electorate in 1972. Others said, echoing Nixon, that evidence against him in the Watergate coverup was based largely on the word of one man, John Dean, a turncoat—hardly enough to convince many members of Congress to start down a road from which there was no turning back. Aside from the Watergate coverup, some of the accusations laid at Nixon's door had to do with his accepting illegal or questionable campaign contributions, and many members of Congress were not exactly pure themselves in that area.

Impeachment was fraught with problems for elected officials, whose careers depended on winning elections. It was difficult for even the most dedicated, serious, and honest members of Congress to view impeachment simply as a search for the truth, a trial in which Nixon's actions alone would be considered. It was only natural that other concerns entered the thinking process, such as, would impeachment help or hinder a congressman's re-election drive?

Ordinarily, a Republican who voted to impeach a Republican President might expect to lose a hard core of constituent support; a Democrat who voted to impeach had little to gain. A Republican who took a stand against impeachment might be threatened by insurgent candidates of his own party and, at the least, stood to lose support from Democratic switch-over voters that was necessary to win a seat in many areas. Democrats who voted against impeachment, it was thought, would be doing so at their peril.

But, since public opinion was volatile and the time was early, there was no certain way of predicting how a stand on impeachment would affect the future of any individual member of Congress. The one thing that was clear was that impeachment was, more than anything else, a headache. So as the impeachment drive began, along with it came cries for Nixon to resign, a solution that would take Congress off the spot. The overwhelming number of congressmen had consistently turned their backs on Watergate until it surrounded them. They were still reluctant to deal with it, hoping Nixon would solve what was becoming their dilemma. The President, however, undertook a counteroffensive, scheduling public appearances before carefully selected audiences in a campaign called "Operation Candor." He began meeting in the White House with groups from Congress, mostly Republicans, and told them the move against him was a partisan one. He said he would not resign under any circumstances.

On November 7, 1973, a highly respected Republican senator, eighty-one-year-old George D. Aiken of Vermont, a former governor of his state and a U.S. senator since 1940, called on members of Congress to realize that pleas for Nixon to resign were dishonorable, and urged them to "either impeach him or get off his back."

In his first major public statement on Watergate, Aiken said:

> . . . the White House has handled its domestic trouble with such relentless incompetence that those of us who would

> like to help have been like swimmers searching for a way out of the water only to run into one smooth and slippery rock after another.
>
> I am speaking out now because the developing hue and cry for the President's resignation suggests to me a veritable epidemic of emotionalism. It suggests that many prominent Americans, who ought to know better, find the task of holding the President accountable as just too difficult . . .
>
> To ask the President now to resign and thus relieve the Congress of its clear congressional duty amounts to a declaration of incompetence on the part of the Congress.

Aiken said he was particularly disturbed by "those who now would have us believe that President Nixon and his associates alone are the ones who corrupted America. If the politics of righteous indignation succeeds in persuading the President to resign and relieving the Congress of its clear duty, how long will it be before our politics is corrupted by competitive self-righteousness?"

Eight days later, on November 15, the House of Representatives voted 367 to 51 to assign one million dollars to the Judiciary Committee to enable it to hire staff to conduct its inquiry. The committee was not yet authorized to make impeachment findings; its function was to recommend whether a true impeachment proceeding should begin. But it seemed clear that if the committee decided to drop its inquiry, sooner or later an impeachment resolution would be brought to the House floor anyway. Ultimately members of Congress would have to deal with the problem.

The inevitable difficulties in having elected officials decide the question of impeachment had been anticipated long ago, when the Founding Fathers decided to put the fate of a suspect President in their hands. In the Federalist Papers No. 65, Alexander Hamilton spelled out the reasoning—and the dangers—in having the legislative body conduct such proceedings. Hamilton said the offenses considered in an impeachment stemmed from the "misconduct of public men, or, in other words, from the abuse or violation of some public trust. They are of a nature which may with peculiar propriety be denominated POLITICAL as they relate chiefly to injuries done immediately to the society itself."

Hamilton saw that regardless of the nature of the charges against the person being impeached, passions would be inflamed and the "whole community" would divide "into parties more or less friendly or inimical to the accused. In many cases it will connect itself with pre-existing factions, and will enlist all their animosities, partialities, influence, and interest on one side or on the other; and in such cases there will always be the greatest danger that the decision will be regulated more by the comparative strength of parties than by the real demonstrations of innocence or guilt."

With the recognition then, that impeachment would be "a national inquest into the conduct of public men," that the difficulties of divorcing justice from politics were enormous, Hamilton asked, "Who can so properly be the inquisitors for the nation as the representatives of the nation themselves?"—the House of Representatives. Impeachment was a "bridle in the hands of the legislative body upon the executive servants of the government."

Hamilton went on to state why the U.S. Senate, not a court, should constitute the jury: "Where else than in the Senate could have been found a tribunal sufficiently dignified, or sufficiently independent? What other body would be likely to feel confidence enough in its own situation to preserve, unawed and uninfluenced, the necessary, impartiality between an individual accused and the representatives of the people, his accusers?"

The problems of factionalism as envisioned by Hamilton came to the fore in the early exploration of whether impeachment proceedings should be instituted against Nixon. Unlikely as it seems, given the nature of the evidence against the President, the Judiciary Committee immediately divided itself along strict party lines.

In its first vote, the committee's twenty-one Democrats all chose to allow Chairman Peter W. Rodino, Jr., of New Jersey to decide what information and which witnesses would be subpoenaed, overriding the vote of all seventeen Republicans who wanted the power to veto any of Rodino's subpoenas. Then, in a second rigidly party line vote immediately following, the Democrats refused to allow the Republicans on the committee the right to issue subpoenas of their own.

Anyone who felt the aim of the Rodino Committee was to seek out the truth about Richard Nixon had to view these votes with great alarm. For while divisions among reasonable people may always occur, it is almost inconceivable that thirty-eight men and women, all of them attorneys, could divide strictly according to party in settling on the proper approach for ferreting out the truth. Defenders of the President, and Nixon himself, seized every opportunity thereafter to claim that the impeachment committee had embarked on a partisan witch hunt.

The question that had to arise from the deliberations of the Rodino Committee was whether the committee, the House of Representatives, and, perhaps, ultimately the Senate, could be counted on to put politics aside and vote up or down on impeachment on the merits of the case.

But certain members of the committee viewed partisanship as a false issue, one that would evaporate as findings for or against Nixon began to come in, and as members of the committee got further soundings from constituents about the depth of feeling toward impeachment.

On January 24, 1974, as one means of dispelling charges of partisanship, Rodino relented on the matter of subpoena power, agreeing to share it with the senior Republican on the committee, Edward Hutchinson of Michigan. At that point the committee was still simply conducting an inquiry to determine whether impeachment proceedings should begin. Rodino and Hutchinson agreed to ask the full House to pass a resolution recognizing the Judiciary Committee as the body that would make a formal impeachment inquiry.

Five days later, the President, at the conclusion of his State of the Union address, extended a challenge to both the new special prosecutor, Leon Jaworski, and the Rodino Committee. Saying that "one year of Watergate is enough," Nixon asserted that he had provided Jaworski "all the material that he needs to conclude his investigations and to proceed to prosecute the guilty and to clear the innocent. I believe the time has come to bring that investigation and the other investigations of this matter to an end."

Nixon said he recognized that "the House Judiciary Committee has a special responsibility in this area, and I want to indicate on this occasion that I will cooperate with the Judiciary Committee in its investigation. I will cooperate so that it can conclude its investigation, make its decision, and I will cooperate in any way that I consider consistent with my responsibilities to the Office of the Presidency of the United States."

He said he would not do anything that "impairs the ability of the Presidents of the future to make the great decisions that are so essential to this nation and to the world."

It was the old Nixon position on the need for confidentiality, now being extended to apply to an impeachment proceeding. Nixon, the prospective defendant, was telling the Judiciary Committee, which was in many ways equivalent to a grand jury, that he, not the committee, would decide what evidence was germane.

About three weeks earlier, I had asked a member of the Judiciary Committee, Democrat Paul Sarbanes of Maryland, what would happen if the President refused to submit material requested by the committee. "I think this constitutional argument to keep from turning over documents is 98 percent hokum," Sarbanes said. "Our role is to exercise ultimate discretion. If the President refuses material, he would be failing to obey a mandate of the Constitution. Secondly, when materials or knowledge are not handed over, by established legal principle you can judge the worst. Failure to turn over material may provoke a constitutional issue strong enough to go to the Senate with all by itself."

On hearing Nixon's State of the Union address, several members of Congress said the President's offer to cooperate was no offer at all and took the same stance that Sarbanes had with me: that refusal to submit material could be an impeachable offense in itself.

On February 6, 1974, the full House voted 410 to 4 to have the Judiciary Committee "investigate fully and completely whether sufficient grounds exist for the House of Representatives to exercise its constitutional power to impeach Richard Nixon, President of the United States of America." The House gave the committee authorization to subpoena any witness and any information "it deems necessary to such investigation."

In the following days, the Nixon position hardened as one of the President's attorneys, James St. Clair, refused to submit material to either the Special Prosecutor or the Judiciary Committee. On February 14, Jaworski complained that some requests for material from the White House had gone unmet since the previous August. He said that during a brief period of cooperation after the firing of Cox, the White House had submitted eleven tapes on Watergate, three that had bearing on the Nixon decision to raise milk price supports, three on possible Nixon interference in the ITT merger, and one on the White House plumbers. But then cooperation had stopped, and requests for twenty-seven additional tapes had been turned down. Jaworski said he had spelled out the need for each of the tapes, that he was not on any fishing expedition.

That same day Judiciary Committee counsel John Doar met with St. Clair in hopes that he could establish procedures to acquire White House data. The meeting was said to be a friendly one, but no procedures emanated from it. At that stage in its inquiry, the Rodino Committee was receiving information and data from the Senate Watergate Committee and from other committees on the Hill that had looked into aspects of the Nixon scandals. But the committee could not count on receiving material from the special prosecutor's office, especially anything that had been the subject of grand jury deliberations, as Jaworski said he did not have the authority to release confidential grand jury records. So the Rodino Committee, now a true impeachment panel, while charged with a more solemn responsibility than any congressional committee in the hundred years since an earlier President was impeached, was being denied material to conduct its inquiry properly. Doar asked St. Clair to submit to him at least the same documents, including tapes, that had been given to the Special Prosecutor, and he set a deadline in early March for the answer, threatening a congressional subpoena for failure to comply.

On March 1, the Watergate grand jury issued its major Watergate indictments, charging H. R. Haldeman, John Ehrlichman, Charles Colson, John Mitchell, Gordon Strachan, Robert Mardian, and re-election committee attorney Kenneth Parkinson with crimes in the coverup. Secretly naming Nixon as an unindicted co-conspirator, the grand jury requested that all the information it had gathered on the President be submitted to the Judiciary Committee, including tapes of conversations. In court, two bulging satchels were given to Judge Sirica as he was asked to decide on the grand jury's request.

On March 5, before Sirica had issued any ruling, the Rodino Committee, having failed to get any response from the White House to its demands, announced that it would subpoena the documents and tapes it sought. Failure to comply could result in a contempt of Congress citation against Nixon. The following day, St. Clair said the President would give the committee the same material that had been offered the Special Prosecutor.

At a press conference that evening, March 6, Nixon was asked whether he would relinquish other material sought by the Rodino Committee. The President said "those matters will continue to be under discussion between White House counsel and Mr. Doar." He said the material turned over to Jaworski included nineteen tapes and over seven hundred documents, and that he felt he had made a "very forthcoming offer" to the Rodino Committee in pledging to respond under oath to written interrogatories and offering to "meet with members of the committee, perhaps the chairman and the ranking minority member of the committee, at the White House to answer any further questions under oath that they may have."

Nixon was still maintaining his right to determine what evidence would be produced against him, a position that neither Doar nor Jaworski could accept. As Doar got the same material that had been submitted to the Special Prosecutor, he continued to press a demand on the White House for forty-two additional tapes, all of them having to do with the latter stages of the Watergate coverup in February, March, and April, 1973. Jaworski went to court, seeking enforcement of a subpoena for sixty-four tapes, including those of conversations in the first days after the June 17, 1972, arrests. He won a favorable ruling from Judge Sirica but the White House said it would not abide by it, and Jaworski then appealed directly to the Supreme Court. On April 11, the Rodino Committee subpoenaed the forty-two tapes which it had originally requested on February 25.

On the 29th of April, as time for a response to the Rodino Committee subpoena was running out, the President went on television to announce one of his striking capitulations, another act in which he cooperated yet did not cooperate at the same time. But this event was far more dramatic than any in the past, even his firing of Archibald Cox. The President told the American people:

> In these folders that you see over here on my left, are more than 1,200 pages of transcript of private conversations I participated in between September 15, 1972, and April 27th of 1973, with my principal aides and associates with regard to Watergate . . . I have been well aware that my effort to protect the confidentiality of presidential conversations has heightened the sense of mystery about Watergate and, in fact, has caused increased suspicions of the President. Many people assume that the tapes must incriminate the President, or that otherwise, he would not insist on their privacy.

Nixon said he was making a major exception to the principle of confidentiality, that he was turning over the transcripts of conversations—but not the tapes themselves—to the Rodino Committee. The transcripts, he said, "include all the relevant portions of the subpoenaed conversations that were recorded." He said he would invite Rodino and the senior Republican on the committee, Hutchinson, to the White House to listen to the full tapes to determine for themselves that the transcripts are accurate and all the relevant information presented.

> Because this is an issue that profoundly affects all the American people, in addition to turning over these transcripts to the House Judiciary Committee, I have directed that they should all be made public—all of these that you see here.

Nixon said he realized that the transcripts would lead to many sensational news stories, that parts would seem contradictory, that they would embarrass him and others. He said that those who read the raw transcripts would see why the principle of confidentiality is essential and must be maintained in the future. He made it as clear as he could that this was his final contribution to those who were investigating him.

The President had given edited transcripts instead of tapes. There were no transcripts at all for eleven of the forty-two tapes that had been subpoenaed. Nixon said that portions of the tapes were unrelated to Watergate and were therefore omitted, so that neither the public nor anyone on the committee but its two chief members could determine the reliability of the tapes. Rodino and Hutchinson were not thought to be expert enough to tell if the tapes had been falsified in some way, and, in all probability, neither of them was expected to be as alert as committee staff members to important material that had been deleted. (Rodino and Hutchinson did listen to the tapes, however, and found some glaring differences from what Nixon had made public.)

On May 1, the Judiciary Committee, in a 20 to 18 vote split almost along party lines, directed Rodino to send this note to Nixon:

> Dear Mr. President:
>
> The Committee on the Judiciary has directed me to advise you that it finds as of 10 a.m. April 30, you have

failed to comply with the committee's subpoena of April 11, 1974.

In the few days following the release of the edited transcripts, the shortcomings in the version of the tapes released by Nixon became readily apparent. It was discovered that two dictationists had transcribed a lengthy, overlapping segment of a conversation between Nixon and Assistant Attorney General Henry Petersen. The typed versions of what they heard were so different that both accounts were inadvertently put, one after the other, in the final edited transcripts—as apt a demonstration as any that the entire package of more than 1,200 pages was worthless insofar as it purported to be an accurate rendition of what was on the tapes.

The transcripts, though incomplete, were seized on by publishers and became overnight best-sellers, with *The Washington Post* and *The New York Times* making immediate arrangements with paperback firms for rapid printing and distribution. A rush, hardcover edition was circulated also. The phrase "expletive deleted" became the latest popular addition to the lexicon of Watergate; "a limited hang out" (a story half told) and "stonewalling" (remaining silent) took their place next to the slang of 1973, the year of "stroking calls," "talking papers," and "that point in time."

Everyone had favorite portions of the transcripts or phrases that stuck in their heads, such as Ehrlichman's reference to John Mitchell as "the big enchilada."

There were bizarre parts, as when Nixon and Haldeman spoke to Ehrlichman about getting his office geared up to tape a conversation. Ehrlichman, who apparently had no idea of Nixon's taping system, questioned the legality of such a procedure although he had taped telephone calls before. Haldeman readily explained the law in detail as he understood it. In the first transcript, that of a conversation on September 15, 1972, Nixon closed a telephone call with Mitchell by saying, "Get a good night's sleep. And don't bug anybody without asking me? OK?" Later on, Nixon lamented his Watergate predicament, saying he was, after all, a law-and-order man.

There was also occasional boastfulness, and sadness as well, with the President expressing concern over family problems that Haldeman was having and talking about how difficult it was for him to turn against Mitchell.

But what struck many people more than anything else was the apparent moral barrenness in the White House, the absolute failure to approach problems through any principled course of action, the hour upon hour of scheming privately while publicly claiming to be above the scandal, and the clear indications that despite his protestations, the President was deeply involved in the coverup.

The question arose that if this was the best face Nixon could put forward through his own edited version of the transcripts, then how much more incriminating might the real tapes be? Gradually an answer came.

Because Nixon had made public his version of some tapes that had been given to the Special Prosecutor, the Rodino Committee staff was able to compare Nixon's editing with the actual tapes that had been turned over to them. They found immediately that in key areas, the President, whether purportedly to remove expletives or to excise material that allegedly did not pertain to Watergate, had, in fact, distorted meaning and left out damaging sections entirely. The best example was a crucial segment of Nixon's March 21, 1973, conversation with Dean and Haldeman. Attorneys for Nixon maintained, even after the release of the tapes, that the President had never approved of the payment of hush money to Howard Hunt, that he had only explored options in discussing blackmail with Dean and Haldeman, and that in the end, he ruled out such payments. The edited Nixon transcript showed this dialogue over whether or not to get money for Hunt:

> NIXON: Would you agree that that's the prime thing that you damn well better get that done?
> DEAN: Obviously, he ought to be given some signal anyway.
> NIXON: (Expletive deleted), get it. In a way that—who is

> going to talk to him? Colson? He is the one who is supposed to know him?

These lines were possibly damaging to Nixon, but one could see where the President might only be sounding out his aide. The Judiciary Committee listened to the tape, however, and heard the expletive that had been deleted. The President's actual words, amounting to a clear order, were, "For Christ's sakes, get it, in a way that, uh—who's going to talk to him, Colson? He's the one who's supposed to know him."

Several committee members were so infuriated over this distortion that they released the corrected account to the press, as well as segments of other conversations in which Nixon's version was at variance in crucial areas with the actual tapes. As they did, presidential aides such as Kenneth Clawson, who had been promoted to the position of White House communications director, charged that the corrections were "leaks" that demonstrated the partisan nature of the Rodino Committee. A new wave of obfuscation began as presidential speech writer Patrick Buchanan challenged the press to address itself to the problem of leaks as a worthwhile subject for news stories.

The audacity of such criticism was unparalleled—the President had put out statements to the nation that were deliberately misleading, doing much of the editing himself. What these congressmen had done was to correct those statements. Yet a claim was made that the congressmen had violated principles of confidentiality.

Later, the Judiciary Committee made public even larger sections of the tapes in which Nixon's version was at variance with what actually had been said. More than ever, the President's own words were incriminating to him.

In the edited version released by Nixon, for example, the March 21, 1973, conversation showed the President saying to H.R. Haldeman and John Dean, in regard to blackmail demands by Howard Hunt: ". . . his price is pretty high, but at least we can buy the time on that." In the Judiciary Committee version, Nixon was heard to say: " . . . his price is pretty high, but at least, uh, we should, we should buy the time on that, uh, as I pointed out to John."

In the tape of a conversation on March 22, 1973, between Nixon, John Mitchell, John Ehrlichman, Haldeman, and Dean, the Nixon transcript omitted an entire section in which the President said, at one point, "I don't give a shit what happens. I want you all to stonewall it, let them plead the Fifth Amendment, coverup, or anything else, if it'll save it—save the whole plan. That's the whole point."

At the White House, Ronald Ziegler criticized the committee for its release of a 131-page comparison of conflicting passages in the transcripts, saying the committee was conducting a "hypoed PR campaign" against Nixon, that "they have chosen the public relations route which will focus the news media only on one section of the tapes." Ziegler said the committee "should release the full body of evidence all together, all at once and not in piecemeal fashion."

Of course, had Nixon not edited the way he did, there would have been no need for the committee to release any comparison of the transcripts. If Ziegler's complaint sounded lame, the fact was that by then, the middle of July, 1974, there were virtually no trump cards left in the Nixon hand. The tapes, even in the form presented by the President, were ruinous to him, and any defense from the White House rang hollow, the mutterings of an emperor trying to convince a citizenry that his clothing was just a little soiled, when they could see that he had none at all.

As time passed, the House Judiciary Committee, which had begun its work in October, 1973, fell far behind its planned schedule. Hoping at first that its work would be completed by April, Chairman Rodino kept pushing the date back, aiming at the last to have its recommendations ready by the end of July. The committee spent weeks listening to the Nixon tapes and hearing witnesses in secret sessions. As they would emerge each day, certain committee members expressed the conviction that the testimony was damaging to Nixon; others would say that it wasn't.

The President's attorney St. Clair developed a strategy aimed at focusing the impeachment debate as narrowly as possible. Maintaining that a President could be impeached only for actions that were criminal offenses, he discarded almost all the vast accumulation of charges against Nixon except for those dealing with the Watergate coverup. Then he singled out the one accusation that had become most prominent in recent months—that Nixon had ordered the payment of hush money to Howard Hunt on March 21, 1973. St. Clair said he could demonstrate that regardless of those words, payment made to Hunt had been arranged before Nixon spoke to Dean, without the President's knowledge. Therefore, he said, Nixon had not been instrumental in seeing that Hunt was bribed to keep silent. Had Nixon been in China, St. Clair said, the March 21, 1973, payment to Hunt would have been made anyway. No other charge against Nixon was as serious as that one. St. Clair maintained. Ergo, the President should not be impeached.

By July, 1974, many of the events dealt here were largely out of the minds of large numbers of citizens; Watergate, as ever, had a tendency to be yesterday's newspaper story. What was remembered was the most recent shock. Reporters covering Capitol Hill returned to their offices saying that if St. Clair could demonstrate what he said he could demonstrate, well . . .

The question, then, was whether Congress would cooperate in St. Clair's strategy or not. It was they, not he, who were to decide Nixon's fate. For many weeks there was no way of predicting what would happen. At just that point, the committee began to release the voluminous testimony it had gathered during its months of work, tracing the pattern of Nixon's behavior from the earliest days of his presidency. As the material became public, the vast majority of members of the House and Senate continued to state that they stood to be judges and therefore should not venture an opinion on the likelihood of a successful impeachment. A few members of Congress attacked the President, at the risk of being labeled partisans. There was a vocal group who, despite the existence of a record two years in the making, said that they saw no evidence of wrongdoing on Nixon's part.

Public opinion and government policy feed on each other. As people clamor, elected officials act. As officials act, people's understanding of events is shaped. In mid-July, 1974, a public that had grown tired of clamoring became somewhat quiet. The Rodino Committee released millions of words of information it had gathered, but not a single sentence explaining the significance of its findings.

Then, on the 19th of July, the committee acted in a striking fashion. The senior counsel to both the Democrats and the Republicans, John Doar and Albert E. Jenner, Jr., urged the committee to endorse sending impeachment of Nixon to the Senate on one or more of several broad impeachment charges:

- Obstruction of justice in the Watergate coverup and related scandals.
- Abuse of government agencies by the President.
- Contempt of Congress and the courts by Nixon in his defiance of subpoenas.
- Failure to observe his constitutional duty "to see that the laws be faithfully executed."
- Denigration of the presidency through Nixon's under-payment of income taxes and the use of federal funds to improve personal property.

The charges were backed up by twenty-nine potential articles of impeachment and a thick summary of the committee staff's findings, containing harsh judgments as to Nixon's conduct in office—both before and after Watergate.

Doar's first proposed article of impeachment read:

> Beginning almost immediately after the burglary and continuing up to the present time, Richard M. Nixon, using the powers of his office, acting directly and personally and through his personal agents at the seat of Government and their immediate subordinates, has made it his policy to cover up and conceal responsibility for the burglary, the identity of other participants, and the existence and scope of related unlawful covert activities.

> The means of implementing this policy have included the subornation of perjury, the purchase of silence of those directly participating in the burglary, the obstruction of justice, the destruction of evidence, improper and unlawful interference with the conduct of lawful investigation by the Department of Justice, including the Federal Bureau of Investigation and the Office of the Special Prosecutor, improper and unlawful misuse of other agencies of the Executive branch, including the CIA, and the release of deliberately false and misleading statements from the White House and by the President.

"For all this, Richard M. Nixon is personally and directly responsible," Doar's report said.

As the House Judiciary Committee moved to bring its findings to Congress, the Supreme Court entered Watergate for the first time when asked by Special Prosecutor Jaworski to decide whether the President could keep from him sixty-four additional tapes that he had requested. The Court was thereby given an uncertain role in impeachment proceedings, as the President's attorneys argued that any material given Jaworski would find its way to the Judiciary Committee despite Nixon's claim that the committee had all the evidence it needed, and his insistence on the need for confidentiality. "In effect court process is being used as a discovery tool for the impeachment proceedings—proceedings which the Constitution clearly assigns to the Congress, not the courts," Nixon's attorneys maintained in a brief in advance of oral arguments in the case.

The brief urged the High Court not to be swayed by the "passing needs of the moment" at the expense "of those enduring constitutional doctrines that have preserved our system of ordered liberty through the ages.

"Of those doctrines, none is more fundamental to our governmental structure itself than the separation of powers—with all of its inherent tensions, with all of its necessary inability to satisfy all the people or all institutions all of the time, and yet with the relentless and saving force that it generates toward essential compromise and accommodation over the longer term if not always in the shorter term."

By attempting to invoke the principle of confidentiality to keep from submitting tapes to the Special Prosecutor and the Rodino Committee, Nixon's Watergate defense became absurdly empty, for while the President chose to rest his public posture on a high constitutional issue, he had, in the Watergate transcripts, shown time and again that he had not the slightest concern with separation of powers or Executive privilege as historic, constitutional matters. The private Nixon was known by anyone who could read the English language as a President who saw confidentiality exclusively as a means of preventing harmful disclosure. In the transcripts he made public, he ridiculed the historic aspects of Executive privilege.

Beginning with his February 28, 1973, conversation with Dean—in which Nixon referred to Executive privilege as the "kind of a line" he wanted to take—there were more than five dozen references to Executive privilege, some of them running for many pages. In every instance the so-called principle of confidentiality was discussed as a tool to save Nixon or his closest associates, and not the "presidency" or future Presidents.

In their February 28, 1973, conversation, for example, Nixon and Dean agreed on a plan to invoke Executive privilege to keep presidential aides from appearing before the Ervin Committee. The aides instead would respond under oath to written interrogatories, and if more information was desired, the aides would answer questions put to them, in the White House, by the chairman and ranking minority member of the Ervin Committee. The idea was that written questions were easier to answer.

In their March 13, 1973, conversation, the transcripts show, Dean and Nixon left no doubt why they preferred interrogatories. Speaking about the possibility that Dean might be called to testify at the Senate confirmation hearings for L. Patrick Gray as permanent FBI director, the young counsel said, "You can handle written interrogatories, where cross-examination is another ball game."

"That's right!" Nixon responded.

In the early part of that day's conversation, while Haldeman was present, Nixon, Dean, and Haldeman talked specifically about using Executive privilege fraudulently. Charles Colson had left the White House to enter private law practice three days earlier, and the discussion opened on whether Colson's severance papers should be amended to state that he remained an unpaid consultant to Nixon. Such a change, Haldeman noted, should be "backdated" so that the Executive privilege claim could be continuous.

If that were done for Colson, the President asked, could it also be done for Dwight Chapin, who had left the White House earlier? Dean said the former appointments secretary didn't have quite the same problem that Colson did, but Haldeman disagreed.

Nixon then said, "Well, can't—that would [be] such an obvious fraud to have both of them as consultants, that that won't work. I think he is right. You would have to leave Chapin." Evidently it was not fraud that disturbed Nixon, only obvious fraud.

On the 20th of March, in a telephone conversation with Dean, Nixon expressed concern that people outside the White House would see Executive privilege for what it was, an attempt to "stonewall" Congress. He asked Dean to circumvent that problem by preparing a statement for the President's use—but not too revealing a statement. The transcripts show the President saying:

> You've got to have something where it doesn't appear that I am doing this in, you know, just in a—saying to hell with the Congress and to hell with the people, we are not going to tell you anything because of Executive privilege. That, they don't understand. But if you say, 'No, we are willing to cooperate,' and you've made a complete statement, but make it very incomplete. See, that is what I mean.

Nixon explained that he wanted such a statement for its effect on Cabinet members and other leaders. "It might just be very salutary.

You see, our own people have got to have confidence or they are not going to step up and defend us. You see the problem there, don't you?"

Dean suggested that at the same time, these Nixon supporters be given a statement explaining Executive privilege, saying, "It is tremendous to have a piece of paper that they know they can talk from."

"Pointing out," said Nixon, "that you are defending the Constitution; responsibility of the separation of powers; and we have to do it." It was no jump at all for the President to go from a request for an incomplete complete statement to a constitutional principle—they were both part of the same defense.

The following day, in the March 21, 1973, conversation in which Dean outlined the cancer growing on the presidency, Nixon asked if it wasn't possible to extend the use of Executive privilege to a grand jury appearance that John Ehrlichman had to make in a criminal case in New York. "Criminal charge, that is a little different," Dean said. "That would be dynamite to try to defend that."

When the Constitution did arise, or any reference to history and principle at all, it was discussed in terms of a "scenario," exclusively as a means through which Nixon, Mitchell, and Dean envisioned hoodwinking Sam Ervin.

> NIXON: It is a record for the future. Maybe you can tell Ervin on the mountaintop that this is a good way to set up a procedure for the future. You know what I mean, where future cases of this sort are involved. We are making a lot of history here, Senator.
>
> MITCHELL: And the Senator can be a great part of it.
>
> NIXON: A lot of history. We are setting a stirring precedent. The President, after all, let's find out what the President did know, talk about the Hiss case.
>
> DEAN: Ervin away from his staff is not very much and I think he might just give up the store himself right there and lock himself in. You know, I have dealt with him for a number of years and have seen that happen.

• • •

Hardly any conversations in the presidential transcripts are without such references to Executive privilege. In the next transcript made public by Nixon, that of a conversation between the President, Haldeman, Ehrlichman, and Ziegler, Nixon instructed his press secretary to use Executive privilege as a tactic to block questioning by reporters, saying, "I would simply stall them off today. Say that is not before us at this time, but let me emphasize, as the President has indicated, there will be complete cooperation consistent with the responsibilities that everybody has on the separation of powers. Fair enough?"

In one conversation, Ehrlichman suggested a court test of the principle of Executive privilege, and Nixon, who had always publicly maintained that the High Court would side with him on the matter, said, "We don't want a court case." Ehrlichman said a court test would delay any appearance of Nixon aides before the Senate Watergate Committee, and that if Nixon lost in court, by then John Mitchell might be indicted and "Mitchell's lawyers are going to somehow move to stop the Ervin hearing."

And finally, when Nixon decided to capitulate on Executive privilege before the Senate Watergate Committee after Ervin remained adamant, he showed no remorse for future presidents. In a late night phone call to Ehrlichman on April 14, 1973, Nixon said, "I think, frankly, let's get off of the damned Executive privilege." He told his aide that to surrender the principle would put the President in the position of appearing forthcoming, suggesting that he wanted the facts out, "and that's that."

Nixon said to Ehrlichman, "We have won lots of things with the Congress. We lose one. But you, in interpreting it, would say we have reached a compromise with the committee, that we limited it to this, to charges of wrongdoing."

At that point, the President waived his power to decide on what was privileged and agreed to Ervin Committee ground rules which said that while aides to the President could assert Executive privilege, the committee itself would make the final decision. Two days later, though, when Nixon became alarmed that Dean might testify against him, the President once more returned to his hard-line position, urging Dean not to report the substance of their conversations, much of which dealt with, as Nixon phrased it, "that damn Executive privilege and all that."

On July 24, 1974, the Supreme Court rendered a unanimous 8-0 verdict that the President had to turn over the sixty-four tapes requested by Special Prosecutor Jaworski. At one point citing the eloquent language of a 1935 High Court case that "guilt shall not escape or innocence suffer," the Court, in a thirty-one-page opinion delivered by Chief Justice Warren Burger, decided:

> We conclude that the ground for asserting privilege as to subpoenaed materials sought for use in a criminal trial is based only on the generalized interest in confidentiality, it cannot prevail over the fundamental demands of due process of law in the fair administration of criminal justice. The generalized assertion of privilege must yield to the demonstrated, specific need for evidence in a pending criminal trial.

That same day, with its final decision considered by many a foregone conclusion, the House Judiciary Committee began its debates—which were televised—to work out the exact language of its impeachment recommendation to Congress.

With the record of Nixon's conduct exposed through his own words, and with the Judiciary Committee's strong findings, it seemed highly unlikely that a large enough number of the members of Congress could combine to rescue Nixon from impeachment. Nixon knew that. He seemed half resigned to the worst, alternately charging that impeachment was partisan-motivated, deploring his "enemies," saying his aides could not get a fair trial in Washington, D.C.

At the same time, he tried to extricate himself from the ever-pulling undertow by rallying public opinion behind him, as though impeachment were an election campaign. As the summer began, Nixon, once more attempting to appear above the fray, flew to the Middle East and then to the Soviet Union for summit talks. One might recall how his trip to Moscow in 1972 had helped enormously in public opinion polls. This time when the President went overseas, it was reported that he was the victim of phlebitis, a blood clot—an ailment that sometimes requires people to undergo extensive periods of rest or run the risk of losing their lives.

When Nixon returned from Russia, then, and after the Supreme Court ruled, the seeds for any possible turn of events had been planted. The evidence against him was being gathered and disseminated. He had a small, staunch corps of defenders who predicted that he would not be impeached. And, with a Congress likely to be importuning him once again, he could resign and attempt to call it "a compromise."

Almost until the end, Nixon fought to dodge impeachment or resignation. His last tactic was to have members of Congress judge him not on evidence of his complicity in one or more aspects of scandal, but on the question of whether the nation could afford to lose him as president. Nixon, the theme went, was needed. The position was formally articulated on July 22, 1974, when the assistant minority counsel to the House Judiciary Committee told committee members, "The question is, did the President do it, and if so, what are the implications of that for the nation in light of all competing interests."

In the last week of July, 1974, as the Judiciary Committee held its final deliberations in lengthy and spellbinding televised sessions, it was apparent that this strategy had failed to move all but a few members of the committee. Nixon had given little in the way of assistance to the Judiciary Committee, generally defying their counsel's requests and subpoenas for evidence. Nevertheless, the committee, working largely from material gathered in earlier investigations by other bodies, presented an overwhelming case against him in the form of three articles of impeachment.

Each article stated that Nixon had violated "his constitutional oath faithfully to execute the office of the President of the United States" and "his constitutional duty to take care that the laws be faithfully executed."

Article One charged that Nixon, "using the powers of his high office, engaged personally and through his subordinates and agents in a course of conduct or plan designed to delay, impede, and obstruct the investigation of such unlawful entry (the Watergate break-in); to cover up, conceal and protect those responsible; and to conceal the existence and scope of other unlawful covert activities."

The article charged that one or more of nine means had been used to implement such conduct, including making or causing false or misleading statements to investigators; withholding evidence; "approving, condoning, acquiescing in, and counseling witnesses" to make false or misleading statements; interfering or attempting to interfere with investigations of the Justice Department, the FBI, the office of the Watergate Special Prosecutor and congressional committees; approving payment of "substantial sums" of money to buy silence or influence the testimony of witnesses or others involved in illegal entry or other illegal activities; attempting to misuse the Central Intelligence Agency; disseminating Justice Department information to subjects of investigations to help them avoid criminal liability; making false and misleading statements to deceive the American people into believing that a thorough and complete investigation had been held, and endeavoring to cause prospective defendants and convicted individuals to expect favored treatment in return for their silence or false testimony.

Article Two charged that Nixon "has repeatedly engaged in conduct violating the constitutional right of citizens, impairing due and proper administration of justice in the conduct of lawful inquiries, of contravening the law of governing agencies to the executive branch and the purposes of these agencies."

The second article dealt with Watergate and also with Nixon's role in other matters that had been uncovered as the great coverup collapsed. Included were charges dealing with abuse of the Internal Revenue Service, the FBI, the Secret Service and "other executive personnel;" the practice of unlawful electronic wiretapping; the creation and continuance of the White House special investigative unit (the plumbers); the failure to act when he knew that aides had behaved illegally, and the misuse of executive power by interfering with agencies of the executive branch.

Article Three held that the President should be impeached for his refusal to comply with Judiciary Committee subpoenas. "In refusing to produce these papers and things," the article stated, "Richard M. Nixon, substituting his judgment as to what materials were necessary for the inquiry, interposed the powers of the Presidency against the lawful subpoenas of the House of Representatives, thereby assuming for himself functions and judgments necessary to the exercise of the sole power of impeachment vested by the Constitution in the House of Representatives."

During the months of closed deliberations of the Judiciary Committee, most members refrained publicly from drawing any conclusions on the evidence the committee staff had assembled. That changed dramatically in the televised sessions as the proposed bill of particulars was drawn, and at the end of each impeachment article, this language appeared:

"In all of this, Richard M. Nixon has acted in a manner contrary to his trust as President and subversive of constitutional government, to the great prejudice of the cause of law and justice, and to the manifest injury of the people of the United States.

"Wherefore, Richard M. Nixon, by such conduct, warrants impeachment and trial and removal from office."

The last article was approved July 30. Subsequently, the committee debated but refused to recommend impeachment on two other charges: Nixon's secret bombing of Cambodia in violation of the constitutional requirement that Congress approve such action, and possible fraud in his payment of personal income taxes.

As the Judiciary Committee completed its televised sessions, it was clear that its thorough and largely bipartisan efforts had made it difficult for most other members of Congress to vote against impeachment without discrediting themselves. The evidence against Nixon was too strong. Still, the vote on impeachment was thought to be treacherous for individual Representatives and Senators in that segments of their constituencies might be angered regardless of how warily they moved. For that reason, and because some leaders felt a Senate trial would be jarring to the nation, a cry emanated from Capitol Hill for Nixon to resign. It was not the first time such a plea had been made, and, at the outset, Nixon responded the way he had in the past; with a firm refusal. It appeared that impeachment would go down to the wire.

It was in such a setting that Nixon was felled by the blow from which there was to be no recovery, the release of new tapes that showed his involvement in dragging the Central Intelligence Agency into the Watergate coverup. "The smoking gun," these tapes were called. Fittingly, as had happened so frequently in the course of the scandal, it was Nixon himself who forced the issue.

The role of the CIA in the coverup has been dealt with at length in this book. Long before the contents of these last tapes became known, from data on the public record, the evidence was overwhelming that within a week of the arrests of five men at Democratic National Committee headquarters, Nixon personally plotted to have the CIA block crucial aspects of the FBI's Watergate inquiry.

The "smoking gun" phrase referred to three of the sixty-four tapes that were ordered made public by the Supreme Court. They were records of meetings between Nixon and Haldeman on June 23, 1972. The tapes demonstrated once and for all that Nixon took part in the Watergate coverup from the outset.

They showed that only six days after the initial Watergate arrests, Nixon and Haldeman discussed strategy to keep the FBI from moving into what Haldeman called "productive areas." As Haldeman spelled out the plan in its details, Nixon issued his approval, saying, "All right, fine." The President then instructed Haldeman on how to elicit cooperation from Richard Helms, the director of the CIA, and from his deputy, Vernon Walters.

The tapes also revealed for the first time that the President knew by June 23, 1972, of the involvement of Gordon Liddy, in the break-in and bugging. Yet five more days were to pass before Liddy was questioned by FBI agents—and then, as is described in this book, it was only through accident that Liddy was uncovered, not because Nixon or any other high officials who knew of his involvement reported him to investigators.

On the first weekend in August, 1974, Nixon met with several of his remaining close advisers and notified them of what was recorded in the June 23 conversations before relinquishing them to investigators. Two of the advisers reportedly said that the material was so damaging that Nixon had no choice but to resign. On Monday, August 5, with the knowledge that the tapes could not be kept from Congress for long, the President made their contents public.

He noted that "this additional material I am now furnishing may further damage my case," and pointed out that portions of the tapes "are at variance with certain of my previous statements." But Nixon still was not ready to give up the fight. He made a last, futile appeal to Congress and to the public, saying he was convinced that the record, "in its entirety, does not justify the extreme step of impeachment and removal of a President. I trust that as the constitutional process goes forward, this perspective will prevail."

Members of Congress felt otherwise. For more than two years, the President had lied to the people about his role in the Watergate cover-up. As he relinquished the last three tapes, he admitted that he had kept them from the House Judiciary Committee with the awareness that they "presented potential problems . . . that those passing judgment on the case did so with information that was incomplete and in some respects erroneous."

To a one, Nixon's strongest defenders on the Judiciary Committee stated publicly that they could no longer support the President. Several of them were near tears in televised interviews in which they expressed the view that they had been betrayed by Nixon. Most of them, and other leaders on Capitol Hill, once more pleaded that the President resign.

By Wednesday, August 7, as the weight of the new evidence sank in, impeachment no longer seemed a difficult matter for any member of Congress. A vote against impeachment might be costly, but not a vote for it. The President's complicity in the great coverup was so amply demonstrated by these tapes that Capitol Hill head counters predicted Nixon could expect no more than fifteen votes from the Senate to keep him in office. He needed thirty-four. The end had come.

from The Final Days

by Carl Bernstein and Bob Woodward

Reporters Bob Woodward (born 1943) and Carl Bernstein (born 1944) broke the story of the Watergate scandal for the Washington Post. *Their 1976 book about Nixon's last days in office includes this account of the president's decision to resign.*

The President left the Oval Office at about eight o'clock and went upstairs to the Lincoln Sitting Room, in the southeast corner of the mansion. It was his favorite room, the smallest in the White House, only about sixteen by thirteen feet, designed and arranged for one person. All the furniture—Victorian chairs, a deep, low couch with high sleigh arms—was uncomfortable except for Nixon's overstuffed brown leather chair and ottoman in the corner. The room was his retreat. He had his music—a stereo and two five-foot shelves of records were within reach. Nineteenth-century prints were arranged over the gray marble fireplace. One was of President Lincoln's last reception. There was another of Lincoln and his son, another of his family.

Now Nixon summoned Kissinger.

Kissinger was expecting resignation, and had had his assistants, Eagleburger and Scowcroft, devise a fourteen-step plan to deal with the transition. It included a statement by Ford at the time of swearing in concerning the continuity of foreign policy, specific presidential messages to thirty-seven countries, and calls by Kissinger himself to fourteen key ambassadors.

For the first time in five and a half years, Kissinger would not be reviewing his plans with Nixon. He was, in fact, supremely relieved that Nixon was finally going. For months, the Secretary of State had been worrying that the world might blow up. But as he walked over and took the elevator to the second floor, he was also angry. Watergate had wrecked his foreign-affairs strategy. The domestic impact was tiny compared to the repercussions abroad. If someone had suggested ten years before to Harvard Professor Henry Kissinger that a superpower could be paralyzed in the nuclear age by a domestic scandal, he would have answered, "Never. Preposterous."

He walked into the alcove. There was the President in his chair, as he had seen him so often. Kissinger really didn't like the President. Nixon had made him the most admired man in the country, yet the Secretary couldn't bring himself to feel affection for his patron. They sat for a time and reminisced about events, travels, shared decisions. The President was drinking. He said he was resigning. It would be better for everyone. They talked quietly—history, the resignation decision, foreign affairs.

Then Nixon said that he wasn't sure he would be able to resign. Could he be the first President to quit office?

Kissinger responded by listing the President's contributions, especially in diplomacy.

"Will history treat me more kindly than my contemporaries?" Nixon asked, tears flooding to his eyes.

Certainly, definitely, Kissinger said. When this was all over, the President would be remembered for the peace he had achieved.

The President broke down and sobbed.

Kissinger didn't know what to do. He felt cast in a fatherly role. He talked on, he picked up on the themes he had heard so many times from the President. He remembered lines about enemies, the need to stand up to adversity, to face criticism forthrightly.

Between sobs, Nixon was plaintive. What had he done to the country and its people? He needed some explanation. How had it come to this? How had a simple burglary, a breaking and entering, done all this?

Kissinger kept talking, trying to turn the conversation back to all the good things, all the accomplishments. Nixon wouldn't hear of it. He was hysterical. "Henry," he said, "you are not a very orthodox Jew, and I am not an orthodox Quaker, but we need to pray."

Nixon got down on his knees. Kissinger felt he had no alternative but to kneel down, too. The President prayed out loud, asking for help, rest, peace and love. How could a President and a country be torn apart by such small things?

Kissinger thought he had finished. But the President did not rise. He was weeping. And then, still sobbing, Nixon leaned over and struck his fist on the carpet, crying, "What have I done? What has happened?"

Kissinger touched the President, and then held him, tried to console him, to bring rest and peace to the man who was curled on the carpet like a child. The President of the United States. Kissinger tried again to reassure him, reciting Nixon's accomplishments.

Finally the President struggled to his feet. He sat back down in his chair. The storm had passed. He had another drink.

Kissinger lingered. He talked on, building a case, pouring his academic talents into a lecture on why Richard Nixon would go down in history as one of the great peacemakers of all time. "You made the tough decisions," he said.

The two men had another drink. Their conversation drifted around to personalities and to the role Nixon might be able to play once he was out of office. He might be an adviser, or a special ambassador. Nixon wondered again if he would be exonerated by history. Kissinger was encouraging; he was willing to say anything. But he was certain that Nixon would never escape the verdict of Watergate.

At last Kissinger got up to leave. Nixon had never really asked as much of him as he had that night. Vietnam, Cambodia, Russia, China—they all seemed easier. Weak in the knees, his clothes damp from perspiration, Kissinger escaped. Though he was the President's only top adviser to survive Watergate, he had never really been consulted about resignation.

As he walked through the West Wing corridor to his office, Kissinger thought he had never felt as close to or as far from Richard Nixon. Never as close to or as far from anyone he had ever known.

Eagleburger and Scowcroft were waiting. It was almost eleven. Kissinger looked somber and drained. He did not shout orders, ask for messages, make phone calls or demand reports. He was clearly upset. To get control over his own tensions, Kissinger began talking about the encounter. The President was definitely resigning, he said.

"It was the most wrenching thing I have ever gone through in my life—hand holding," Kissinger added. The President was a broken man. What a traumatic experience it had been, what a profound shock to see a man at the end of his rope. He was convinced that historians would at least treat Nixon better than his contemporaries had, but it might take some time before that particular revisionist history would be written.

Scowcroft mentioned that he thought it significant that the President had turned to Kissinger for sustenance in his most awful moment. Not to Haig, not to any of the others.

"Henry," Eagleburger said, "at times I've thought you're not human. But I was wrong. I've never seen you so moved."

The phone rang. It was the President.

Eagleburger picked up an extension to listen. That was the custom—Kissinger rarely took a call alone. Eagleburger was shocked. The President was slurring his words. He was drunk. He was out of control.

"It was good of you to come up and talk, Henry," the President said. "I've made the decision, but you must stay. You must stay on for the good of the country."

Eagleburger could barely make out what the President was saying. He was almost incoherent. It was pathetic. Eagleburger felt ill and hung up.

The President had one last request: "Henry, please don't ever tell anyone that I cried and that I was not strong."

from Turmoil and Triumph

by George P. Shultz

Washington in late 1986 was rife with rumors that members of Ronald Reagan's (in office 1981–1989) administration had traded arms for Americans held hostage in Iran. Secretary of State George P. Shultz (born 1920) was horrified to find that the rumors were true.

The presidency of Ronald Reagan was in deep trouble, whether the president and his White House staff realized it or not. I had to drive that point home to them. I somehow had to bring an end to arms sales to Iran in exchange for hostages, however dressed up the deals were in the strategic guise of a change in relations with Iran. I had to break through the disposition to stonewall the public and Congress: that was a sure road to a disastrous cover-up. And I had to get policy on Iran and on antiterrorism back on track, into my hands and away from the NSC staff. A tall order, but I was convinced that my success in this fight was essential to save the Reagan presidency.

My dilemma was that while the White House clearly had taken us down the wrong path, the president was still surrounded by people who were asserting—here in November 1986, *after* the revelation of efforts to trade arms for hostages—that a further hostage release was imminent. I did not want to abort the possibility of a release, but I was battling to shut this operation down. What bothered me immediately was a comment made on television by Vice President Bush. His close friend and adviser, Nick Brady, had telephoned me Saturday night, November 8, 1986, to ask whether I planned to resign. I didn't answer but told Brady, "What concerns me is Bush on TV saying it is inconceivable even to consider selling arms to Iran for hostages. The vice president was in one key meeting that I know of, on January 7, 1986, and he made no objection to the proposal for arms sales to Iran, with the clear objective of getting hostages released in the process. Cap and I were the only voices of dissent. The reality of whatever happened is just emerging. Who knows what will be revealed? The vice president could get drawn into a web of lies. If he blows his integrity, he's finished. He should be very careful how he plays the 'loyal lieutenant' role now."

The next morning, Sunday, November 9, Nick Brady came to my house to talk about what I had said on the telephone. Shortly before he arrived, the vice president's assistant for national security matters, Don Gregg, telephoned Nick Platt to say that Bush was worried. "What is Shultz's disposition?" Bush wanted to know. He had apparently heard from Brady of my warning that his television statement did not square with the proposal put forward during the critical January 7 meeting we had both attended.

After Nick Brady and I watched "This Week with David Brinkley," I turned off the television and said to Nick, "The vice president should not rush out with statements until he knows all the facts or he'll get himself in the glue." Bush, I said, had been perfectly aware that arms sales to Iran—along lines that Cap and I had argued was an "arms-for-hostages deal"—had been proposed in the administration and that he had, on at least one occasion to my knowledge—in the January 7,1986, meeting—not objected to the proposal. So it would not square for him to say to the media that such a step was "inconceivable."

Not long after Nick left, Vice President Bush telephoned to invite O'Bie and me to dinner that night. We couldn't accept because of an earlier obligation, but we went over for a drink with him and Barbara in the late afternoon. I put my views to him: I didn't know much about what had actually transpired, but I knew that an exchange of arms for hostages had been tried on at least one occasion. And I knew such an action would never stand up in public. Bush admonished me, asking emphatically whether I realized that there are major strategic objectives being pursued with Iran. He said that he was very careful about what he said.

"You' can't be *technically right*; you have to be right," I responded. I reminded him that he had been present at a meeting where arms for Iran and hostage releases had been proposed and that he had made no objection, despite the opposition of both Cap and me. "That's where you are," I said. There was considerable tension between us when we parted.

(I was astonished to read in the August 6, 1987, *Washington Post*, the account of an interview by David Broder during which Vice President Bush said, "If I had sat there and heard George Shultz and Cap express it [opposition to Iran arms sales] strongly, maybe I would have had a stronger view. But when you don't know something, it's hard to react. . . . We were not in the loop." Cap called me. He was astonished, too: "That's terrible. He was on the other side. It's on the record. Why did he say that?")

That evening, Bud McFarlane telephoned me. He told me that he had made no trip to Tehran that I didn't know about. I didn't know what prompted his call and did not want to discuss the matter with him.

Every few hours the mood of the crisis seemed to shift and to worsen: The issue on Monday, November 10, changed to the constitutional implications. The *Washington Post* ran the headline: "Hill Probes of NSC Planned; Arms Deal With Iran Seen as Attempt to Circumvent Congress." The view was emerging that what had happened was a back-room operation run by staffers who, given their positions in the bureaucracy, would not be subject to congressional or public scrutiny.

Early that same day, Poindexter finally telephoned me. There would be a meeting at 11:30 a.m. with the president at which Poindexter would brief Vice President Bush, me, Cap Weinberger, Bill Casey, and Ed Meese on what "really" was going on.

"Good idea," I said, "but my opinion hasn't changed. We should shut the operation down. I thought that it had been shut down last May or June." Poindexter and Casey had both explicitly told me that.

Poindexter said that in August 1986, "Rafsanjani's nephew" got in touch with the White House and had been "a valuable channel" ever since then. "Rafsanjani wants to end the [Iran-Iraq] war," Poindexter told me. He went on to elaborate on his theory that in Rafsanjani's public revelation of the McFarlane trip to Tehran, in which he incorrectly stated facts of which he had personal knowledge, Rafsanjani was sending a signal to the United States that he was still "with us."

After he hung up, I recalled an old Bernie Kalb line, "Is that what they told you, Missy?" an old Asia hand's way of noting hopeless gullibility.

With everyone alert to the slightest nuance, reports and rumors were flying in. The State Department's Near East bureau picked up a report that the release of Father Jenco in July 1986 had been arranged by Oliver North in return for arms valued at $24 million. The corridors of the State Department buzzed with rumors of several such schemes. It was insane if true. All along, the only sensible approach had focused on getting *all* the hostages out at once *without any trade of arms* in exchange. To let the terrorists sell hostages to us one by one was to create a hostage-taking industry. I could scarcely believe that Casey, Poindexter, and North could be so foolhardy and gullible, but now I did believe it.

Most incredible of all were the rumors reaching us on this morning of November 10 that an arms-for-hostages operation was still under way at this very moment. An Iranian aircraft reportedly had been expected in Vienna to pick up an arms shipment, but it had not come on time, and "the Iranians are no longer answering Ollie's telexes." I decided to collect all the facts I could find in order to put them in front of Ronald Reagan to open his eyes and get him to order a halt to the continuation of this madness.

The latest swap was supposed to produce the hostages Terry Anderson and Thomas Sutherland and the remains of Beirut CIA Station Chief William Buckley. Iran also, as part of the rumored deal, was supposed to deliver a Soviet-made T-72 tank to our base on Diego Garcia Island in the Indian Ocean. If the arrangement worked, so we heard, President Reagan would authorize a military operation to rescue three other hostages, presumably those held in the Hezbollah prison that Ambassador Bartholomew had reported on in March.

North was saying that Iran, as part of this effort, had agreed eighteen months ago to cease terrorist acts against the United States and that they had kept that deal. That is why, I was told, Poindexter had put out the statement that the American arms embargo was in effect "as long as Iran advocates the use of terrorism." It was a rhetorical trick. It was also preposterous. Frank Reed had been kidnapped in Beirut on September 9, 1986, Joseph Cicippio on September 12, 1986, and Edward Tracy on October 21, 1986, and the other hostages were still being held.

Incredulous as I was about everything Poindexter and others reported, I saw that he and North were continuing their efforts—undaunted by the disasters of their own making. They had entangled themselves with a gang of operators far more cunning and clever than they. As a result, the U.S. government had violated its own policies on antiterrorism and against arms sales to Iran, was buying our own citizens' freedom in a manner that could only *encourage* the taking of others, was working through disreputable international go-betweens, was circumventing our constitutional system of governance, and was misleading the American people—all in the guise of furthering some purported regional political transformation, or to obtain in actuality a hostage release. And somehow, by dressing up this arms-for-hostages scheme and disguising its worst aspects, first McFarlane, then Poindexter, apparently with the strong collaboration of Bill Casey, had sold it to a president all too ready to accept it, given his humanitarian urge to free American hostages.

"Ultimately," I said, "the guy behind it, who got it going, and the only guy who can stop it, was and is Ronald Reagan." Perhaps the most important achievement of the administration was President Reagan's restoration of the faith and confidence of the American people in the integrity and strength of the presidency. Even Arthur M. Schlesinger, Jr., had said so on television a few weeks previously—now this.

I consulted Abe Sofaer, State's legal adviser, about the legal aspects of such arms transfers. The president could provide an exception to any executive order, Abe said, but he would have to do so in a recognized, regular manner. The president could not, however, override statutes, and specifically, one prohibiting arms exports to any nation that the secretary of state had designated as a supporter of international terrorism. Iran was on the terrorist list. Abe said he had checked with the White House counsel, Peter Wallison. "They say they haven't the foggiest notion what is going on," Abe told me.

Calls were flooding in. Nearly everyone I knew had a view on whether I should resign or not. A terse message came in from Shimon Peres in Israel: "Hello. Don't go."

At 11:30 on November 10, the president's national security group gathered in the Situation Room. The president opened. He had watched the Sunday talk shows, he said, and we were being taken apart without justification—because what we were doing was right, and legal, and justifiable. We were trying to turn around a strategic situation in the Persian Gulf area, to move Iran toward a constructive role, to help the Iranians with their problem with the Soviets. And, of course, he added, we wanted the hostages back.

Poindexter then made a long presentation. There had been a "finding" on January 17, 1986. CIA director Bill Casey had been told, presumably by the president, not to brief Congress on it. The finding emphasized, Poindexter said, our strategic objectives toward Iran.

Potential moderates in Iran would be given credibility with the military there by getting an arms relationship with us. That, Poindexter suggested, was why we had to give arms to Iran before expecting to get hostages freed in return.

"This is the first I ever heard of such a finding," I exploded. Cap was equally astounded.

This all started, Poindexter maintained, when Lieutenant Colonel Oliver North tried to find out about Israeli arms shipments to Iran: he stumbled onto an Israeli warehouse in Portugal and challenged the Israelis to explain it. Their reply was that they had to develop a relationship with the Iranians because Israel was concerned about Jews in Iran. This led, said Poindexter, to a "Ghorbanifar-Kangerlou [the Iranian intelligence chief] channel" and an operation that culminated in Bud's trip to Tehran in May 1986. None of this achieved anything, Poindexter said, so that channel was closed.

Subsequently, Poindexter went on, another channel more directly related to the Iranian government was opened through the nephew of Rafsanjani. As a result of discussions in this channel, the Iranians had pursued the release of the hostages in many ways, Poindexter told us, including through Anglican emissary Terry Waite and Lebanese contacts. A number of meetings had been held in Europe and the United States. The Israelis sold 500 TOWs to Iran. Poindexter had learned about this sale after the fact. Then, Poindexter said, we agreed to replenish the Israeli TOW stockpile. Two hundred and forty Hawk missile battery parts also were shipped, followed by a second shipment of 500 TOWs just the previous week, for a total of 1,000 TOWs. These were small amounts, defensive in nature, Poindexter said, and designed to establish good faith. They could not affect the outcome of the Iran-Iraq War, he said. I was astonished to learn of all these arms sales.

"So what are the results?" Poindexter asked. No more American hostages had been taken for over a year; Iran had stopped terrorist attacks, he said. "Well, there were three hostages taken recently," Poindexter corrected himself, "but there is a special explanation for that." The special explanation, I reflected, must be that the additional hostages can be traded for more arms! His tale was ludicrous.

We have achieved, Poindexter went on, solid contact with Rafsanjani. We have convinced Iran that it can't win the war, that the hostages have to be returned, and that the Soviets are a threat to them. Poindexter then sketched for us his view of the political scene in Iran: there were conservatives and clerics opposed to Khomeini; among them was Foreign Minister Velayati; in the middle of the road was Rafsanjani: the revolutionary guards were with him. In other words, Poindexter said, some of the radicals were changing—becoming more moderate. The most radical elements, Poindexter said, were for war, terrorism, revolution. Those radicals were the ones who sent armed pilgrims into Saudi Arabia during the Haj; and they were the ones who were linked to Hezbollah in Lebanon and who were responsible for the last three hostage takings. Khomeini's heir apparent, Ayatollah Montazeri, was an "independent player." In other words, the Iranian political situation was fluid and susceptible to influence in a way that would be positive for us, said Poindexter.

As for American policy, Poindexter said, there was no problem. The moderate Arabs knew that our policy was unchanged. We assured Iraq of our neutrality. And the Saudis, he said, had their own contacts with Iran. Egypt supported our contacts with Iran. Only Jordan had not yet been reassured. As for our European allies, Poindexter said, they all traded with Iran anyway, so they couldn't complain about what we were doing.

I started asking tough questions about Poindexter's preposterous assertions. I could see immediately that Poindexter, and the president, regarded me as a problem. I asked about the 500 TOWs that Poindexter said had been shipped the previous week. He replied that the shipment had been arranged by Oliver North and CIA operative George Cave at a meeting in Europe with the Israelis. North had reported to Poindexter that another two Americans would be released by the end of this week. "So if the 500 TOWs plus other items have been supplied to Iran in the context of hostage releases," I asked Poindexter, incredulously, "How can you say this is not an arms-for-hostages deal?"

The president jumped in, asserting, "It's not linked!"

Poindexter undercut him. "How else will we get the hostages out?" he asked me in an accusing tone. In that flash of candor, Poindexter had unwittingly ripped away whatever veil was left to the rationale of a "changed Iran" as the reason for our arms sales.

I responded that as we crossed the line of conspiring with the Israelis on arms sales to Iran, we gave Israel a clear field, and they would then supply Iran with equipment that really mattered.

CIA director Bill Casey then produced a draft statement to be released to the press. The purpose was to say that all the president's advisers were fully aware of this operation and supported it. "Everyone must support this policy," the president said. That I was *not* prepared to do. President Reagan was being ill served by advisers who were putting forth schemes for arms-for-hostages swaps—which this was—despite the refusal to call it that. I continued to ask questions about the structure of arrangements, which always came down to a trade of arms for hostages. Poindexter was furious at me.

"Our policy is what we *do*, not what we *say*," I argued forcefully. The session ended with a dangerous electricity in the air. At the meeting, Cap had said that he agreed with my position, but he was not as vehement now as I had seen him earlier. As I returned to the State Department, I felt that I had become the most unpopular man in town. I was in a quandary, however, because of Poindexter's assertion that hostages would be released in a few days. I feared doing anything that might block an imminent release. I was thoroughly frustrated.

What Poindexter had described was absolutely outrageous. The arms transfer could not be justified. I could not support this program in public, and I could not acquiesce with its continuation. President Reagan, in his desire to free the hostages, had allowed himself to be sold a bill of goods. Poindexter had fabricated a high-toned rationale for a sordid swap, and the president had accepted it. "Iran is playing us for suckers," I said, "and we are paying extortion money to them."

My overriding responsibility would have to be to get the president to understand the true nature of this terrible operation and to order it stopped. That would not be easy, for President Reagan simply did not seem to grasp what was actually going on. I would have to marshal my arguments carefully and powerfully so that he could not brush them aside. I went to Andrews Air Force Base and boarded my plane for the Organization of American States General Assembly in Guatemala City, scheduled for the next day, November 11. Not long after we reached cruising altitude, a telephone call came to the aircraft from the Oval Office. A press release had been prepared; the White House wanted to read the proposed release over the phone and have me agree to it. The president, Vice President Bush, Casey, Meese, and Weinberger all had already cleared it, I was told. The message was written down by a member of my staff:

> The President today met with his senior national security advisers regarding the status of the American hostages in Lebanon. The meeting was prompted by the President's concern for the safety of the remaining hostages and his fear that the spate of speculative stories which have arisen since the release of David Jacobsen may put them or others at risk. During the meeting the President reviewed ongoing efforts to achieve the release of all the hostages as well as our other broad policy concerns in the Middle East and Persian Gulf. As has been the case at a number of meetings with the President and his senior advisers on this matter, there was unanimous support for the President's decisions. While specific (garble) [decisions] at the meeting cannot be divulged, the President did ask it be reemphasized that our policy of not making concessions to terrorists remains intact.

> At the conclusion of the meeting the President made it clear to all that he appreciated their support and efforts to gain the safe release of all hostages. Stressing the fact that hostage lives are at stake, the President asked his advisers to ensure that their departments refrain from (garble) [making] comments or speculating about these matters.

"That's a lie," I said in disgust. "It's Watergate all over again." I asked the USAF communications specialist to get Poindexter on the phone for me. It took a while, and the patched-in voice at the other end was faint, but we could understand each other. "I have your message, and it is not accurate," I said with stony anger.

I told him that I could not accept the release as drafted. I did *not* support this operation and I would *not* join in lying about it. "It says there was unanimous support for the president's decisons. That is not accurate. I can't accept that sentence. Drop the last word [decisions]." There was sharp disagreement. Poindexter said he would change the sentence to read "there was unanimous support for the president." I said that helped. "Eliminate 'in a number of' before 'meetings,' " I added. Even so, I said, it's misleading. I won't object to the statement, but I am very uncomfortable with it.

"*That,*" Poindexter replied, "is most unfortunate" and hung up.

"They are distorting the record," I said afterward, "and there's no end to it. They are lying to me and others in the cabinet right now." I knew that Oliver North had not stumbled on an Israeli warehouse in Portugal; this effort had begun much earlier; Bud McFarlane was working at it in May 1985. Bud always gave me the impression that as national security adviser, he wanted to be like Henry Kissinger, to do big and dramatic things *secretly*. As Henry brought off "the opening to China," so Bud had the idea of an "opening to Iran." McFarlane hoped to bring off this coup, run secretly out of the NSC staff, and hand to the president the triumph of "winning Iran back to the West." But Kissinger had dealt with *officials* of the Chinese government and did not violate any U.S. laws in doing so; this operation with Iran, on the contrary, was conducted with disreputable international arms merchants and shady operators. And somewhere along the line Oliver North and Bill Casey had become involved, and hostages had come to dominate the whole scheme. The Iranians must have learned, no doubt with help of media hype, that the president would do just about anything to get hostages released.

As my plane droned on, I said that unless this operation was stopped now, it would ruin a great presidency and make a shambles of American policy. "I will have to keep fighting the operation and refuse to be part of it." Back on August 5, 1986, reflecting my sense of difference with the president on the Philippines, my disagreement with him the previous January on arms sales to Iran, the unease I felt in the national security community over my refusal to go along with lie detector tests applied as a routine tool of management, and the constant sniping I felt from low-level White House operatives, I had handed the president a letter starting, "I hereby submit my resignation as Secretary of State."

President Reagan had said that he would not accept my resignation, that he would work with me to straighten out our problems and that we *were* on the same wavelength. I asked him to put the letter in his desk drawer for future discussion, and he did. So the president had my letter of resignation and could pick it up at any time. As we began our final approach into the Guatemala City airport, I knew that I would have to make a hard and unwelcome statement to the president.

The situation was beginning to remind me of Richard Nixon's attempt to get me to use the Internal Revenue Service to go after his "enemies list." I wouldn't go along with that then, and I wouldn't go along with an arms-for-hostages deal now. On occasions like this, you look for allies to help prevail on the president. But I felt alone. What had been going on here was a staff con job on the president, playing on his very human desire to get the hostages released. They told the president what they wanted him to know and what they saw he wanted to hear, and they dressed it up in "geostrategic" costume. And they kept me as well as others who had constitutional responsibilities to advise the president in the dark. A responsible staff should have kept the president fully informed and should have continuously warned him of the legal and constitutional problems created by the actions taken or not taken. They should have called his attention repeatedly to the violations of his own policies and warned him that the intelligence about Iran was fragile at best and obtained from parties with strong interests and biases of their own.

I recalled a brief incident a few days earlier that had puzzled me at the time, but now seemed to have meaning: I had been over in the West Wing of the White House and by chance had an extra minute on my hands. I dropped in on Poindexter to leave a paper on the Middle East with him. I stuck my head in his outer office and asked his secretary whether the admiral was in. "Yes," she said, "and he's alone. Go right in." I knocked, opened the door, and surprised Poindexter, who was huddled in a meeting with Oliver North, NSC staffers Howard Teicher and Alton Keel, and a bearded man I did not recognize. I excused myself and left. I could not understand how they could have been in there without the secretary, whose desk was only a few feet away from Poindexter's office door, knowing of it.

I asked my secretary, Lora Simkus, who once had worked at that same NSC office desk, if there was another entrance to Poindexter's office. "No," she said, "only one, and the women who sit in that outer office, Wilma and Flo, are perceptive people with long experience over there; they would certainly know who was in that office with Poindexter." Was I being given a message that something was wrong?

On the Guatemala trip I drafted and redrafted and redrafted yet again the case I would make to the president, to try to convince him to halt this operation—permanently. I wanted to awaken him to the reality of what was taking place. I would have to persuade him that something was deeply wrong and that he had a big problem on his hands. I had to warn him that his staff was "rearranging the facts."

When I returned to Washington on Wednesday, November 12, I talked to Charlie Wick, the U.S. Information Agency director. Wick was a pal of the president and Nancy from way back. I went over my views, and Wick agreed with me entirely. He said he would try to get to Nancy Reagan first, and then to the president, to persuade them to pay attention to what I would be saying.

At two o'clock that afternoon, the president met with key members of Congress. Vice President George Bush, John Poindexter, Cap Weinberger, Don Regan, Ed Meese, Bill Casey, and I were there. We met in the Situation Room, which was highly unusual for a meeting with the congressional leadership.

Poindexter opened with a long discussion about our strategy toward Iran. He was vague to the point of prevarication when it came to mentioning hostages. He did not give any sense that arms transfers to Iran might have been linked to the hostages, but admitted that arms had been sent. He read out the January 17 "finding" on policy toward Iran but said nothing about its origin. Poindexter said the operation had been conducted throughout by "a representative" of his and a representative of Bill Casey's.

Senator Robert Byrd turned to me. "The press says you didn't agree with this policy." I replied that I made a practice of not revealing the advice that I gave the president. The president wrote something on a pad and pushed it over to me. "Thank you," it said.

Senator Byrd saw through Poindexter's presentation. "Iran is a terrorist country. You are selling arms. You want others *not* to sell arms. It's selling arms for hostages," he said, "and it's a bad mistake." The meeting then trailed off into a pointless wrangle between Jim Wright and Cap Weinberger over arms control talks with the Soviets.

Afterward, I got Don Regan alone and went through the problem with him. Don was from the world of finance, and I figured he should know how to make a tough decision when one had to be made. I told him that the president was in deep trouble. He had to help me get Ronald Reagan out of the line of fire and turn this mess over to me to clean it up. We discussed how a presidential speech or press statement might terminate the whole operation and put Iran policy and terrorist policy back in my hands.

Leaks from the Situation Room session with the leadership flowed out immediately. NBC-TV reported that at the session the president had admitted for the first time that arms had been transferred to Iran, and arms-for-hostages became an even hotter media story. The lid had now come off.

Poindexter's threatening insistence that any public revelation would jeopardize further hostage releases was now irrelevant. Bud McFarlane, in an op-ed piece published November 13, 1986, in the *Washington Post* sought to explain his role by saying that his model indeed had been Kissinger's approach to China in the early 1970s. George Will's column in the *Post* that day dealt with me: "Given the passion Shultz has invested in the principle of not dealing with terrorists, he may now feel like resigning not because he was responsible for what was done, but because he was not. In any case, someone should sober up Uncle Sam before he staggers into another of the world's sharp edges."

There was truth in that. My past position—being cut out—was, if humiliating, explicable in terms of my not knowing what took place; my present position—being cut out of what the president was treating as a major American foreign policy effort—was not sustainable. I would have to get the president to see that grave mistakes were being made, get control over the mess, or go.

On November 13, in a nationally televised address, President Reagan stated that he had authorized a small shipment of arms to Iran, but not as part of a trade for hostages: "That no concessions policy remains in force, in spite of the wildly speculative and false stories about arms for hostages and alleged ransom payments. We did not—repeat—did not trade weapons or anything else for hostages, nor will we."

The president's speech convinced me that Ronald Reagan still truly did not believe that what had happened had, in fact, happened. To him the reality was different. I had seen him like this before on other issues. He would go over the "script" of an event, past or present, in his mind, and once that script was mastered, that was the truth—no fact, no argument, no plea for reconsideration, could change his mind. So what Reagan said to the American people was true to him, although it was not the reality. He had stated publicly that our policy was no arms for hostages. If no more arms were sent, then I could work with that renewed statement of policy.

I telephoned Don Regan: stop the NSC staff effort; transfer the president's policy as stated in his speech to me, and I will try to put our policy and our behavior back together, I said.

Regan seemed to agree. He seemed eager to get the operation out of the hands of the NSC staff, away from the president and out of the White House. He asked me once more to go on one of the Sunday talk shows. I agreed and accepted one of the flood of requests for me to be interviewed on television.

I knew that I was engaged in all-out diplomacy with my own president and his administration, aimed at gaining the authority to do the job I had been hired to do. Everything now depended on getting the arms-for-hostages operation stopped and getting the policy as a whole under control and back to the State Department.

The president's November 13 speech did not have many takers; the story he recounted was not believed. The *Wall Street Journal* on November 14 quoted Senator Pat Moynihan, who said that the secret Iran negotiations were "the worst handling of an intelligence problem in our history." Barry Goldwater, in the same paper, said: "I think that's a dreadful mistake, probably one of the major mistakes the United States has ever made in foreign policy." And others heard in the president's speech an underground message that he was still willing to trade. There was chaos in the White House. Don Regan, interviewed on TV, said no more arms for hostages; Poindexter, on television, suggested that there would be further arms transfers.

In my regular sessions with the president, when I tried to get him to focus on demanding issues elsewhere in the world—Soviet relations, arms control, the Middle East—he could not concentrate. Poindexter, who in earlier days had been eager to join me whenever I saw President Reagan, was now arrogant and aloof. Poindexter almost had to be dragged into the Oval Office when I was there, and when I spoke, he feigned boredom, doodled, and looked out the window. I was getting a strong message.

I recalled how I had resigned as Nixon's secretary of the treasury. Nixon had put on a wage-price freeze in 1971. I opposed it. He did it again in 1973. Herb Stein, chairman of the Council of Economic Advisers, had said to him, "Mr. President, you can't walk on water twice." In a rare flash of humor, Nixon replied, "I can if it's frozen!" I opposed the freeze the second time but again defended it in public. Then I handed in my resignation. Nixon refused it. So I just dropped out for a while—no public appearances. Finally, I went to White House Chief of Staff Alexander Haig and said, "I'm not showing up for work tomorrow, so you better get a new secretary of the treasury." And he did—Bill Simon.

But this time I wasn't going to drop out. I would fight to get the Reagan presidency back on track, and if I couldn't, I'd go. No successor could function in this job, I felt, unless this terrible situation was put right.

I went to see President Reagan at 1:30 p.m., Friday, November 14. Poindexter was there. I told the president that it was time for me to go but that for the next few weeks I would try to get him through this crisis and then be on my way. The president again said he didn't want me to resign. "I want you to stay. I want to talk later about it." He still believed that what had been done was right and was not a trade with terrorists for hostages. That evening, in my office at the State Department, I watched "World News Tonight." ABC's "Person of the Week" was Oliver North. A poll indicated that 57 percent of the American public felt that Reagan had gone back on his vow of no deals with terrorists; one by one, fact after fact set out by the president in his speech was taken apart and discredited by the television report. It was a sad day for the Reagan administration. For the first time, the president had gone before the American people to make his case and try to clear things up, and they had not believed him. That was devastating to him, I knew.

I also wanted to talk to the president about human rights in Chile and the idea that we would vote against a proposed World Bank loan to that government. Our action would be a signal to Chilean President Augusto Pinochet and to the people of Chile. The president did not agree to this slap at the anti-Communist dictator. He and I argued. I knew a lot about the Chilean economic program because economists trained at the University of Chicago, known in Chile as the "Chicago boys," had been the architects of their successful use of free market ideas. But I opposed Pinochet's regime of political repression. The president raised the idea, possibly to provoke me, of a State visit by the Chilean dictator. It was a measure of how far apart we were. There had been a time when the president would simply have trusted my judgment on such an issue, but not since the fall of Ferdinand Marcos. Poindexter was snide, challenging every point I made, conveying the impression that I already was off the administration rolls.

The program I agreed to appear on was CBS's "Face the Nation" on Sunday, November 16. On Saturday, I was to go to Camp David with Margaret Thatcher to see the president. I wanted to have some time there to go over with the president what I would say on television, with the aim of getting control of the policy shifted away from Poindexter and back to State. I drafted a paper for the president to approve. I proposed to state on "Face the Nation":

- The president's counterterrorism policy is a good policy. I support it.
- But the way it has been conducted in the past is under intense scrutiny. All the record will come out for everyone to judge.

For the future:

- Policy toward Iran will be directed and conducted by the State Department;
- Our policy to end the Gulf War continues. There will be

no arms transfers to Iran or Iraq as long as they remain intransigent;

• We are working night and day to get the hostages released. But we will not pay for them. A consensus exists in the administration that this is the right policy: concessions to terrorists only produce more hostages;

• We do not want a relationship of permanent hostility with Iran. The president's policy provides a way to go forward toward a constructive situation. That will be done quietly and in recognized, structured State Department channels. The president wants it this way, and we have indications that Iran does, too.

At Camp David I was not able to get even a moment alone with the president for a serious discussion. So I handed the paper to Don Regan, saying that I proposed to express administration policy "this way" on television tomorrow. He read my notes.

"I understand," Don said, "but we are not in a position to do what you're asking for."

Sunday, November 16, was a gloomy, gray day. A camera crew was a now-familiar presence stationed outside my house, waiting for me to emerge—perhaps to announce my resignation. State Department colleagues Hill, Bremer, Platt, and Redman came over early. This was my first television appearance since the "revelation." Jerry Brewer, director of State's anti-terrorist efforts, referring to Margaret Thatcher's presence at Camp David, pointed up the absurdity of what the White House had done. "Maybe you should tell Mrs. Thatcher that as the Irish Republican Army does not conduct terrorism against Americans, we have decided to open a quiet dialogue with them, and as a signal of our serious intent, we are making some token arms shipments to them."

"Don't tell me things like that," I said, laughing, "I might use them."

Our discussion continued. My main fight was with an NSC staff that had developed an operational capability and a fervent will to use it—

often unwisely. With authority, ambition, and power, the NSC staff could operate without anyone's full knowledge, even the president's, and was not subject to congressional oversight. Laws that limited the behavior of regular government agencies could be read as not applying to the NSC staff. And there was the bizarre situation of the NSC adviser having his own spokesman and appearing in the media: Poindexter would be interviewed on NBC's "Meet the Press" at about the same time as my appearance on "Face the Nation." Here we had, as a primary foreign policy figure of the administration, the NSC adviser—who is not even subject to confirmation by the Senate and is not obliged to testify before Congress. The NSC staff had turned into a "wildcat operation." There used to be a "passion for anonymity"—no longer. Arthur Burns always took the position "Either you are a private adviser and have nothing to say publicly, or else you are a public figure. You cannot have it both ways." If Poindexter was to be on "Meet the Press," then he had no reason not to testify before congressional committees. When Poindexter explained something, he was frequently pedantic, pedagogical, and patronizing: once Poindexter had lectured me, "You see, George, the Arabs don't like the Israelis." I could imagine that when he had briefed the president on this operation, he would have been pretty dogmatic.

Lesley Stahl, the moderator of "Face the Nation," was a solid, tough questioner. She was relentless that morning. "I don't want to badger you," she said once, pursuing her point.

"No, you can badger me," I came back. I wanted to set straight where I stood. "It is clearly wrong to trade arms for hostages. So that is our policy . . . it isn't the right thing for governments to trade arms or anything else for hostages, just because it encourages taking more."

She persisted: "Will there be any more arms shipments to Iran, either directly by our government or through any third parties?"

"It's certainly against our policy," I answered swiftly.

"That's not an answer," she asserted. "Why don't you answer the question directly? I'll ask it again. Will there be any more arms shipments to Iran, either directly by the United States or through any third parties?"

"Under the circumstances of Iran's war with Iraq, its pursuit of terrorism, its association with those holding our hostages, I would certainly say, as far as I'm concerned, no," I responded.

"Do you have the authority to speak for the entire Administration?" she followed up.

"No," I said, looking her straight in the eye.

On that stark note, the program ended.

Afterward, Lesley gripped Nick Platt's arm. "I need a drink."

"I never should have come on," I told her.

"We were all amazed you did," she replied. I felt I had done as good a job as possible for the president. But I had thrown down the gauntlet in my final exchange. I felt I had to do it. Now it was up to the White House to respond.

When I returned home, I was in a rather gloomy mood. I almost expected a telephone call from the White House—"you're out." I felt I was alone and without support from others at the top level of the government to stop further arms deals. Bob Strauss called about my appearance on "Face the Nation": "You were somewhere between A+ and fabulous," he said. I felt a little better.

On Monday morning, press and television accounts were laden with reports on arms to Iran. Andrea Mitchell, on NBC's "Today," reported that Poindexter indicated more arms sales were to come, while Shultz opposed more arms "but can't say it won't be done against his advice." The *Washington Post* headlined on November 17: "Shultz Sees No Benefit for U.S. In Further Iran Arms Shipments; Disapproval of Deal Is Undisguised." The *New York Times* headlined: "Shultz Declares He Opposes Giving More Arms To Iran; Officials Appear Divided; Secretary Says That He Can't Speak for Administration on Issue of Shipments."

That afternoon, I was to deliver a major speech at the University of Chicago, setting out the achievements at the Reykjavik summit and pointing toward future steps in negotiations with the Soviets. I flew off to Chicago half-expecting to be ousted from office before returning to Washington that evening.

When I got back to the capital, I was met by Nick Platt. "The White House blinked," Platt said. My public declaration on "Face the Nation" finally flushed out of the White House the statement earlier that day from spokesman Larry Speakes that I *did* speak for the administration and that "The President has no desire, the President has no plans, to send further arms to Iran." The president and the secretary "are in complete accord on this," Speakes said. Poindexter had argued, I learned, for a response of "No comment." Later when the president was asked directly whether he was going to make any more arms shipments to Iran, he replied, "We have absolutely no plans to do any such thing." In this peculiar way the whole issue had come to a head in public and shifted the weight of the argument in my direction. The White House simply could not stand up to saying publicly that we would continue to sell arms to Iran.

Reviewing the intelligence analyses from the CIA that evening, I read through a piece on the "power struggle" in Iran that was wholly at odds with the briefing that Poindexter had given in the Situation Room a few days before: Khomeini was firmly in power, and Rafsanjani was carrying out the ayatollah's resolute policy of opposition to the United States; recent events in Iran suggested that no Iranian leader other than Khomeini has the power to initiate a rapprochement with the United States or even to offer such a suggestion for debate. So much for the wooing of the Iranian moderates. Doubting the reliability of CIA material on Iran, I could not, however, credit this as a serious piece of analysis, even though it matched my own views on the situation in Tehran. The thought crossed my mind that perhaps someone in the CIA had "blinked," too.

Bernard Gwertzman of the *New York Times*, who had an uncanny ability to get inside a story, wrote on November 18, in a front-page article headlined "All Eyes on Shultz," that "Secretary of State George P. Shultz appears to have swayed White House policy on Iran in his direction, at least for the moment."

I wasn't so sure. The damage to the Reagan presidency continued to mount. Former Presidents Ford and Carter spoke harshly of the Iran operation. A poll taken by the *Los Angeles Times* showed that only 14 percent of the American people believed the president was telling the truth in his speech. A cabinet crisis was building, the media seemed to agree, and the president would have to fire some people or be seen as no longer in charge.

In one sense I felt that, bit by bit, I was edging the White House staff back into line, but the NSC staff was fighting back. Bob Pearson, a foreign service officer assigned to the White House, passed the word that my "Face the Nation" appearance "had not hit the applause meter" over there. The NSC staff, he said, "thinks State has kicked over the traces, is off the train, and should not be allowed to criticize the president." Poindexter was said to be furious over foreign service reporting that other nations, especially those in Europe and the Middle East, were appalled at what the United States had done. Resentment ran deep.

The media played my "Face the Nation" appearance as an act of defiance, suggesting that I had shaken some sense into the president and his White House staff, but noting that the NSC staff—as though they were some autonomous entity—was proceeding with the operation, and was determined to knock me off.

from Dutch

by Edmund Morris

Ronald Reagan (in office 1981–1989) appointed Edmund Morris (born 1940) to be his official biographer during his second term. The resulting work was a controversial blend of biography and fiction. Here Morris chats with Reagan before the November 19, 1986 press conference about the Iran hostage crisis.

CONVERSATION IN THE OVAL OFFICE,
NOVEMBER 18, 1986

The following conversation is reproduced at length as a testament to the President's mental and emotional state before his disastrous press conference of November 19, 1986.

EM: Do you wish you had stuck to breeding horses?

RR: No. These last couple of weeks I've had difficulty controlling my temper, which I think is a wise thing to do. But I've never seen such a concerted campaign of dishonesty with results that can be tragic for some people as has been going on here. And I'm just amazed at the lengths that they've gone, and the phony staging, even. One network-news broadcast in the evening—and while Mr. Rather was talking—it was the pictures they were using. But they weren't even using the pictures about what they were talking about. For example, he was talking about weapons and so forth, but they had on the screen F-14s flying and zooming and so forth. And then: cut to a man, obviously an Iranian, throwing rifles into an open-back truck, piled high with these AK-47s—the Russian rifle—but all of this, if pictures speak a thousand words, and people are going to go away with the impression that these were the weapons we were dealing in.

EM: I was at the American Book Award ceremony last night, and George Will was the speaker. . . . He was on the subject that the news these days requires visual images. You can't photograph and show on the news a peace initiative that took six months [*sic*]. But you can show a picture of an F-14. And they'll always go for the image, rather than a long story that requires time and space.

RR: It's been quite a two weeks! And I imagine tomorrow night will be kind of exciting, with the press conference. The hell of it is, I am still bound to a certain extent on how specific I can answer because of—well, oh, Terry Waite explained it last night on television . . . hostages fear for their lives. I remember when I was on the Rockefeller Commission . . . (*Long anecdote about open debate compromising covert sources*)

EM: Mr. President, the Chief [Donald Regan] was telling us at lunch about what David Jacobsen told you, that they tortured him, that they strung him up and lashed him out "from his feet down to his nuts." Is there anything more you can remember Jacobsen saying?

RR: Well, no, (*distressed*) he told about that, but at the same time, he told us that these people, the guards, were actually people, and he said that actually they could be pretty friendly at times. . . .

EM: Sir, are you also feeling angry at the Iranians in the sense that, out of the goodwill of your heart, you wanted to make a gesture toward them, and you expected, I presume, a fairly clean exchange. [But] you found yourself forced into a continuous barter arrangement—

RR: Well, no, that didn't bother me. We weren't going to—the thing was so simple and, of course, the first hostage did come, from a hostile—from a side we were avoiding in Iran. (*He begins to flounder*) But we told them that we could not do this as long as Iran was sponsoring terrorism. And they told our people that even Khomeini had written a piece disavowing support for terrorism, that they were not terrorists. . . . They wanted some evidence they could use on their own associates, of our good faith. So this was the arms thing. But when they told us that, we said, "Well, look, we want a little more than just your word for it, that you're through with terrorism, and there's some pretty good evidence to that effect. But what about the hostages?" Well, the truth is, Iran cannot order the Hezbollah to give up those hostages. But we *do* know that . . . the Hezbollah does not feel hostility toward Iran and yes, there is a way they can be appealed to by Iran and would want to be of help. So, when we said this they succeeded in getting three out. And we have every reason to believe that the other two [*sic*] would be home by now, if it hadn't been—(*he hesitates*)

EM: For all this—

RR: (*sadly*)—what was made public.

EM: Mr. President, I'm kind of interested to know what made you take this Initiative. Was it something in your heart, was it compassion towards families of these hostages, and if so, what made you tip over the brink?

RR: (*clears throat unhappily*) Well, this was a two-track thing, and we have been exploring every channel we could to find a way to get at freeing these hostages. But the other thing was very much on our minds for quite some time. . . . Suddenly, like a door had been open, and we began to explore in this direction . . . it was evident that the kidnappers [had], however tenuous it might be, a tie with Iran, that opportunity was offered. But to say "a deal involving some kind of ransom" is utterly ridiculous. (*He is thinking of some sarcastic words by former President Carter on television this morning, and becomes vehement*) What if . . . in all our searching, it was never off of my mind: you see, you say, "What's in my heart?" Yes, I campaigned on this thing about terrorism, and I still mean it, but what I also campaigned, and I said a number of times, "I have a belief: if there is any excuse for a government, the kind we have in this country, it is

[this]—any place in the world, even the least among us as citizens, a person is being unjustly denied his God-given Constitutional rights—life, liberty, and the pursuit of happiness—it is the responsibility of the government to go to his aid. . . . I feel, as strongly as anyone in the world, you cannot ransom with a kidnapper. You just make that a thriving business. But you *do* explore how you can get them back. Now that doesn't rule out if you can do it by force. (*Long, wistful anecdote about the effectiveness of Italian anti-terrorist commandos*) I don't care how much Mr. Carter wants to snipe at me as he did on TV this morning on this one. But there's a great difference when you've hostages that are being held by a government . . . and if he wants to talk about ransom—how the hell did we did get *them* back? We ransomed them—grant you, it was their money, but it was money we had frozen, since the overturn of the Shah, hundreds of millions of dollars—we said, "We'll give your money back. . ." (*He is unable to continue for anger*)

EM: I'm just wondering if there was a little personal pressure on you, that made you decide to go that final inch. Was it simply strategic, [or] had you met with the families?

RR: Oh, I had met with the families the time the hostages were taken, and tried to keep them apprised of what we were doing, and yet, in many instances, we couldn't say specifically, "We're talking to a man who is going to do this or that." And I can't tell you how many heartbreaking calls we had, where sometimes people we had counted on couldn't come through, couldn't deliver. . . . We thought we were going to have some action and then! (*snaps fingers*) It just blew up. . . .

EM: Do you mind if I ask a pretty tough one?

RR: All right.

EM: We have stated as fact that we gave them 261,000 pounds of arms—that's the content of one plane—in exchange, and simultaneously gotten three hostages back. Now, a cynical Arab fundamentalist mind might say, Well, that works out to 87,000 pounds per hostage. So in the future, whenever we need another 87,000 pounds of arms, we kidnap another American. I'm wondering whether you ever felt you might have set a precedent—whereby other hostages might become the victims of your compassion for these three.

RR: No. And there again, this is where I say, the *press* has cost us so much. *They're* the ones—just as they're still insisting that we traded Daniloff for the spy, when we didn't. (*This is true enough: what he had done was trade the spy for Daniloff. Reagan fulminates on about the press, as all Presidents have done before him, and gradually reverts to Topic A.*) . . . What if you found a fella over there that came to us with a plan of rescue and said, "I can rescue the hostages, I can get them out, but there's going to be a cost associated that's more than I can do, and it's gonna cost me *x* amount of money to spring 'em." Now, are you paying ransom? Or are you *hiring* someone to get your hostages out for you? And I think of this thing that we did was kind of in that framework. Our payoff was to people who believed that they could do something we couldn't. . . . But nothing was given to them or offered to them. What would you do? So . . . (*He runs dry*)

The President's essential decency, passion ("What's in my heart?"), obstinacy, and moral astigmatism are all apparent in this interview—as is his tendency to put a film frame round everything, and believe the best of barbarians, as long as they do not hail from the Evil Empire. He can no more comprehend that he has broken the law of the land (a specific embargo against selling arms to Iran) than he can accept a positive biopsy. By changing the word *has* to *had*, he rids himself of disease; by *hiring* intermediaries rather than *paying* them, he retains his honor; by so intensely *feeling* the injustice of hostage-taking, he makes hostage-trading respectable.

Nothing, not even a forced admission to the contrary on national television, will ever shake his certainty that he did the right thing by Benjamin Weir, Father Jenco, and David Jacobsen, at an eventual cost of $3.1 million each, and permanent damage to his own reputation.

from The Presidency of George Bush

by John Robert Greene

John Robert Greene (born 1955) describes how George Herbert Walker Bush (in office 1989–1993) used his diplomatic skills and experience to rally support for the Desert Shield *operation against Iraq.*

On 2 August 1990, with Saddam claiming that Iraq was responding to calls from a revolutionary government working for the overthrow of the emir, some 140,000 Iraqi troops and 18,000 tanks rolled into Kuwait. The 16,000-man Kuwaiti army was hopelessly outmatched. Within three-and-one-half hours, the invaders had reached the kingdom's capital at Kuwait City; within twelve hours, it had fallen to Saddam. Although the Iraqis failed to capture the emir, who had fled to Saudi Arabia (Saddam hoped to put him on trial as a war criminal), the Iraqi leader not only controlled Kuwait but also 21 percent of the world's oil supply. Saddam proclaimed that Kuwait had ceased to exist and that it had become the "Nineteenth Province, an eternal part of Iraq."

Bush certainly knew the terrain—his Zapata Oil Company had built Kuwait's first offshore oil well in the 1950s—and he responded quickly. Within hours of the invasion, Bush followed the advice of the NSC Deputies Committee and signed an executive order freezing the approximately $100 billion in Iraqi property and assets in the United States and overseas, an action somewhat offset, as it were, by the fact that the Iraqis were able to plunder Kuwait at will and by all reports did so. Bush also moved the *USS Independence* Carrier Battle Group (two carriers, one guided missile destroyer, two frigates, and one ammunition ship) into the Persian Gulf from the Indian Ocean.

Immediately, Bush's predilection for personal political diplomacy took over. Within hours of learning of the invasion, on 3 August, he worked the phones and spoke to every leader of the Western Alliance, building what soon became known as a coalition of world leaders against Iraqi aggression. The United Kingdom, France, West Germany, Japan, and seven other nations quickly joined the United States in freezing Iraqi assets. Keeping an appointment to speak on cold war diplomacy at the Aspen Institute, Bush nevertheless continued to work the phones from Air Force One. Egypt's Mubarak and Jordan's Hussein, who apologized for inadvertently misleading Bush regarding Saddam's intentions, urged him not to act precipitously, still holding out hope for an Arab solution. In Aspen, Bush met with British prime minister Margaret Thatcher, who, in a joint press conference following their meeting, was unequivocal: "What happened is a total violation of international law."

Saddam undoubtedly was stunned by the surprising unity in the international community against his actions. For the first time since its inception, thanks to a timely shove by an American president who had also served as UN ambassador, the United Nations lurched forward and gave the strongest show of unanimity in its forty-five-year history. The Security Council met within hours of the invasion; by the end of that evening, UN Resolution 660—denouncing Iraq's invasion, calling for its immediate withdrawal, and promising sanctions if it did not comply—had been unanimously passed (with one abstention: Yemen). It was only the fifth time in its history that the Security Council had issued such a threat. On 6 August the UN passed Resolution 661, calling for a complete prohibition of trade with Iraq and authorizing nonmilitary measures to enforce the sanctions. Yet had the

UN not acted, the upcoming scenario might well have been the same. Scowcroft was clear in his memoirs: "Never did we think that without its blessing we could not or would not intervene." But the UN had indeed provided Bush with significant political cover; on both votes, the United States was supported by the Soviet Union.

The Soviet Union was key to Bush's coalition. It was the first test of the new partnership that had been forged at Malta. Bush needed Gorbachev either on his side or scrupulously neutral, if for no other reason than to ensure that there would be no trouble in the Security Council. For his part, Gorbachev was reluctantly creaking into line with the rest of the international community against his former client in Iraq. But he was facing mounting opposition. Despite the promise of a trade pact with the United States, Gorbachev's hard-line opponents, particularly in the Soviet military, were still seething over what Gorbachev had conceded to get that pact: agreements to end the Lithuanian embargo and to tolerate a unified Germany. Gorbachev's cold warriors were also concerned about the possibility of a permanent American presence in the Middle East and argued for sending Soviet aid to Saddam.

But by the end of 1990, the Soviet economy had further crumbled into disarray. The food situation was getting close to desperate, and Gorbachev was forced to once again ask Bush for aid. He knew that if he was ever to hope for any further American economic support, he would have to join Bush's coalition against Iraq. Besides, he and his closest advisers saw Saddam's invasion as both foolhardy and as a violation of international law. Thus, Gorbachev had to walk a tightrope during the crisis, torn as he was by his own belief in the necessity of joining the coalition and the demands of his military hard-liners to help Saddam.

On the day of the invasion, Baker had just left the Soviet Union after a visit with Foreign Minister Eduard Shevardnadze and was on his way to Mongolia for a previously scheduled state visit. While in Mongolia, Baker worked out the details of a joint statement with Shevardnadze.

On 3 August Baker joined the foreign minister on the tarmac of Vnukovo II airport, just outside Moscow. In their statement, the Soviet Union took the unprecedented step of joining with the United States in calling for "an international cutoff of all arms supplies to Iraq."

Shevardnadze's announcement was a critical, if not the most important, moment in the whole of the Persian Gulf crisis. It was now clear to the world that Saddam could not count on the normal U.S.-Soviet cat-fighting over Middle East policy to help him to quietly consolidate his gains. Over the next several weeks, largely due to the cajoling of Baker, the Soviet Union joined in the UN resolutions. However, the Soviets continued to couch their support with calls for Bush to resist using any kind of force in the region. It was, as Bush later called it, a "new world order." For the first time since 1945, the United States and the Soviet Union were fighting on the same side.

Out of gratitude to Gorbachev's response, as well as from a desire to keep the coalition together, Bush agreed to travel to Helsinki on 5 September for a third summit with Gorbachev. Bush was even willing to appear as the supplicant, and during the summit he agreed to an international conference on the Middle East, an implicit admission that after the conflict, in a stunning reversal of over forty years of policy, America would agree to a Soviet presence in the Middle East. Terrified at the prospect of completely losing the support of the Soviet Union just as the Americans were threatening a counterstrike, Saddam sent his foreign minister, Tariq Aziz, to Moscow to try to soften up Gorbachev. It was to no avail. At Helsinki, Bush and Gorbachev issued a joint statement: the two nations would act "individually and in concert" to see to it that Saddam unconditionally withdraw from Kuwait, "even if that cannot be accomplished by peaceful means." With the Soviets on board, it would be impossible for Saddam to find any European allies. The *New York Times* called it "Bush and Gorbachev, Inc."

After the fall of Kuwait, Bush's attention immediately turned to protecting Saudi Arabia. There was ample reason for Saddam to invade that nation—if he took Saudi Arabia, he would control 40 percent of the world's known oil reserves. From the opening moments of the crisis, Bush was inclined to place American troops in Saudi Arabia to protect that nation. But the Saudis had every reason to be skeptical of American promises of protection; they had heard it all before. After the fall of the Shah of Iran in 1979, Jimmy Carter had promised to send F-15s to Saudi Arabia as a show of power and then had reneged. Saudi memories were also fresh of Reagan's withdrawal of the marines from Lebanon in 1984. And there were concerns about an American presence in their nation, particularly around their holy sites. But Bush held some cards of his own. Saddam had lied to Saudi King Fahd about his plans for Kuwait, as he had lied to Jordan's Hussein and Egypt's Mubarak. Further, Bush had built up a close relationship with King Fahd during his years as CIA director. Perhaps most important was that military intelligence showed the distinct possibility that Saddam's next move would indeed be against Saudi Arabia.

On the afternoon of 3 August, Bush told Scowcroft to invite Prince Bandar to the White House to make a case for allowing American troops to deploy in Saudi Arabia. After the meeting had begun, Bush came into the office. He told Bandar that the Kuwaitis had not asked for help until it was too late and that Fahd should not wait until the last minute. Bush then ordered Colin Powell to fully brief Bandar on Schwartzkopf's two-tiered plan. Powell did so, and he also showed the Saudi ambassador secret satellite photos that demonstrated that Saddam had increased his military strength in Kuwait to the point where an attack against the Saudis was a real possibility. When Bandar asked how many men the Americans were thinking of placing in Saudi Arabia, Powell replied "about one hundred thousand," an understatement of Schwartzkopf's estimate. Still, Bandar was stunned by the force that Bush had in mind; he smiled and replied to Powell, "Well, at least it shows you're serious." Bandar then excused himself to dispatch the news to his uncle, King Fahd.

The next day, during an NSC meeting at Camp David, Bush was more fully briefed on an expanded version of Schwartzkopf's plan. He was also informed that intelligence reports strongly suggested that the

Saudis continued to be disinclined to accept any long-term American presence on their soil. As Scowcroft's notes of the meeting show, Bush was clear: "Our first objective is to keep Saddam out of Saudi Arabia. Our second is to protect the Saudis against retaliation when we shut down Iraq's export capability. We have a problem if Saddam does not invade Saudi Arabia but holds on to Kuwait." The meeting led to Bush's approval of the plan, subject to the approval of the Saudis. After the meeting, according to Bob Woodward, Bush met with Scowcroft alone and decided to immediately send Cheney and Schwartzkopf to present the Pentagon's plan to Fahd.

Whether the next event was a result of Scowcroft's convincing Bush, as Woodward's reporting implies, or of Thatcher's prompting, as Powell implies, remains an open question. On Sunday, 5 August, after disembarking from his helicopter from Camp David, Bush announced to the press that "this will not stand, this aggression of Kuwait." Powell was astonished; this clearly changed the focus of the American response from giving up on Kuwait and protecting Saudi Arabia to protecting Saudi Arabia by evicting the Iraqis from Kuwait. It is, of course, highly possible that Bush's statement was designed primarily to impress the Saudis with the irreversibility of the American commitment. If that was one of the goals of Bush's statement, it worked. The next day, Cheney and Scowcroft arrived in Riyadh to explain the extent of the American commitment to Fahd. The delegation was astounded at the king's immediate positive reply.

On Wednesday, 8 August, Bush addressed the nation, announcing the deployment of the Eighty-second Airborne Division as well as two squadrons of F-15 fighters to Saudi Arabia. He later remembered that as he prepared his speech, he wanted to make it clear to the American people that "this time I wanted no appeasement." Proclaiming that "a line has been drawn in the sand," Bush said that what the Americans sought was nothing less—or more—than "the immediate, unconditional, and complete withdrawal of all Iraqi forces from Kuwait." He also stated, "The mission of our troops is wholly defensive . . . [but] they will defend themselves, the Kingdom of Saudi Arabia, and other friends in the Persian Gulf." By the end of August, there were 80,000 coalition troops in Saudi Arabia, part of what was by then code-named DESERT SHIELD. Saddam immediately reinforced his own army to a strength of some 200,000; on 21 August Bush responded by calling up 40,000 reservists to help transport troops, the first call-up of the reserves since the Tet Offensive of 1968. On 19 November Saddam added 250,000 more troops, giving him a ground contingent of approximately 680,000 men. The *Washington Post* severely understated the case when it noted that "a happy ending does not appear imminent."

In the weeks that followed Bush's announcement of DESERT SHIELD, the allied coalition became both larger and more fully committed to the American cause. Much of this was due to Saddam, who had embarked on a program of "Zionizing" the conflict. In an attempt to win Arab support, he intimated that he would withdraw from Kuwait if Israel would withdraw from its occupied Palestinian territories. But Saddam had worn out his welcome with his Arab neighbors. After a 10 August meeting of the Arab League, both Syria and Egypt joined forces against Iraq. In fact, it was Mubarak, who felt personally betrayed by Saddam, who made the first reference to the Iraqi leader as "the new Hitler, since he has become a danger to the region, to the Arabs, and to the world."

Yet the key to keeping Arab support on the side of the budding coalition against Saddam—and the most difficult task that Bush had in the entire war—was keeping Israel out of the coalition. There had never been any love lost between Bush and the Likud government of Yitzhak Shamir. Baker and Bush held the prime minister responsible for holding up the Middle East peace process by continuing to build settlements on the disputed territory of the West Bank, even as the Palestine Liberation Organization (PLO) had taken a major step in 1989 by acknowledging Israel's right to exist. However, from the point of view of Washington, Israel could not be a part of the coalition. If it entered the war, neighboring Arab states would be forced to decide whether to declare war on the hated Israel, a quandary that Saddam hoped would present itself. But Shamir turned out to be the voice of reason in his cabinet. In the days after the invasion, he promised that Israel would restrain itself unless attacked.

Bush was also shrewd enough to understand that he needed to win commitments of financial support from the coalition, if for no other reason than that the cost of American intervention was incredibly expensive; one estimate suggests that by the end of August, the Americans were spending $28.9 million a day to keep U.S. troops in Saudi Arabia. There were also early warning signs of the recession to come, not only in the United States but also abroad. In terms of financial underwriting, Bush concentrated his efforts on Germany and Japan. Neither nation could be expected to commit troops; both had constitutions, drafted by the United States after World War II, that severely constrained what they could do with their troops off their own soil. Moreover, there were domestic political considerations. Germany was only weeks away from its first elections as a unified nation since 1945, and in Japan leaders of several of the minority parties argued against sending aid of any kind. But the two countries could afford a financial commitment, and both Helmut Kohl and Toshiki Kaifu eventually convinced their respective governments to send money. By the end of the operation, Kuwait, Saudi Arabia, and the United Arab Emirates (UAE) paid for 62 percent of the costs; Germany, Japan, and Korea another 26 percent. Over 70 percent of the foreign commitment came in cash. In addition, Bush asked for, and on 10 April 1991 received, a supplemental defense appropriation from his own Congress of $15 billion in budget authority to support DESERT SHIELD.

If persuading the world community to support American intervention in the Gulf financially was an act of political legerdemain—and it was—convincing the other members of the coalition to send troops for the purpose of ousting Saddam from Kuwait was actually much easier. The hawkish Thatcher's support came effortlessly (in the words of Freedman and Karsh, "Fighting aggressors can appear as almost a national calling in Britain"). Squadrons of Tornado fighters and the Seventh Armored Brigade were sent to Saudi Arabia. Even France, which had been closest to Iraq of any Western nation, eventually sent 4,200 troops.

As coalition troops began to arrive on Saudi soil, they were particularly vulnerable to Iraqi attack. One estimate suggested that it would take until the end of September for the troops to be ready to withstand an assault. War, then, could not come too soon. Yet on 22 August it almost did. Saddam challenged the UN embargo policy by sending an Iraqi tanker, the *Khaneqan*, toward Yemen, one of Saddam's few remaining allies. An American frigate fired warning shots across the bow of the tanker; Saddam warned of "grave consequences" if any more shots were fired. Bush originally favored an immediate retaliation, and Powell, Cheney, and Scowcroft agreed. Baker protested, however, pointing out that the Soviet Union made it clear that it was not in favor of an attack on the tanker. Baker won; he called Shevardnadze and said that Bush would not fire on the ship, but only if the Soviets agreed to a new UN resolution that would allow the coalition to enforce the embargo—by force, if necessary. Gorbachev agreed. Bush allowed the tanker to pass (Thatcher, angry at what she perceived to be Bush's weakness, told the president on the phone, "This is no time to go wobbly") and pressed the UN to be more definitive in its statement on the embargo. On 25 August that body passed UN Resolution 665, giving the coalition the right to search, and if necessary disable, ships that were suspected of attempting to run the embargo.

In his memoirs, Bush claims, "I don't know exactly when I became resigned to the fact that it would come to war." Observers of the Bush administration, both contemporary and historical, have also struggled with this question, trying to decide when Bush's intentions turned from a defense of Saudi Arabia and toward a plan for expelling Saddam Hussein from Kuwait, in Operation DESERT STORM.

Bush's actions during fall 1990 strongly suggest that he never really thought that economic sanctions would work and that from the beginning of the crisis he was planning to use DESERT SHIELD troops in an offensive manner to dislodge Saddam from Kuwait. Powell himself cites an instance in mid-August when Bush turned to him and said, "I don't know if sanctions are going to work in an acceptable time frame"; Powell concluded that Bush "did not sound like a man willing to wait long for sanctions to work." Indeed, throughout Powell's account, Bush is depicted as a person who is simply waiting for the right moment to launch an offensive attack. This conclusion is made even more certain by the tone of the four chapters in Bush's memoirs dealing with DESERT SHIELD. Bush relates that as early as 23 August, when he was fishing with Scowcroft at Kennebunkport, he "asked impatiently when we could strike." Scowcroft remembers that from the very beginning of the crisis, with Bush's approval, he undertook to push the NSC to take a tougher stance on the issue of the possible use of force to dislodge Saddam. Apparently Bush never doubted that he would be sending more troops; the mindset of "incrementalism" had taken over: Schwartzkopf would have enough men to do the job. In Cheney's words, Bush had adopted the post-Vietnam, "don't-screw-around school of military strategy." Indeed, Bush admitted as much to the American people on 10 September, in a speech to a Joint Session of Congress, when he quietly but pointedly said, "Iraq will not be permitted to annex Kuwait. That's not a threat or a boast. That's just the way it's going to be." On 22 September Bush wrote in his diary: "I am wondering if we need to speed up the timetable."

Nevertheless, Bush had to deal with the fact that by October, the economic sanctions as set by the United Nations showed signs of working. Saddam had control of 20 percent of the world's oil supply, but he could not sell any of it anywhere; indeed, on 10 September he began giving it away to any developing nation who dared to run the blockade. His hopes of affecting the world market had also fallen flat. The oil lost by Kuwait was made up for, and rather quickly, by increased production from Saudi Arabia, Venezuela, the United Arab Emirates, and Nigeria. The coalition could keep food from Iraq—a nation that imported 75 percent of its food-stuffs—but it could not be seen to be starving children as a war aim.

No one knew for sure how soon the sanctions would begin to affect not only Saddam but the members of the coalition. The Western economies, including that of the United States, were already on shaky ground. The recession that played such a large part at the end of the Bush administration was only a few months away, and even before the invasion the economy had already begun to show signs of a slow-down. It was doubtful whether the economies of the Arab members of the coalition would survive the two years that some analysts predicted it would take for the sanctions to bring Saddam to his knees; indeed, the CIA was telling Bush that the sanctions might never work.

Since the beginning of the crisis, Bush had been meeting regularly with a group that was dubbed the Gang of Eight—Dan Quayle, James Baker, John Sununu, Brent Scowcroft, Richard Gates, Dick Cheney, and Colin Powell. Baker and Powell urged the president to continue the containment route, at least until that time when economic sanctions and diplomacy had been given enough time to work. But Scowcroft, Gates, and Cheney advocated an offensive option that would expel Saddam from Kuwait. That military option had been in the pipeline since early August. On 8 August, the day that Bush announced the deployment of DESERT SHIELD, Schwartzkopf asked for assistance in developing an offensive plan. That initial plan, code-named Operation INSTANT THUNDER, called for the targeting of key Iraqi military and technological installations for air bombardment. It also called for an intensive air bombardment of Iraqi command and communications and then a ground war, with coalition troops attacking straight into the teeth of the Republican Guard. Nevertheless, the prediction of the planner was succinct: "National leadership and command and control destroyed. Iraq's strategic offense and defense eliminated for extended period." Powell was briefed on the plan on 11 August, and he ordered it to be expanded to include options for expelling Hussein from Kuwait, should it come to that.

The plan was presented to Bush from 6 to 8 October, but it satisfied no one. It virtually guaranteed high losses, and the military felt that they were being pressured into providing an offensive option too soon, before the DESERT SHIELD troops were even safely in place; the civilians in the room saw only poor planning. Ordered to present a new offensive strategy that would guarantee success, Schwartzkopf returned with a plan that called for the doubling of the DESERT SHIELD troop commitment. These reinforcements would be necessary to guarantee the success of the bold plan, which called for an initial attack against the heart of Saddam's forces and then a strike against the Iraqi flank to the west—a "left hook"—that would encircle the fleeing Iraqi army.

When presented in October with the revamped INSTANT THUNDER plan, Bush immediately favored reinforcing the DESERT SHIELD troop commitment. But politically, his hands were tied; the congressional elections were coming up, and Bush did not want to send more troops to the Gulf until they were over. He approved the doubling of forces on 31 October but did not announce it until after the election. On 8 November Bush revealed that he was doubling the American force in Saudi Arabia from 230,000 to more than 500,000 troops in order to create an "offensive military option." Bush also added more than 1,200 M-1 tanks to those already in Saudi Arabia. The new reinforcements, in numbers approximately equal to those stationed in Europe at the height of the cold war, represented the largest American military deployment since the Vietnam War.

Bush justified his decision to move toward an offensive option on the grounds of saving the world from a brutal bully. By the end of 1990, he was making regular comparisons between Saddam (whose name he continually mispronounced, a serious slight to an Arabic male and one that it is possible Bush did deliberately) and Adolf Hitler. He also frequently used terms like "rapist," "evil," and "madman" to describe the Iraqi leader. Bush used the Wilsonian rhetoric of righteousness; in his 1991 State of the Union Address, he bluntly asserted, "Our cause is just. Our cause is moral. Our cause is right."

Yet Bush's most impassioned utterance in this regard was part of an interview, first broadcast to the American people on 2 January 1991. British journalist David Frost had been given access to Bush for a program analyzing the first two years of his presidency. Not surprisingly, the crisis in the Gulf dominated the program—particularly since on the day he was interviewed, Bush had read an Amnesty International report that outlined a host of Iraqi atrocities. Bush told Frost that the report "should be compulsory reading [for] anyone who thinks we have all the time in the world." He then listed several examples from the report, the most gruesome of which was the torture and rape of a handicapped child. As he continued, Bush's lips tightened and his face flushed with anger. He called Saddam "primeval" and "the rapist of Kuwait" and promised that "we will prevail. There's no question about it."

Bush was completely sincere in his hatred of Saddam; it was easy for him to equate the Iraqi dictator's actions to those of the 1940s' dictators whom he had risked his life to defeat. But there was an equally important national security reason for Bush's actions, one that James Baker highlights in his memoirs: "We *had* responded to a clear violation of international law . . . and we *were* dealing with a megalomaniacal personality. But it was also true that we had vital interests at stake. . . . We had to make sure we could maintain a secure supply of energy."

For half a century, the United States had clearly stated that keeping the Middle Eastern oil pipeline flowing—and keeping the price of crude as low as possible—was in its vested national security interests. Yet Bush did not articulate the economic ramifications of Saddam's actions nearly as well, or as passionately, as he expressed his belief that Saddam was basically an evil man. Bush left the oil argument up to Baker to explain, which the secretary of state did on several occasions. The most notable came after a 13 November press conference, when Baker declared, "We cannot permit a dictator such as this to sit astride that economic lifeline. And to bring it down to the level of the average American citizen, let me say that means jobs." Baker later argued that it was the "rhetorical confusion" of the administration—sending too many mixed messages in an attempt to justify the military actions—that played into the hands of a growing movement in opposition to DESERT SHIELD. Just as likely is the explanation that Baker never should have mentioned the oil issue publicly, for that was the aspect the antiwar activists pounced on.

The announcement of troop reinforcements, and the administration's heated rhetoric about Saddam's actions costing American jobs, brought a wave of antiwar protests both in the United States and around the world. In New York City, a parade of marchers six blocks long rallied at Times Square, chanting "Hell, no, we won't go—we won't fight for Texaco." A group that called itself Out Now ran an advertisement in the liberal magazine the *Nation*; they asked for contributions for future ads so that they might continue to broadcast their message: "Must we trade body bags for oil? Why not Give Peace a Chance? Speak Out Now—Remember Vietnam. . . . Out Now—Bring Our Troops Home."

More troubling from a political point of view was the fact that many Republican conservatives, who presumably would support the president's actions, were instead opposing the move toward war, claiming that Bush was involving the nation in another Vietnam-like morass for no real purpose. Chief among these critics was conservative columnist and television talk-show host Pat Buchanan. In August 1990, the former Nixon speechwriter had written an editorial, "How the Gulf Crisis Is Rupturing the Right." In it, he claimed that "neoconservatives" like Bush supported a war "that has quagmire written all over it. . . . Saddam Hussein is not a madman; he is no Adolf Hitler; while a ruthless menace to his neighbors, he is no threat to us. . . . Have the neocons thought this through?" And Buchanan was by no means the only conservative critical of Bush's policies. In January 1991, the Cato Institute ran a conference "America in the Gulf: Vital Interests or Pointless Entanglement?" The papers presented make it clear that the participants overwhelmingly sided with the latter interpretation.

The public support for Bush's actions, which had been high at the beginning of the crisis, slowly ebbed throughout the fall. In August Bush's popularity rating had been at 75 percent in favor of the job he was doing as president; by October it had dropped to 59 percent, and immediately after the congressional elections it was at 50 percent. This drop was caused not only by his moves toward an offensive option but also by his decision to support a tax increase. With Bush's tumble in the polls, the opportunity presented itself for the Democratic Congress to make some political hay before the November election. The Senate Armed Services Committee, chaired by Sam Nunn, began a series of hearings on the Gulf crisis. They gained instant notoriety because of the testimony of a young girl who claimed to have seen Iraqi soldiers snatch Kuwaiti babies from the incubators in the hospital where she worked, leaving them to die on the floor. The witness, however, was the daughter of the Kuwaiti ambassador to the United States who had been prepared for her testimony by an American public relations firm.

As the administration prepared to expel Saddam from Kuwait, no one helped Bush's cause more than Saddam himself. Foremost was his taking of hostages. Saddam's treatment of the thousands of Western civilians (including over 3,000 Americans) living in Kuwait or Iraq, whom he refused to allow to leave after the outbreak of the crisis, can only be described as bizarre. Although calling them "human shields," they were nonetheless treated well, housed in hotels in Baghdad, and then paraded in front of television cameras with Saddam so that they might testify to the humaneness of their treatment. The strategy, if it was one, backfired. Westerners were appalled at pictures of five-year-old British hostage Stuart Lockwood, riveted with fear, standing next to Saddam as the Iraqi leader patted his head and asked him, "Are you getting your milk, Stuart, and your corn flakes, too?" Thatcher mocked Saddam for "hiding behind women's skirts." For his part, Saddam ignored the rumbling of world opinion against him, and on 22 September he issued a statement urging all Iraqi citizens to prepare for "the mother of all battles." The UN responded on 29 November by passing Security Council Resolution 678, giving him a deadline: it agreed to support the use of "all necessary means" by the coalition forces to expel Saddam from Kuwait if he did not withdraw his forces by 15 January 1991.

• • •

The day after the UN vote, Bush surprised many observers when he announced that he was willing to go the "extra mile for peace," and he offered to send Baker to Baghdad and to receive Iraqi foreign minister Tariq Aziz in Washington. The decision was less a diplomatic move than it was a political one. Baker's political radar told him not only that there was a great deal of support in the country for the idea but also that even if Saddam spurned the invitation, as the administration seems to have assumed, then the mere act of extending the olive branch would help defuse the rapidly growing antiwar feeling at home. As Baker recalled, it would show that "we weren't cowboying this."

The plan almost backfired on Bush when Saddam found reasons to reject each American request for a meeting. On 14 December, in remarks to the press on his way to Camp David, Bush chided his opponent: "It is simply not credible that he cannot, over a two-week period, make a couple of hours available for the secretary of state on an issue of this importance—unless, of course, he is seeking to circumvent the United Nations deadline." Eventually, Saddam agreed to a meeting between Baker and Aziz in Geneva on 9 January 1991.

The meeting was both tense and confrontational. Baker presented Aziz with a letter from Bush, to be delivered to Saddam. Dated 5 January, it was stark and blunt. Bush told Saddam that "we stand today at the brink of war between Iraq and the world," a war that "can only be ended by Iraq's full and unconditional compliance" with UN Security Council Resolution 678. Bush also made it clear that the time for negotiating was over and that if Saddam used chemical or biological weapons—which he had done against Iran—or if he destroyed any of the Kuwaiti oil fields, "the American people would demand the strongest possible response." Bush closed the letter by saying that he had not written "to threaten, but to inform." Aziz, who apparently believed that the meeting was for the purposes of negotiation, refused to accept the letter from Baker. Clearly, Baker had not come to negotiate but to deliver Bush's ultimatum. Baker wanted to make sure that Saddam understood the gravity of the situation; he looked at Aziz and quietly declared, "Don't let your military commanders convince you that your strategy against Iran will work against us. You are facing an entirely different kind of force. . . . Because of the superiority of our forces, we will dictate the terms of the battle, not you." Aziz responded, "We accept war." After the meeting broke up, Baker told the press, "Regrettably, I heard nothing today that suggested to me any Iraqi flexibility."

The final hurdle to war was on Capitol Hill, where the Congress stood poised to claim authority given it under the War Powers Act and to debate Bush's authority to send troops into combat. Bush decided to co-opt the process and to formally ask Congress for its support before such a debate could begin. This decision was made despite the advice of C. Boyden Gray, who believed that "as a question of international law, we were on solid ground deploying the troops" (a conclusion heartily shared by Bush), and of Cheney, who did not want to take the risk that Congress would reject the measure. But Bush was adamant; as he later remembered, he wanted "to send a signal to Saddam Hussein that it wasn't just a trigger-happy president" but that he had the American nation behind him. And there was another consideration; as Gray remembered, "If it went sour, [Bush] wanted Democrats with him. . . . He wanted a unified government. . . . It's a military, constitutional, moral, and political thing."

The debate was civil, but lines had been drawn. Antiwar resolutions were introduced in both houses of Congress, and for most of 10 and 11 January, the debate on the issue was nonstop. Senate majority leader George Mitchell (D-ME), who with Nunn had sponsored the antiwar resolution in the Senate, argued that although "it may become necessary to use force to expel Iraq from Kuwait . . . because war is such a grave undertaking, with such serious consequences, we must make certain that war is employed only as a last resort." Edward Kennedy proclaimed that "there is still time to save the president from himself." In the House, minority leader Robert Michel argued, "Either we stop [Saddam] now, and stop him permanently, or we won't stop him at all." Several times, debate had to be suspended because visitors in the gallery were shouting antiwar slogans. The vote in both chambers promised to be close.

But Baker's gamble in Geneva paid off; the administration was able to say that it had gone the extra mile and been spurned. Both the House and the Senate voted on 12 January. In the House, the conservatives who had abandoned Bush on the budget only weeks before returned to the fold; the vote was 250 to 183 against an antiwar resolution. In the Senate, the vote was closer. Mitchell and Nunn worked hard to hold the Democratic ranks together. However, minority leader Bob Dole did a better job of holding the Republican feet to the fire. The final vote was a razor-thin 52-to-47 defeat of the antiwar resolution. Nine Democrats, including Al Gore Jr. of Tennessee, had defected to support the president; only two Republicans, Charles Grassley of Iowa and Mark Hatfield of Oregon, voted no. Following the defeat of the antiwar proposals, both houses voted, by the same tally, in favor of House Joint Resolution 77, the Authorization for Use of Military Force Against Iraq.

As with the earlier support of the UN, however, the vote of Congress was, though welcome, hardly deemed by the White House to be absolutely necessary. In a later interview, Bush made it clear that "I know I would have" ordered troops into combat, even without a resolution of support from Congress. From the earliest moments of the crisis, the die had been cast.

Three days after the congressional vote of support, Bush signed National Security Directive 54: "Pursuant to my responsibility under the Constitution as President and Commander in Chief, and under the laws and treaties of the United States, and pursuant to H[ouse] J[oint] Resolution 77 and in accordance with the rights and obligations of the United States under international law," the president was initiating military hostilities against Iraq. The directive was clear in its statement of war aims:

> a. To effect the immediate, complete, and unconditional withdrawal of all Iraqi forces from Kuwait.

b. To restore Kuwait's legitimate government.
c. To protect the lives of American citizens abroad, and
d. To promote the security and stability of the Persian Gulf.

Bush was also clear about when those military operations would end: "Only when I have determined that the objectives set forth . . . above have been met."

On 31 December 1990, after he left a family celebration at Camp David, Bush wrote a letter to his children.

> I hope I didn't seem moody. I tried not to. . . . I have thought long and hard about what might have to be done. As I write this letter at year's end there is still some hope that Iraq's dictator will pull out of Kuwait. I vary on this. Sometimes I think he might; at others I think he is simply too unrealistic—too ignorant of what he might face. I have the peace of mind that comes from knowing that we have tried hard for peace.
>
> I look at today's crisis as "good vs. evil"—yes, it is that clear. . . . Principle must be adhered to—Saddam cannot profit in any way at all from his aggression . . . and sometimes in your life you have to act as you think best—you can't compromise, you can't give in.
>
> So, dear kids, better batten down the hatches.

At 3:00 a.m. Iraqi time, 17 January 1991 (7:00 p.m. eastern standard time, 16 January in the United States), one day after the deadline set in UN Resolution 678, Operation DESERT SHIELD turned into Operation DESERT STORM. The first strikes came from AH-64A Apache antiarmor attack helicopters, which flew into Iraq and knocked out key early warning radar systems. They were followed by attacks by

F117A bombers—the Stealth bomber—and F-15C fighter bombers, which struck at targets in the heart of the city of Baghdad. Within the first fourteen hours of the war, over 1,000 sorties were flown, and forty-five key targets in the capital city were hit. The bombing runs were supported by Tomahawk missile attacks from destroyers in the Gulf—one of the support carriers was Bush's old ship, the USS *San Jacinto*. That first night, Americans were glued to their TV screens, as CNN, which had three reporters holed up in a hotel in Baghdad, broadcast terrifying live shots of Tomahawk missiles descending upon the city, then exploding only yards from where the reporters were stationed.

After five-and-one-half weeks of near constant air bombardment, and several attempts by Saddam to end the war without withdrawing from Kuwait, the land war began on 24 February. Feinting an amphibious marine landing just outside Kuwait City, the First and Second Marine Divisions and the Tiger Brigade of the Twenty-second Armored—already some ten miles inside Kuwait before the attack order was given—smashed into the teeth of the Iraqi front-line defenses. However, the marines moved so quickly that they engaged the Iraqis in Kuwait City before they could be joined by the Twenty-eighth Corps and the Seventh Corps advancing from the west (neither Gen. Norman Schwartzkopf in the field nor Gen. Colin Powell at the Pentagon thought that the army was advancing anywhere near fast enough). As a result, within twenty-four hours Iraqi troops poured out of Kuwait City, taking the road north to Basra. On 27 February, more than 1,500 coalition tanks, led by the Seventh Corps, shattered the heart of the Republican Guard defensive position at the Battle of Medina Ridge (tank commander to his forward positions: "Understand we are engaging the Medina Division?" Response: "Negative sir. We are *destroying* the Medina Division"). In about forty minutes, 300 Iraqi tanks were lost; one American was killed. The next day—six weeks after the beginning of the air war, and exactly 100 hours after the beginning of the ground war—a cease-fire was declared. On 3 March at Safwan, Iraq, Schwartzkopf met with the Iraqi military leadership and dictated the terms of the cease-fire. The Americans had lost 148 killed in action and 458 wounded (more Americans were murdered in the United States during that 100-hour period than were lost in combat in Iraq); the rest of the coalition lost some ninety-two soldiers. Iraqi reports, although still disputed, suggest some 22,000 Iraqi dead.

My purpose here is not to offer a full military history of the Persian Gulf War. Indeed, the literature on the subject is vast, and beginning with Rick Atkinson's exceptional *Crusade: The Untold Story of the Persian Gulf War*, surprisingly good, given that at this writing much of the government material on the war continues to be security classified. My goal, rather, is to look at the impact of the war on the nation as a whole and on the Bush administration in particular.

With that in mind, several points need to be made. First, the point that is the most often made on the Gulf War: the outcome was never in doubt. Outnumbered and with no air support, Saddam knew that he could not win. The only strategy open to him was to dig in his lines and hope that he could repel the coalition advance long enough for the American people to tire of the war, just as they had in Vietnam. However, this strategy played right into the coalition's hands. With superb intelligence, the coalition knew that the Iraqi forces were dug in; thus, the Iraqis were sitting ducks. When the bombardment began, it was so easy for the coalition forces that airmen christened a new sport: "tank plinking." Moreover, this entrenched Iraqi army was so chained to its eastern trenches that when the ground assault came, the army had no chance. After the left hook began, reports circulated of American tanks simply rolling over and burying Iraqi soldiers who had no way out of their trenches.

Over the five-and-one-half weeks of the air bombardment, the coalition flew more than 100,000 sorties. Saddam's tiny air force was both unable (most of the 800-plane air force was destroyed on the ground early in the offensive; during the entirety of the conflict, a total of seventy-six American planes were shot down) and ultimately unwilling to respond. Few Iraqi sorties—toward the end of the bombardment, virtually none—were flown to meet the allied offensive.

American Stealth bombers were never touched by Iraqi defenses, and they operated at will over Baghdad. During the ground war, the marines advanced so quickly against only token opposition that they reached Kuwait City before the flanking attack could catch up with them. When the left hook finally met the Republican Guard, there was absolutely no contest. Iraqi T-72s were simply no match for the new American M1-A1s; coalition soldiers called it a "turkey shoot."

Added to this situation was the fact that the Iraqi military leadership was completely incompetent. Let one example suffice: the Iraqis marked their way through their own minefields with concertina wire in a path that was clear to the invading coalition tanks. As one tank commander put it, "Once we found that, the only thing missing was a neon sign saying 'start here.' " Iraqis surrendered by the thousands, chanting "M-R-E" (the American serviceman's slang for "Meals Ready to Eat") and flashing victory signs rather than white flags (final military guesstimates say that the coalition captured some 80,000 Iraqi prisoners of war). The president's Office of Communications was so optimistic about a quick victory that on 14 January, a full three days before the war began, it sent Chief of Staff John Sununu a full plan, including the setup for lights and teleprompters, the length of the address, and sequencing for the "presidential announcement of the liberation of Kuwait." The staff was overly confident, but not wrong. For the Americans, Operation DESERT STORM was always a no-lose proposition. Another key point that had long-lasting effects for Bush's New World Order was the role that Israel played during the Gulf War. Saddam's only real offensive weapons were Scud missiles, 14,000-pound liquid-fueled rockets, with an accuracy of one mile (to improve its range, the Iraqis welded two rockets together). For all intents and purposes, the Scud was useless as a tactical weapon and useful only for inflicting civilian terror. On the second night of the war, Saddam began to indiscriminately lob Scud missiles into Israel. Property damage occurred, but initially there were no fatalities. Certain members of Yitzhak Shamir's cabinet, most notably Minister of Defense Moshe Arens and Minister of Housing Ariel Sharon, argued for immediate retaliation.

Key to Bush's success at holding together the coalition had been his ability to keep the Israelis out of the conflict. With the launching of the Scuds, however, Bush had to up the ante. The DELTA FORCE, a counterterrorist commando unit, was infiltrated into Iraq to try to ferret out and destroy any Scuds as well as their launchers. Bush also sent two Patriot missile batteries to Israel, the largest airlift of American military weaponry to Israel since the 1973 Yom Kippur War. And he agreed to inform Shamir in real time, by way of the newly installed secure satellite line between the White House and Tel Aviv, code-named HAMMER RICK, of any confirmed Scud launchings toward Israel. Iraq continued to lob Scuds into Israel; a total of forty were fired at Israel and forty-six at Saudi Arabia. The total death toll from this counterattack was 31 dead and 400 injured. Israelis lived with gas masks within their reach: puppet performers on the children's television program *Kippy of Rechov Sumsum* also wore gas masks to calm the fears of their little viewers. But Shamir did not retaliate. A grateful Bush remembered Shamir's restraint in the months following the war, with important ramifications for the Middle East peace process.

During the war, the American press stressed the impact of the new technology on both strategy and offensive capability. It was dubbed the Nintendo War, after a popular video game of the time; and stories abounded of the technological marvels that gave the United States an overwhelming military superiority—the term "unbeatable" was omnipresent in press reports of the conflict. Certainly since World War II's mass-destruction bombings of Germany and Japan, the air force had developed technologies of precision guidance that allowed it by 1990 to pinpoint its targets with amazing accuracy. Few people who watched the drama unfold on television were not awed by pictures taken from within the cockpit of an F-15 fighter, showing a missile zoom down an airshaft and destroy a building.

The surgical nature of America's air power might have given the impression to many observers that the war was bloodless. It often seemed to the American public that the key to the war was the skill of a military technician who sat behind a computer, punched in coordinates, and launched missiles that simply erased the enemy from memory. American bombardiers apparently never missed. Bush himself perpetuated this perception, calling the bombing "fantastically accurate"; Schwartzkopf's chief of staff, Robert Johnson, declared, "I quite truthfully cannot tell you of any reports that I know of that would show inaccurate bombing."

It is now clear, however, that the Americans were far less accurate with their precision bombing than was portrayed by either Washington or Riyadh. Rick Atkinson recounts that of the 167 laser-guided bombs dropped by F-117s during the first five nights of combat, 76 missed their targets completely, a fact that was not acknowledged to the press by either the Pentagon or the White House. One bizarre example of this inaccuracy was an F-15 attack on what was purported to be seven mobile missile launchers. When the cockpit tape was played back for CIA analysts, however, they immediately saw that the destroyed targets were not missile sites; some thought them to be oil tankers, others believed them to be milk trucks (the error was not revealed to the public). There were other examples. On 22 January, coalition bombing destroyed what CENTCOM claimed was a factory that made biological weapons; Iraqi claims at the time, broadcast by CNN's Peter Arnett, suggest that the factory actually made baby formula.

Along with accusations of targeting errors came reports of problems with the Patriot missile. A postwar army investigation claimed that the greatest single loss of American life in the war—twenty-eight American soldiers killed—resulted from a Scud hit on an army barracks. The Scud had sneaked through coalition defenses due to a computer failure that shut down a Patriot missile's capacity to intercept it. The problems of the Patriot were kept from media and public scrutiny, as was the astoundingly high number of coalition deaths resulting from errant bombardment by their own forces. Thirty-five coalition soldiers, 23 percent of the total, were killed by friendly fire—"fratricide," in military parlance. In comparison to past wars, this percentage was much higher, and it took the Pentagon some five months to inform their families of that fact.

The "bloodlessness" of the war can also be challenged by the number of civilian deaths. The most publicized tragedy took place on 13 February. The coalition had been closely monitoring a building in the Al Firdos section of Baghdad that had been labeled Public Shelter Number 25. But the allies believed that the bunker had become, in the words of the attack plan that sealed its doom, an "activated, recently camouflaged command-and-control bunker." Available evidence suggests both that the coalition had evidence that showed this assessment to be true but that this evidence—a newly camouflaged roof, captured radio messages, and a new protective fence—was hardly irrefutable. Nevertheless, the bunker was destroyed, killing 204 civilians, many of them children, who had been sleeping in an air-raid shelter in the bunker. Administration and military planners remain convinced to the present day that somewhere in the bunker there had been a command-and-control center. But the tragedy, quite aside from the human loss, took on a political life of its own. In order to avoid any further public-relations disasters, CENTCOM was ordered to choose its bombing targets in Kuwait rather than in Baghdad. Some analysts argue that this decision lengthened the air war and gave Saddam badly needed time to regroup.

In a postwar study, the group Human Rights Watch evaluated the civilian death toll during the war and largely exonerated the American military: "In many if not most respects the allies' conduct was consistent with their stated intent to take all feasible precautions to avoid civilian casualties." The evidence suggests that this assessment was quite accurate. Nevertheless, one must also agree with Atkinson's assessment: "The sanitary conflict depicted by Bush and his commanders, though of a piece with similar exaggerations in previous wars, was a lie."

This lie was perpetuated, although not willingly, by the press. Unlike in Vietnam, where television shots of ravaged bodies became daily fare for the nightly news, in the Persian Gulf the military constricted the operations of the some-1,600 reporters to the point where they got little film footage other than what the central command wanted them to have. The U.S. Armed Forces Joint Information Bureau decided which reporters actually got to visit, and film, the front. The wire services and a few newsmagazines, television networks, and radio outlets were given priority in the field, and even those lucky enough to get into the pool were most often fed information by the armed services and taken only where the army wanted them to go. Other reporters were, in their parlance, "corralled" behind the lines, left to file their stories largely from watching CNN reports and from attending official military press conferences. As one reporter put it, "For most journalists, coverage of the war has been by invitation only." As a result, Americans saw more video clips of successful bombing raids than they saw human beings in combat; they saw virtually no casualties and heard few references to coalition errors.

The press, smitten with the impressive show of American technological might, did little to challenge the situation. The general tone of the coverage—particularly on television, and especially on CNN, the most watched network during the conflict—makes it clear that reporters largely accepted CENTCOM's line at face value. Reports such as those from the *New York Times* on 21 January claiming that American Patriot missiles "intercepted most or all of [the Scuds] and knocked them from the sky before they could hit their targets" were the norm. With remarkably few exceptions, the Gulf War was sanitized for popular consumption.

Perhaps the biggest controversy arising from the Gulf War revolved around Bush's decision as to when it would end. His decision to stop it before the left hook had completely encircled the Iraqis, thus completely cutting off their path of retreat, was for him an easy one. He had been clearly told both by Powell and Cheney that Saddam's capability to make war had been obliterated by the end of the first day of the ground war, and Powell argued for ending the fighting as soon as possible. The road out of Kuwait City north to Basra—the line of retreat for the occupying Iraqi army—became known as the Highway of Death. As coalition forces bombed the fleeing Iraqis at will, Bush found himself appalled at the slaughter. NSC Deputy Robert Gates recalled that Bush used the word "unchivalrous" to describe the infliction of any further carnage on the Iraqis. Powell summarized the situation: "You don't do unnecessary killing if you can avoid it." Bush agreed with him. Put simply, when faced with the choice between any further bloodshed or ending the war ahead of schedule, Bush did not hesitate to end the war.

Powell remembers that when he got the news, Schwartzkopf responded, "I could live with that." Atkinson reports that Schwartzkopf "seemed neither upset nor surprised" at Bush's decision (when one of his staffers asked why they were not being allowed to encircle the enemy completely before the cease-fire, Schwartzkopf replied, "Because that's what the commander in chief wants. The president says we've accomplished enough"). In his memoirs, Powell writes that "every member of [Schwartzkopf's] policy-making team agreed" with the decision. Scowcroft later agreed: "There was no dissent." In a later interview with David Frost, however, Schwartzkopf asserted that Bush had been too hasty: "Frankly, my recommendation had been, you know, continue the march"—an assertion that made Powell, in his words, "mad as hell." Schwartzkopf's statement, made during the 1992 presidential campaign, gave fodder to Bill Clinton and Ross Perot, both of whom charged the administration with ignoring the supposed recommendation of its field general to end the war one day later, a recommendation that, as it turned out, was never made. The tempest prompted Powell to issue a statement on 27 August 1992, which read in part, "General Schwartzkopf and I both supported terminating DESERT STORM combat operations at 12 p.m., 27 February 1991 (EST), as did all the president's advisers. There was no contrary recommendation. There was no debate. . . . Those who claim that another twelve or twenty-four hours of fighting *without a cease-fire* would have fundamentally changed the residual capability of the Iraqi army are mistaken."

Indeed, if anyone was responsible for letting Saddam's army "escape," it was Norman Schwartzkopf. During the cease-fire meeting at Safwan, his generosity to the Iraqis was pronounced. He promised that American forces would not long remain in Iraq, but he went even further. Through his generals, Saddam claimed that he needed to keep his armed helicopters because the Americans had destroyed most of the bridges and roads. Without obtaining the permission of Washington, Schwartzkopf acquiesced. The cease-fire allowed the Iraqis to continue to fly armed helicopters over their territory, an arrangement that soon came back to haunt other Iraqi opponents. To be fair, everyone in the White House did not initially see the danger in Schwartzkopf's largesse. Scowcroft wanted to reverse Schwartzkopf's decision, remembering in a later interview, "I didn't care whether the country was administered that way or not and it gave [Saddam] a great loophole." However, Scowcroft was overruled.

On 6 March 1991, Bush went before a joint Session of Congress, each member having been given a miniature American flag to wave. In the most dramatic moment of his presidency, Bush turned to face the Kuwaiti ambassador, sitting in the House gallery, and announced to a standing ovation: "Ambassador Al-Sabah—Kuwait is free." Bush then recalled the CNN footage of an American soldier who was guarding several Iraqi prisoners, softly and carefully telling them, "You're all right." When Bush remembered that moment, to thunderous applause, he took out his handkerchief and dabbed his eyes. At the end of the talk, he gave Colin Powell a hug.

Certainly, one outcome of the war was a tremendous surge of patriotism, typified for many Americans by the near-constant radio airplay of Lee Greenwood's signature song, "God Bless the U.S.A." For others, it was the pageantry of the 8 June victory parade held in the streets of Washington. Norman Schwartzkopf was immediately enshrined as the first American military hero since Eisenhower; Dick Cheney and Colin Powell were christened overnight as presidential contenders. Fred Barnes, one of Bush's most severe critics, declared in his column in the *New Republic*: "I can't think of another president who could have pulled this off." For George Bush, these accolades were quite quantifiable; those people expressing faith in the Bush administration increased from 43 percent in September 1990 to 67 percent at war's end.

When I asked Brent Scowcroft if the United States won the war with Iraq, he did not hesitate for a moment when he answered in the affirmative. Yet he later mused that "very few geopolitical problems are solved by any one action." Despite the many bits of evidence that pointed to an overwhelming American victory in the Persian Gulf War, by mid-1991 one point had begun to gnaw at many Americans. Despite the success of the coalition at expelling Saddam Hussein from Kuwait, he was still very much alive and in control of Iraq's destiny. He had also escaped with a full one-third of his army intact.

It is important to note that nowhere in his public statements—or anywhere in the available records of the administration or in the memories of any of the individuals present in the decision-making loop—did George Bush (or the United Nations, which specifically and carefully avoided any such reference in any of its resolutions on the crisis) ever call for the overthrow of Saddam from his position of power in Iraq. For Bush, the potential political ramifications of an operation designed to catch and overthrow Saddam were staggering. Uppermost in the president's mind was the Panama Syndrome; how could an army that could not catch one Panamanian dictator dislodge Saddam Hussein? Moreover, such a strategy would necessitate marines fighting in the streets of Baghdad, guarantee thousands of coalition casualties, and ensure a protracted military commitment, possibly an army of occupation after the war, none of which was acceptable either to the Pentagon or Bush, for whom "escalation"—reminiscent of Vietnam—was abhorrent. Also important was the same issue that had guided Bush's temperate response to the fall of communism in Eastern Europe in 1989: a completely smashed Iraq, leaving a power vacuum in the Gulf area that either Iran or Syria could quickly exploit, was not in the best interests of the United States. Thus, throughout the conflict, the president's goal, as clearly stated in press briefing notes dated 2 August 1990, was to "get

Iraq out of Kuwait and Kuwait back to the status quo ante." As Scowcroft bluntly put it, getting Saddam out of power was "never a goal—only a hopeful byproduct." Privately, Bush reportedly told his aides that he hoped "some kind of Ceaucescu scenario" would befall the Iraqi dictator. But the hoped-for coup did not emerge. Indeed, Saddam had expanded his power base by declaring that he had stood up to everything the Americans could throw at him, and he had survived. Bush and Scowcroft had both hoped for a Battleship *Missouri* surrender, reminiscent of the Japanese unconditional surrender to the Allies on an aircraft carrier at the end of World War II. This, due to Schwartzkopf's miscalculations at Safwan and to Saddam's survival, they did not get; and ethnic minorities in Iraq soon paid the price.

Sensing an instability in Saddam's regime, Shi'ite Muslims, a religious minority located in southern Iraq and longtime vocal critics of Saddam's claim that he headed the one, true branch of the Muslim faith, rose up in revolt in early March. Saddam and his helicopters were brutal in their response, and the Shi'ites suffered terrible losses. Citing earlier promises of American support, the Shi'ite rebels fully expected American help. They did not get any. Robert Gates was blunt: "Therein lay Vietnam, as far as we were concerned."

The same fate awaited the Kurds, an ethnic minority living in the north of Iraq who had been systematically denied a political homeland of their own for almost a century. Bush may well have inadvertently called for a Kurdish uprising when he said that "the Iraqi military and the Iraqi people should take matters into their own hands, to force Saddam Hussein, the dictator, to step aside." Regardless, Saddam used his helicopters to wreak havoc on the Kurds, who tried to flee to refugee camps in nearby Iran and Turkey. When they pleaded for Western assistance, however, they were spurned.

According to one source, during one Oval Office meeting on the subject, Powell spelled out a "precise military case against" intervention. In his memoirs, Powell was clear: "Neither revolt had a chance. Nor, frankly, was their success a goal of our policy." More interested in getting American troops home from the Gulf than in embroiling them in another conflict, postwar America took on a decidedly isolationist tinge. Newspaper editorials were clear in their advice: "Iraq: The Limits of Sympathy"; "A Blood Bath Beyond Our Grasp"; "Caution on New War With Iraq"; "The Quicksand in Iraq." Baker paid a pro forma visit to a Kurdish refugee camp but spent only seven minutes there.

Perhaps the greatest legacy of the Gulf War was that it rejuvenated the peace process in the Middle East. In his diary, Bush wrote that despite Israeli intransigence, "We kicked Saddam Hussein and solved their security problem in the area . . . [so now] they're going to have to move on the peace process." Thanks to Baker's postwar shuttle diplomacy, all affected parties—including, in a breakthrough of gigantic proportions, the Israelis, the Syrians, and the Palestine Liberation Organization—agreed to the international conference on the Middle East that Bush had promised Gorbachev in Helsinki. But the Soviet leader was not a major factor at the conference. He had just survived a coup attempt and was but a month away from resignation when the conference convened in Madrid on 30 October 1991. Indeed, little of substance emerged from Madrid; little had been expected. But its symbolic effects were nevertheless earth-shattering. For many observers, the conference was the most tangible sign of Bush's New World Order—for the first time in decades, age-old enemies had all sat together and talked in the same room.

from The Natural

by Joe Klein

Joe Klein (born 1946) wrote a best-selling novel (Primary Colors) *whose main character was based on Bill Clinton (in office 1993–2001). Klein's non-fiction book on Clinton's presidency includes a discussion of the Lewinsky scandal.*

The plan was that the President would speak to the nation on the evening of August 17, after he'd testified to the grand jury, and apologize for what he had done. He did speak, and he did apologize, sort of. But it was a grudging apology. In fact, the real emotion in the speech wasn't contrition, but an assault on Starr. Clinton explained that he had "misled" the public because of personal embarrassment, out of concern for his family, but also because:

"The independent counsel moved on [from the Whitewater investigation] to my staff and friends. Then into my private life. And the investigation itself is under investigation. This has gone on too long, cost too much, and hurt too many innocent people . . .

"Even presidents have private lives. It is time to stop the pursuit of personal destruction and the prying into private lives and get on with our national life."

The sentiments were worthy—but, as always with Clinton, the body language was far more important than the words: His tone was angry, unapologetic, ungracious. It was, perhaps, his least effective public moment in the White House—and the most embarrassing four minutes that an American President had suffered through since Richard Nixon's maudlin resignation speech. But it was nothing compared to the embarrassments to come.

It is possible, indeed probable, that nothing Clinton could have said that night would have staunched the insanity of the next six months—the release of Starr's gratuitously prurient "report" of the details of the Lewinsky affair, the televising of Clinton's grand jury testimony, the Republicans' futile and nihilistic impeachment of the President. But there were those who believed that a more heartfelt, emotional Clinton apology on August 17 would have rallied public opinion and further isolated Starr, forcing a more circumspect Starr Report and causing the Republicans to think twice about impeachment. The cool, defiant nature of the speech was certainly out of character for this most emotionally astute of presidents—and this was largely attributable to the fact that Clinton's communication machine had, for once, broken down.

Just before the President went on the air at 9 p.m., in the same White House Map Room where he had been questioned by Starr, Tim Russert, NBC's Washington bureau chief, reported that he had spoken with White House aides who said the purpose of the speech would be "candor, contrition, and, they hope, closure." He said the President was going to offer a fulsome apology to the nation, that he would be a "good cop" and not attack the independent counsel—the dirty work would be left to his staff. "The President will take a big step," Russert said, "but it will not be the end of this."

Russert had been misled by his White House sources. Aides—particularly Paul Begala and Rahm Emanuel, who had written a more contrite and less combative draft—had obviously been engaged in wishful thinking. They had briefed the press for the speech they *hoped* Clinton would deliver. That briefing constituted an astounding breach of "message discipline" at a crucial moment.

Another important advisor who may have chosen the moment to

pursue a personal agenda was the First Lady. "It's your speech, say what you want," the First Lady was reported to have said—and most commentators took this to be a form of encouragement, that Hillary Clinton had wanted her husband to deliver a defiant, avenging message. A second popular theory was that this was the speech that the president *thought* his wife wanted him to deliver. But the truth of the matter was far more brutal.

Under normal circumstances, Mrs. Clinton's role would have been to calm her husband, saying, "You're too angry—stop yourself," when he came out "seething" from his grand jury testimony. But she rather pointedly chose not to do that. When she said "It's your speech, do what you want," during a last-minute, prespeech strategy session in the solarium, she was really telling the President, "I don't want to have any part of this."

And so, for once, the President stood before the country without staff or spouse to tamp down his wilder impulses. It wasn't pretty. But the results would have probably been just as grisly if the President had had the benefit of his usual spin team. He might have seemed less angry, more contrite, but he would still have been stuck with his untenable verbal fudgery: that his previous denial of a sexual relationship with Lewinsky, delivered under oath in the Paula Jones sexual harassment case, had been "legally accurate." In other words, Bill Clinton had decided to acknowledge the most hilariously absurd and mingy rumor that had been floated during the eight months of Lewinskyiana: that he believed oral sex was not sex.

The only possible response of a loyal Clintonite to such a remarkable proposition was silence, and pained silence was the most favorable reaction that the President received as the reality of his statement was absorbed during the next forty-eight hours. Privately, the White House staff was aghast. More than a few of his closest advisors—especially those who had vehemently defended the President on television during the past eight months—felt personally betrayed. There was some disingenuousness in that: Within the Clinton inner circle, the long-standing assumption about Monica Lewinsky had been the same as the general assumptions about Paula Jones and Gennifer Flowers and, more recently, Katherine Willey, who claimed that Clinton had groped her in the Oval Office—that the President had undoubtedly glanced their way, and had perhaps done a bit more than glance, but the actual facts probably didn't bear much resemblance to the stories the women were telling.

In this case, though, they had. The reality of the Lewinsky affair was astonishing in its selfishness, crudeness, and banality. It had happened in the White House. With an intern. It involved acts—and the President had now admitted as much—more exploitative than romantic. Dee Dee Myers, Clinton's first-term press secretary, was not merely upset that the President hadn't told the truth. "I never believed," she wrote in *Time*, "that Bill Clinton would actually risk his presidency—a job he had studied, dreamed about, and prepared for since he was a kid—for something so frivolous, so reckless, so small."

This was an expurgated version of what some of Clinton's oldest friends were saying privately. "I'm mad as hell," a former high-ranking administration official told me the day after the President's speech. "Here you had the most tactical, risk-averse President we've ever had—all that polling and market-testing before he'd even propose the tiniest of Dick Morris's 'bite-sized' social programs. And at the same time, for reasons that are inexplicable to me, he takes these huge, absurd personal risks and throws it all away. You know, you hear the same comment over and over from working people, 'He's an asshole.' Well, I'm with them."

On the day after Clinton's appearance, Starr called Dick Morris to testify before the grand jury. It was brilliant choreography. Afterward, Morris announced to the press that Clinton had consulted him in January, after the Lewinsky story broke, and had asked him to poll the possibility of an apology. Morris claimed to have found that the public would tolerate a confession of adultery, but not an admission that he'd lied in his Paula Jones deposition. This nauseating revelation, which was almost lost in the torrent of news, seemed to encapsulate all the worst aspects of the Clinton administration: The President was a man who would actually poll whether or not he should tell the truth. (In his book *A Vast Conspiracy,* Jeffrey Toobin later revealed that Mark Penn had been testing possible language for Clinton's apology speech.)

Within days, various staff members—and the President himself, who knew that he'd screwed up—began to think about taking another run at an apology, in an interview, perhaps, or in response to a question at a press conference. "He can still finish the conversation," one aide said. And he tried. And tried. In interviews, in speeches, at prayer breakfasts. He apologized to the Lewinsky family, to his family, to the members of his Cabinet, to the Democratic Party, to the American people. At times, he did so with tears in his eyes.

Meanwhile, the president was at work on another, far more questionable, strategy to turn the nation's attention away from the Lewinsky scandal. For nearly two weeks before Clinton's grand jury date, the Administration had been planning an assault on the guerrilla infrastructure of Osama bin Laden, the Saudi millionaire who, according to the White House, had masterminded the bombings, on August 7, 1998, of United States embassies in Kenya and Tanzania. Early on the morning of August 20, three days after his testimony, Clinton approved a cruise-missile attack on a pharmaceuticals factory in Sudan and on a guerrilla camp in Afghanistan, both of which were said to have been linked to bin Laden.

The attacks were ineffective, to say the least—and a rather suspicious use of presidential power besides. It remains an open question whether the pharmaceuticals factory had any link at all to bin Laden, and sending cruise missiles against a desert camp was the most oafish sort of overkill. Indeed, these attacks had a distressing similarity to the plot of the movie *Wag the Dog,* which had opened—uncannily—about the same time as the Lewinsky scandal did. In the film, political consultants concoct an imaginary war in Albania to distract attention from a presidential sex scandal involving a young "Firefly Girl." And there were suspicions, even among the President's own foreign policy team, that the scandal had influenced Clinton's decision to go after bin

Laden: "This is a man who has always had a very difficult time making up his mind about taking military action," said a ranking foreign policy expert. "This time, he was very decisive. I believe it was the right thing to do, but you can't tell me it was unrelated to the domestic political situation."

The funny thing was, it sort of worked. Pentagon officials suddenly were stealing airtime from prosecutors on the evening news. The overwhelming, and rather surreal, assessment was that the President had done the right thing. The public supported the bombings. And so did many Republicans. Moreover, Clinton's decisiveness gave pause to those who had been saying that his presidency was crippled, unable to function, lacked the "moral authority" to act in a crisis. Senator Orrin Hatch, Republican of Utah, who had called the president a "jerk" after the Monday night speech, quickly "applauded" the President's actions and hoped that more would follow.

And so began the most lurid month in the history of the American presidency, a month punctuated by the release of the Starr Report and the televising of Clinton's grand jury testimony in mid-September, a deranged time when even the most level-headed members of the political and journalistic communities seemed to come unhinged. In the midst of the mayhem, the internet magazine *Salon* released a story that the rest of the press—in an inexplicable spasm of responsible behavior—had passed on: Congressman Henry Hyde of Illinois, the Republican chairman of the Judiciary Committee, who was to preside over the impeachment hearings, had had an adulterous liaison forty years earlier. "Ugly times call for ugly tactics," *Salon*'s editor explained, creating an instant epitaph for an era.

For a time, the President seemed to be in desperate trouble. The word spread—and no one was quite sure how it spread—that his grand jury testimony was an embarrassment: He had been successfully cornered, lost his temper, stumbled, seemed foolish. Democrats grew nervous, even moderate Democrats. A few days before Clinton's testimony was broadcast, Representative Jim Moran of Virginia, who was one of the President's closest allies in Congress, told CNN: "There is some hemorrhaging going on within the Democratic party. . . . The President has to come up with a way, in my opinion, to stop this." What sort of way? "I'm just not creative enough to think of a way other than resignation," Moran said. "But maybe he can."

And then, on Monday, September 21, the scandal reached its apogee. A nation gathered around its television sets expecting to see the President of the United States make a fool of himself, turn purple, scream like a banshee, and storm out of the room.

But Bill Clinton didn't turn purple. On my television, he seemed sort of salmon pink, with several shiny patches of sweat on his forehead; aside from that, he was the same Bill Clinton we'd always seen in public—which is to say, charming, mesmerizing, and wicked smart. A bit too smart, at times. The testimony contained one of the monumental Clinton howlers: "Well, it depends on what your definition of 'is' is." It also contained one of the more improbable arguments in the history of human sexuality—that oral sex isn't really sex. But apart from those moments, Clinton did about as well as could be expected under the circumstances. He was at once gallant and brutal about Lewinsky; he was credibly remorseful about his actions; he was appropriately indignant about the motives of the prosecutorial army that had been pursuing him; his decision not to discuss sexual details seemed eminently rational. Indeed, the testimony proved to be a rare and unexpected event: It was subtle, complicated, enigmatic, slow-moving—by its very pace, it defied the prevailing hyperbole and tamped down the scandal.

When it was over, the fever had broken. The cable-news hysteria subsided. There was a new, oddly subdued air to the endless commentary. And even the Republicans seemed taken aback. How on earth had Clinton survived *that*? At the White House press briefing, a few hours after the tape had been aired, Mike McCurry was asked: "Can the President use something like this"—the taped testimony—"to turn it around and perhaps pull in some support?"

McCurry smiled. "I don't know how you use a day like this to rally support," he said.

By the time *Larry King Live* rolled around that night, with a special two-hour extravaganza, the mood shift was palpable. Most of the guests thought the President had had a "good day." The White House seemed revitalized, and its spin operation was back in gear. The President's speechwriter, Paul Begala, who had gone to ground in disgust and anger over Clinton's behavior, suddenly reemerged as Larry King's guest—a chirpy presidential cheerleader once more. "Is this something that we impeach a president over?" he asked, adding that the prosecutors had been fundamentally unfair: "There were eighty-some-odd questions about sex and zero about Whitewater."

At the beginning of the Clinton administration, Begala had invented a new, acronymic term of opprobrium—BAU, meaning Business As Usual. BAU was originally a bad thing; the Clinton administration was anti-BAU, they were going to be fundamentally, radically different from the Republican fuddy-duddies who'd gone before. Now Begala was celebrating, with no small relief, a return to BAU, Clinton style—blithely spinning, attacking Starr, and seeming very pleased with himself.

The public loved the Lewinsky show, for a time. The ratings of the all-news networks soared. Newspapers and magazines did well, too. The vast popularity of the soap opera was, in a way, a precursor of "reality" shows like *Survivor*, which would suddenly, and perhaps not coincidentally, become hot just as Clinton was leaving office. But the ratings only held for the prurient stage of the drama; the story was, in effect, over after Clinton's testimony was aired. The distended impeachment hearings were judged wasteful and unnecessary by the folks—the worst sort of television, a foregone conclusion.

And when it all had been digested, public opinion had shifted not a whit. The President's job approval ratings remained very high, in the 60 percent range—he would leave office with the highest sustained job approval ratings of any President since John F. Kennedy. His personal approval ratings were lower, of course. It was difficult to imagine any civilian answering in the affirmative if asked, "Do you approve of the President's personal behavior?" Of course, many secret sympathies were undoubtedly harbored, especially among those Clinton's age, who had navigated themselves—shakily—through the uncertain moral shoals of the late twentieth century. Americans have a quiet appreciation of rogues, and a sophisticated ability to distinguish rogues from scoundrels, and Clinton had been judged the former.

Even in the white heat of the scandal, in the days after his grand jury testimony, overwhelming numbers—two thirds, according to most polls—opposed impeachment; a solid majority favored an alternate punishment option: censure by Congress (a legislative slap on the wrist). When asked how they'd vote if the 1996 election were to be held again, the results were almost exactly the same as they'd been: 46 percent said Clinton, 36 percent said Dole, 11 percent said Perot. It was as if the name "Lewinsky" had never been heard in the land.

Although, not quite so: The Republicans suffered, grievously. They lost five seats in the congressional elections that fall, which was very rare for a midterm election during a President's sixth year in office. Newt Gingrich suffered an appropriately Jacobin fate, becoming a target of his own hotheads. He resigned as Speaker after the elections, left the House of Representatives, and soon left his second wife, Marianne, and married a young woman with whom he'd been having an extramarital affair. His reign had lasted exactly four—entirely disastrous—years. Gingrich's successor, Robert Livingston of Louisiana, also resigned after rumors spread that he, too, had experienced moments of untoward humanity with women not his wife in the past.

The press suffered more subtly, but no less profoundly, than the Republicans did. A Harris Poll showed that journalists were now held in the lowest public esteem of any professional group, lower even than lawyers.

This mystified Washington. William Bennett, the former Reagan Education Secretary who had built a cottage industry out of books that compiled stories about "virtues" (he was also the younger brother of the President's lawyer, Robert Bennett), now hustled forth with a new book called *The Death of Outrage,* and made a national tour lamenting the moral insensitivity of the American people. The editorial pages of both the *New York Times* and *Washington Post* had sounded, in the midst of the scandal, every bit as intemperate as the editorial page of *The Wall Street Journal.* Just before the testimony was broadcast, the *Washington Post* had proposed that "invoking the majesty of the impeachment clause against behavior such as this is somehow to cheapen the clause"—in other words, the President lacked the stature to be impeached. This had become the conventional wisdom among the Washington Establishment: Why didn't he have the class to resign?

It was nearly impossible to find a political commentator who had anything measured to say about Bill Clinton. Even the normally understated dean of political columnists, the *Washington Post's* David Broder, had mournfully concluded: "Like Nixon, he has done things of importance for the country, but in every important way, he has diminished the stature and reduced the authority of the Presidency. He may hold on, but when he said of the investigation of his activities, 'This has gone on too long,' the words could equally apply to his own tenure."

How, then, to explain the contrast between the intensity of outrage in Washington and the laissez-faire attitude toward the President's immorality among the citizens of the most religious of Western democracies? It seemed an unprecedented disparity, and quite fascinating. It was especially entertaining to watch the commentariat—which had been predicting for months that the public would soon share its anti-Clinton obsession—try to explain why that hadn't happened. But then, the public reaction defied illogic. Americans had judged the Lewinsky affair a delicious, disgraceful, exploitative, and ultimately *private* act of consensual sex. This seemed a sophisticated, level-headed, almost Continental reaction—but also a rather cynical one. The President was assumed, from the start, to be promiscuous. Starr was assumed to be political (and found to be a charmless fanatic). Politicians were assumed to be liars. The media were assumed to be craven and sensationalist.

Clinton had, as Broder maintained, surely disgraced the presidency, but that was only part of the story: Washington had disgraced itself. Twenty-five years of self-destructive, internecine stupidity had finally borne its fruit: The public was disgusted—in a vague, bored way—with almost everyone associated with public life.

In the end, I found two theories—one historical, the other spiritual—that helped explain the witless intensity of Washington's reaction to the Lewinsky scandal.

Years earlier, the Yale historian Stephen Skowronek had described Clinton, Richard Nixon, and Woodrow Wilson—as well as Andrew Johnson, John Tyler, Grover Cleveland, and Dwight Eisenhower—as Third Way presidents. The nomenclature was unintentionally ironic: Skowronek's "third-way" was different from Clinton's. Skowronek defined this sort of President as one who tended to appropriate his opponents' agenda and get it enacted after sanding off the rough edges (Wilson appropriated Theodore Roosevelt's Progressive program; Eisenhower was the first Republican to accept the assumptions of Franklin Roosevelt's New Deal). Such presidents are often mistrusted by their own party, and they are inevitably detested by the opposition, but they also tend to be quite successful: Each of Skowronek's Third Way presidents who chose to run for a second term won reelection (except Cleveland, who lost and then won again four years later). Success, however, was usually fleeting—"no 'third way' has ever outlasted the president who articulated it," Skowronek wrote years before Al Gore failed in his attempt to succeed Clinton.

Furthermore, the price of Third Way success was often a dangerously personal political atmosphere: "While other leaders might appear weak or even incompetent," Skowronek continued, "third-way presidents are often judged moral degenerates, congenitally incapable of rising above nihilism and manipulation." Even Woodrow Wilson—that perfect Presbyterian—was, Skowronek notes, subjected to an amazing assault by his predecessor, Theodore Roosevelt, who "mercilessly derided Wilson's adroit, unscrupulous cunning, his pandering to those who love ease . . . his readiness to about-face . . . his lack of all conviction and willingness to follow every gust of opinion."

Certainly, Clinton's political hermaphroditism had something to do with the excessive hatefulness that crippled his opponents. But beneath the politics, a more primal and even theological melodrama was at work: a temple riot, of sorts—a disturbance among the national priesthood, a scapegoat sacrifice. The Stanford University literature and religion scholar René Girard, whose book *Violence and the Sacred* explores the intense societal purposes of the scapegoat ritual in the ancient world, told me that Bill Clinton was a classic scapegoat—which is not to say that he was wrongly accused. Quite the opposite, in fact. In the ancient world, a scapegoat personified the pathologies of his society and his times. "In Greek mythology, the scapegoat is never wrongfully accused," Girard said. "But he is always magical. He has the capacity to relieve the burden of guilt from a society. This seems a basic human impulse. There is a need to consume scapegoats. It is the way tension is relieved and change takes place."

It seems likely, in retrospect, that Bill Clinton was a compendium of all that his accusers found most embarrassing, troubling, and loathsome about themselves, especially those who came of age, as he did, in the deep, narcotic prosperity that enveloped the nation after World War II. On the most superficial level, his excesses reflected the personal excesses—sexual and material—of his generation. Deeper down, his poll-obsessed administration often seemed the triumph of marketing over substance—which reflected nagging doubts about a nation dominated by a virtual economy of "concepts" and cyber-processes, rather than the substantive assembly lines that had provided the illusion of economic stability in the past. Finally, there was the free-range fudgery: Clinton had escaped military service in Vietnam. He had never sacrificed for his country. He had never been tested by adversity. He (and his doppelgänger, Gingrich, and his successor, George W. Bush) were relative dilettantes compared to the generation that preceded them—the generation of Bob Dole and Bob Michel and George H.W. Bush. A certain generational callowness needed to be exorcised.

But the Lewinsky affair was a scapegoat sacrifice that didn't work. There was no catharsis; the scapegoat escaped. And the tension remained in a society troubled by a vague, aimless emptiness—a tension attributable, perhaps, to the spiritual toll taken by the most spectacular prosperity in the history of the world.

In the end, Clinton's symbolic identification with the pathologies of his era may be destined to overwhelm the real accomplishments of his time in office.

In Four Days, A National Crisis Changes Bush's Presidency

by David E. Sanger

and Don Van Natta, Jr.

The New York Times *ran this article by reporters David E. Sanger and Don Van Natta, Jr. on Sunday, September 16, 2001. The piece portrays George W. Bush's (in office 2001–present) early efforts to respond to the September 11th terrorist attacks.*

President Bush was sitting in a second-grade classroom in Sarasota, Fla., on Tuesday morning, his eyes and his smile fixed on 7-year-olds showing off their reading skills. But his mind was clearly fixed on the news he had heard just moments before: a passenger jet had crashed into one of the World Trade Center towers.

At 9:05 a.m., the White House chief of staff, Andrew H. Card Jr., stepped into the classroom and whispered into the president's right ear, "A second plane hit the other tower, and America's under attack."

The president blanched. But he stayed put, occasionally arching his eyebrows at the children. "Really good readers, whew," he said. "This must be sixth grade."

Minutes later, 900 miles to the north, a squad of Secret Service agents burst into the West Wing office of Vice President Dick Cheney, grabbing his arms, his shoulders and his belt. "They literally propelled him out of his office," one witness said. The agents all but carried Mr. Cheney down to the White House's deepest sanctum, the Presidential

Emergency Operations Center, a tubelike structure designed to withstand a nuclear blast. Another hijacked plane was bearing down on Washington, the agents said, and the White House was almost certainly its target.

In the course of the next four days, George W. Bush was transformed into a president at the helm of a White House, and a nation, in crisis.

On Monday night, he was laughing over dinner with his brother Jeb at a seaside Florida resort, posing for pictures with the restaurant staff and dodging questions from reporters about looming battles over the vanishing budget surplus. By this morning, with downtown Washington locked down by the military, he was conducting a war council at Camp David and demanding that countries around the world, starting with the Arab world, declare whether they were allies in the war on terrorism.

As he rode Marine One from Andrews Air Force Base to the White House on Tuesday evening, Mr. Bush watched the smoke billowing from the jagged gash in the Pentagon and seemed to recognize how profoundly his young presidency had been transformed.

"The mightiest building in the world is on the floor," he told an aide riding with him. "That's the 21st-century war you just witnessed."

President Bush awoke around 6 a.m. on Tuesday at the Colony, a tennis resort in Longboat Key, Fla.

Eager to start his day with exercise, he took his motorcade to a nearby golf course and ran hard for four and a half miles. He returned to his hotel for a shower and his daily intelligence briefings, which apparently included reference to heightened threats of terrorism. Then he took the 20-minute ride to the Emma E. Booker Elementary School, the second event in two days staged to galvanize support for an education bill languishing in Congress.

He arrived just before 9. Right before the event, Karl Rove, one of his most trusted aides, whispered news of what appeared to be a chilling accident, a plane crash into the upper floors of the North Tower of the World Trade Center. Mr. Bush was briefed by phone by Condoleezza

Rice, his national security adviser, calling from the White House. He decided to go ahead with the short school event.

But as beepers lit up with the news, reporters and a few of Mr. Bush's senior staff members slipped across the schoolyard to watch the disaster unfold in a classroom where the television networks had set up their equipment and monitors. They had just assembled when the second plane, United Airlines Flight 175, slammed into the South Tower.

A minute later, Mr. Card whispered the news in the president's ear.

"It was a surreal moment," Mr. Card recalled late this week. "It was immediately obvious that it was neither an accident nor a coincidence."

Mr. Bush has not said why he lingered in the room for another six minutes, but it was a testament to either his calm or his acting ability. But at 9:12, he abruptly retreated, speaking to Mr. Cheney and New York officials.

Hurriedly Mr. Bush wrote a statement on a yellow pad with a black felt-tip pen. At 9:30, he appeared in a large media room, where charts about the education budget had been whisked away. With children, teachers, and Florida Republicans jammed into the room, he faced the cameras, noticeably shaken.

"Today we had a national tragedy," he said. "Two airplanes have crashed into the World Trade Center in an apparent terrorist attack on our country."

Then, lapsing into some informal language, he vowed "to hunt down and to find those folks who committed this act. Terrorism against our nation will not stand." He said he was returning to Washington immediately.

But as he spoke, panic had spread in the White House. Mr. Cheney was swept into the Presidential Emergency Operations Center, along with his wife and Ms. Rice and other senior staff members. They were told, administration officials say, that American Airlines Flight 77 was bearing down on the White House. Bomb squads were already racing through the upper floors of the Old Executive Office Building, screaming, "Get out, get out, this is real!"

In only minutes Mr. Bush and his agents raced back to Air Force

One, which hastily departed Sarasota at 9:55. No one aboard—White House aides, flight crew members or Secret Service agents—claimed to know the plane's destination. By then, the jetliner possibly headed for the White House had taken out one side of the Pentagon, and another seemed on the way.

Moments after he was aloft, Mr. Bush opened a line to Mr. Cheney and kept it open. "That's what we are paid for, boys," Mr. Bush told the vice president, according to the account of an aide. "We are going to take care of this. When we find out who did this, they are not going to like me as president. Somebody is going to pay."

By 10:30, a call had come to the White House that "Air Force One is next." What sent chills through the White House is that the caller had used code words that showed familiarity with how the president moves about the country.

"To get bound into the secure facility and hear the code name for Air Force One, there's something headed for Air Force One—I don't think you can underestimate, at that moment, that you're sorting lots of information and you're trying to deal with the consequences," Ms. Rice said.

And then there were the false reports that only heightened the anxiety: a car bomb at the Pentagon, a transponder code from an aircraft coming across the Pacific from South Korea that suggested a hijacking was under way, four flights from the Atlantic that Mr. Cheney and Ms. Rice were warned might be hostile.

"They pretty quickly made the decision to scramble aircraft," one witness to the discussions said.

But in the White House Situation Room and at the Pentagon, the response seemed agonizingly slow. One military official recalls hearing "words to the effect of, 'Where are the planes?' "

The Pentagon insists it had air cover over its own building by 10 a.m., 15 minutes after the building was hit. But witnesses, including a reporter for *The New York Times* who was headed toward the building, did not see any until closer to 11.

As they worked, Mr. Cheney and Ms. Rice, still in the tunnel command center, saw the horrifying collapse of the second twin tower.

"There was just a momentary pause in activity," one witness said. "Just total silence. But no one talked about it, not even an 'Oh, God.' They just went back to work."

At 10:41, with Air Force One headed toward Jacksonville to meet jets scrambled to give the presidential jet its own air cover, Mr. Cheney was urging Mr. Bush to avoid a quick return to Washington. He wanted the president at Offutt Air Force Base outside Omaha, which he knew from his days as secretary of defense had an extraordinarily sophisticated strategic command communications center.

At 11:45, the plane landed at Barksdale Air Force Base in Shreveport, La., an intermediate stop. A White House official asked the small pool of reporters in the back of the plane to keep their cellphones off because the signals could allow someone to identify the plane's position.

White House officials told reporters that they could say only that the president was at "an unidentified location in the United States," a requirement that was lifted after reporters learned that local television stations had already reported the landing.

Mr. Bush appeared before the reporters for just two minutes, declaring, "Freedom itself was attacked this morning by a faceless coward."

But he looked nervous, and the tape of the appearance was jumpy and grainy. "It was not our best moment," one administration official conceded.

Mr. Bush may have thought so too; he told his aides: "I want to go back home as soon as possible. I don't want whoever this is holding me outside of Washington."

But Mr. Cheney and the Secret Service urged Mr. Bush to stay away, and Mr. Card said, "Let's let the dust settle."

At the time, administration officials said, there had been two reports of international flights that were unaccounted for, and two domestic flights were seen as possible threats.

"That's a potential of four missiles in the air, and we were concerned that if Air Force One landed in a predictable place, one of those planes could hit it on the ground," said a senior administration official, who spoke on condition of anonymity. The official added that the hijackers had shown "they had the capacity to fly planes into still objects."

From Louisiana, Air Force One flew northwest, to Offutt. Mr. Bush disappeared into what looks like a small cinder-block bunker that leads to an underground site, where he convened the first meeting of his National Security Council, via teleconference.

Ms. Rice recalled that the president opened the meeting by saying firmly that the day's terror amounted to "an attack on freedom, and we're going to define it as such."

"And we're going to go after it," she recalled him saying, "and we're not going to lose focus. And we're going to minister to the country and deal with the horrors that people are experiencing and the consequences, and we're going to get through our period of mourning. But we're not going to lose focus and resolve on what happened here and what this means for the United States of America, in its leadership role, to mobilize the world, now, to deal with this scourge."

The meeting ended shortly after 4 p.m., and again Mr. Bush insisted that he return to Washington. Political aides and the communications staff also wanted him to return, but the Secret Service again cautioned that he should not. This time, Mr. Bush insisted that he had to deliver a prime-time television address from the Oval Office, not a bunker.

Back in Washington, Republicans were anxious that Mr. Bush had not yet returned to the capital. Late Tuesday afternoon, a Bush supporter and fund-raiser said: "I am stunned that he has not come home. It looks like he is running. This looks bad."

Mr. Bush arrived at the White House around 7 p.m. At 8:30, he addressed the nation, saying, "None of us will ever forget this day, yet we go forward to defend freedom and all that is good and just in our world."

Republican advisers to the administration said the speech fell flat, that it failed to meet either the magnitude of the day's events or the nature of the task ahead. But one senior White House official, sounding defensive, said: "The point was not to be eloquent. It was to say I'm here, I'm safe, I'm alive."

As soon as it was over, Mr. Bush joined the others at the Presidential Emergency Operations Center for his first in-person briefings by the Central Intelligence Agency and the Federal Bureau of Investigation.

Sometime overnight or Wednesday morning, Mr. Bush, Mr. Cheney and Secretary of State Colin L. Powell, just back from Latin America, made a critical decision: to describe the terrorism as "acts of war," and to declare, "We will rally the world." Mr. Bush's advisers insist this was not a response to criticism of his performance the previous day, but several administration officials acknowledged that the words of war he used before the cameras in the cabinet room that morning should have been uttered in his address before the nation the previous night.

A longtime Republican supporter of Mr. Bush said, "They recognized that people thought he wasn't fabulous on television, and they set out to change that."

An administration official, asked about the use of the war phraseology, said it was Mr. Bush's "own decision to say it publicly that morning." If so, it was highly coordinated: Mr. Powell used it repeatedly in five separate talk-show appearances early that morning, and the language escalated all day.

Mr. Bush then began doing what his father had done after Saddam Hussein invaded Kuwait: dialing leaders around the world and beginning to build a coalition of nations. Later that afternoon, the president visited rescue workers and fire personnel at the Pentagon. It was the first time he spoke without notes, and he seemed far more comfortable.

On Thursday morning, he spoke again without notes but in a different forum. He let reporters into the Oval Office and stood behind the desk. After placing a call to Mayor Rudolph W. Giuliani and Gov. George E. Pataki of New York, the president surprised at least two White House aides by holding an impromptu news conference and answered a half-dozen questions, far more than usual.

One reporter asked the president if he had said a prayer for himself, and the emotional toll of the crisis became evident.

"Well, I don't think of myself right now," he said. "I think about the families, the children." He paused, and his eyes filled with tears. "I'm a loving guy. And I am also someone, however, who's got a job to do and I intend to do it. And this is a terrible moment. But this country will not relent until we have saved ourselves, and others, from the terrible tragedy that came upon America."

Mr. Bush left the Oval Office. Afterward, he visited a local hospital. But then a second scare spread around the White House. A wider perimeter was set up; the East Wing was temporarily evacuated, along with the Capitol. Ronald Reagan National Airport, which had temporarily opened on Thursday, was closed again.

As a precaution, Mr. Cheney was moved to Camp David full time on Thursday. The Secret Service did not want the president and the vice president to be in the same place. An administration official declined to describe the exact nature of the threats, except to say they were "credible" and "serious."

Some younger members of the White House staff were rattled and talked privately about the frightening but also reassuring sight of military guards cordoning off Lafayette Park.

While Mr. Bush moved from one strategy session to another, the White House staff began planning a national Day of Remembrance for Friday, with the president as the featured speaker at Washington National Cathedral.

Alongside him were his father and mother, and three former presidents: Bill Clinton, Jimmy Carter, and Gerald R. Ford. The pressure was on. This was the kind of event at which Mr. Clinton had excelled, and the comparisons would be clear to a nation looking for the right tone from a new president. Inside the hall, Mr. Bush seemed dwarfed by the massive limestone columns, but on television he took on a larger presence, and seemed to find his footing.

"Today we feel what Franklin Roosevelt called the 'warm courage of national unity,' " Mr. Bush said. "In every generation, the world has produced enemies of human freedom. They have attacked America because we are freedom's home and defender. And the commitment of our fathers is now the calling of our time." He glanced at his own father, a World War II pilot.

From there it was off to New York. This time Air Force One took off with close air cover and landed at an air base in New Jersey rather than one of the New York airports.

"The people who knocked these buildings down will hear all of us soon," he declared over a bullhorn, as thousands of rescuers in lower Manhattan cheered, "U.S.A.! U.S.A.! U.S.A.!"

An aide said the bullhorn moment, like others this week, was spontaneous. "It was one of the most chaotic scenes I have ever seen," the aide said. "The president wanted to speak and someone spotted the fireman who was standing on that spot high above the workers." Nina Bishop, who was helping coordinate the visit, found a bullhorn and thrust it into the president's hand. "It just happened," the aide said.

By 11 p.m., the president's helicopter could be heard landing at Camp David. This morning, Mr. Bush tried to regain a semblance of his ordinary schedule. He rose at 5:30 a.m., walked his dogs, Barney and Spot, and went running inside the Camp David grounds, his first run outside since that sunny morning in Sarasota.

Then he joined Mr. Cheney, Ms. Rice, Mr. Powell, and other members of his security team for an all-day war council.

He seemed far steadier than he had early in the week. He told the cabinet what he had seen in New York, calling the scene "the signs of the first battle of war." On Tuesday morning, in his first public statement about the attacks, the president had called the suicide hijackers "folks." Today, he called them "barbarians."

"This is a great nation; we're kind and peaceful," Mr. Bush said. "But they have stirred up the might of the American people, and we're going to get them."

acknowledgments

Many people helped make this Anthology.

At Thunder's Mouth Press and Avalon Publishing Group:
Thanks to Ghadah Alrawi, Tracy Armstead, Will Balliett, Sue Canavan, Kristen Couse, Maria Fernandez, Linda Kosarin, Shona McCarthy, Dan O'Connor, Neil Ortenberg, Paul Paddock, Susan Reich, David Riedy, Simon Sullivan, and Mike Walters for their support, dedication and hard work.

At the Portland Public Library:
The librarians helped me collect books from around the country.

At The Writing Company:
Clint Willis shared his experience and creativity. Nate Hardcastle answered countless questions. Kate Fletcher helped with research. Mark Klimek, Taylor Smith, and March Truedsson were fun to be around.

At Davidson College:
Dr. Ralph Levering provided encouragement and ideas.

Finally, I am grateful to all the writers whose work appears in this book.

permissions

We gratefully acknowledge everyone who gave permission for written material to appear in this book. We have made every effort to trace and contact copyright holders. If an error or omission is brought to our notice we will be pleased to correct the situation in future editions of this book. For further information, please contact the publisher.

Excerpt from *Patriarch: George Washington and the New American Nation* by Richard Norton Smith. Copyright © 1993 by Richard Norton Smith. Reprinted by permission of Houghton Mifflin Company. ✥ Excerpt from *Polk and the Presidency* by Charles A. McCoy. Copyright © 1960 by University of Texas Press. Reprinted by permission of the University of Texas Press. ✥ "The Words That Remade America: Lincoln at Gettysburg" by Garry Wills. Copyright © 1996 by Garry Wills. Reprinted by permission of the author. ✥ Excerpt from *Theodore Rex* by Edmund Morris. Copyright © 2001 by Edmund Morris. Used by permission of Random House, Inc. ✥ Excerpt from *Roosevelt: The Soldier of Freedom* by James MacGregor Burns. Copyright © 1970 by James MacGregor Burns. Reprinted by permission of Harcourt, Inc. ✥ Excerpt from *Truman* by David McCullough. Copyright © 1992 by David McCullough. Reprinted with the permission of Simon & Schuster Adult Publishing Group. ✥ Excerpt from *The Crisis Years: Kennedy and Khrushchev, 1960-1963* by Michael R. Beschloss. Copyright © 1991 by Michael R. Beschloss. Reprinted by permission of HarperCollins Publishers, Inc. ✥ Excerpt from *Counsel to the President: A Memoir* by Clark Clifford. Copyright © 1991 by Clark Clifford. Used by permission of Random House, Inc. ✥ Excerpt from *The Great Coverup: Nixon and the Scandal of Watergate* by Barry Sussman. Copyright © 1992 by Barry Sussman. Reprinted by permission of Seven Locks Press. ✥ Excerpt from *The Final Days* by Carl Bernstein and Bob Woodward. Copyright © 1976 by Carl Bernstein and Bob Woodward. Reprinted with the permission of

bibliography

The selections used in this anthology were taken from the editions listed below.a In some cases, other editions may be easier to find. Hard-to-find or out-of-print titles often are available through inter-library loan services or through Internet booksellers.

Bernstein, Carl, and Bob Woodward. *The Final Days*. New York: Simon & Schuster, 1976.

Beschloss, Michael R. *The Crisis Years: Kennedy and Khrushchev, 1960-1963*. New York: HarperCollins, 1991.

Burns, James MacGregor. *Roosevelt: The Soldier of Freedom*. New York: Harcourt Brace Jovanovich, Inc., 1970.

Clifford, Clark. *Counsel to the President: A Memoir*. New York: Random House, Inc., 1991.

Greene, John Robert. *The Presidency of George Bush*. Lawrence, KS: University Press of Kansas, 2000.

Klein, Joe. *The Natural: The Misunderstood Presidency of Bill Clinton*. New York: Doubleday, 2002.

McCoy, Charles A. *Polk and the Presidency*. Austin, TX: University of Texas Press, 1960.

McCullough, David G. *Truman*. New York: Touchstone, 1992.

Morris, Edmund. *Dutch: A Memoir*. New York: Random House, Inc., 1999.

Morris, Edmund. *Theodore Rex*. New York: Random House, Inc., 2001.

Sanger, David E., and Don Van Natta, Jr. "In Four Days, A National Crisis Changes Bush's Presidency". First appeared in *The New York Times* September 16, 2001.

Shultz, George P. *Turmoil and Triumph: My Years as Secretary of State*. New York: Charles Scribner's Sons, 1993.

Smith, Richard Norton. *Patriarch: George Washington and the New American Nation*. New York: Houghton Mifflin, 1993

Sussman, Barry. *The Great Coverup: Nixon and the Scandal of Watergate*. Arlington, VA: Seven Locks Press, 1992.

Wills, Garry. "The Words That Remade America: Lincoln at Gettysburg". First appeared in *The Atlantic Monthly* June 1996.